487306

Drury, W.   16.95   B/NORTON
  Norton I.

WACO-McLENNAN COUNTY LIBRARY
1717 Austin Avenue
Waco, Texas   76701

MAIN

NORTON I
Emperor of the United States

NORTON I

Emperor of the United States

William Drury
Foreword by Melvin M. Belli

DODD, MEAD & COMPANY
NEW YORK

Copyright © 1986 by William Drury

All rights reserved

No part of this book may be reproduced in any form
without permission in writing from the publisher.
Published by Dodd, Mead & Company, Inc.
79 Madison Avenue, New York, N.Y. 10016
Distributed in Canada by
McClelland and Stewart Limited, Toronto
Manufactured in the United States of America

Designed by Erich Hobbing

First Edition

Library of Congress Cataloging-in-Publication Data

Drury, William, 1918–
Norton the First.

Bibliography: p.
Includes index.
1. Norton, Joshua Abraham, 1819–1880. 2. United
States—Biography. 3. San Francisco (Calif.)—
Biography. I. Title.
CT275.N75D78   1986   979.4′61′0992 [B]   85-29244
ISBN 0-396-08509-1

1 2 3 4 5 6 7 8 9 10

For Peggy

Contents

Foreword by Melvin M. Belli   ix
Acknowledgments   xiii
Prologue   xvii
Chapter 1   Death of a Guttersnipe   1
Chapter 2   The Tailor's Tale   9
Chapter 3   Boy on a Broomstick Horse   14
Chapter 4   The Oof Bird's Nest   26
Chapter 5   Perchance to Dream   35
Chapter 6   The Edge of Hell   43
Chapter 7   Over the Edge   51
Chapter 8   Fitch the Kingmaker   57
Chapter 9   Thunder in the East   64
Chapter 10   Colonel Moustache   69
Chapter 11   The Bummers   80
Chapter 12   Fifty Cents a Night   87
Chapter 13   Emperor of the West   96
Chapter 14   The Feud   103
Chapter 15   The Emperor's Secretary   110

Chapter 16   Lazarus Redivivus   120
Chapter 17   In Durance Vile   124
Chapter 18   Railroad to Renown   130
Chapter 19   The Bridge to Nowhere   140
Chapter 20   Possible Dreams, Reachable Stars   148
Chapter 21   Birth of a Legend   158
Chapter 22   Old Queen Cole   165
Chapter 23   Don't Call It 'Frisco   172
Chapter 24   Captain Stormfield's Daughter   180
Chapter 25   Emperor of the World   188
Chapter 26   The Palace of Truth   194
Chapter 27   The Controversy   202
Epilogue   205
Appendix A   The Clampers   207
Appendix B   The King and Huck Finn   214
Sources   221
Bibliography   223
Index   227

Foreword

by

Melvin M. Belli

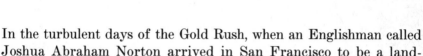

In the turbulent days of the Gold Rush, when an Englishman called Joshua Abraham Norton arrived in San Francisco to be a landowner and a merchant prince, his first place of business was an adobe cottage at the corner of Montgomery and Jackson streets. The cottage vanished in the fire that ravaged the city in 1851, and a banker named William T. Sherman, better known today as the Civil War general who put Atlanta to the torch, bought the site in 1854 and built his bank on the spot, a solid structure of granite and brick that fire could not easily destroy. Just fifty paces to the south of it, another building was erected at the same time, also of brick. Both were built to last; even the terrible earthquake of 1906 could not topple them. They stand there still. Sherman's bank now houses several small business enterprises, and the building nearby, at 722 Montgomery Street, has been my office for years.

My building and Sherman's are almost the oldest in the city, but there is one even older, adjoining Belli's Building at 728 Montgomery, and that, too, is part of my law office. It is called Caesar's Annex, named for my grandfather, Caesar Belli, and it was put up in 1849, the year that Norton came to town with the gold miners, when it served as the birthplace of Freemasonry in California, as a plaque on its facade attests. That brick building also escaped the fire that demolished so much of a city largely constructed of wood.

But some parts of Belli's Building itself date back to an earlier day, when it was a warehouse. The architects who restored it for me—keeping everything of historical value intact—found traces of loading docks, doors, and windows, scorched by the flames of 1851. I have a photograph that shows the walls still standing after the fire and before the builders of 1854 put up the walls that surround me now. In December 1857, the new structure became a music hall, known as The Melodeon. A theatrical journal, *Variety*, said of it then:

> The Melodeon, with songs, dances, recitations, good wines, cigars, brandy and "lager" for such as like it, is the most attractive place of amusement in San Francisco. The winning sweetness of the Misses Mandeville on the stage holds even the ruder portions of the audience spellbound, save when applause must follow their vocal efforts; whilst Johnson's rollicking humor would cause a dying miser to smile, or make a Turk leave his prayers at "Muezzin Call."

San Franciscans had need of Johnson's rollicking humor in those days to heal their cares, having just come through the second vigilante uprising in five years, which was caused when a County Supervisor shot and killed the editor of the *Evening Bulletin* not far from the door that is now mine. For that he was lynched by the vigilantes. Joshua Norton, who had been a vigilante in 1851 (albeit a reluctant one), took no part in this second rebellion, for by then he was well on his way to madness and so perhaps had more sense.

Three years later, having lost his reason completely, he proclaimed himself Emperor of the United States.

When I sit at my desk I am conscious of history, knowing that the old brick walls around me have heard the voices of men discussing the latest outrage by the Committee of Vigilance of 1856 or possibly laughing together over some story in the *Alta California* about Norton the First. However, I must confess that, until Bill Drury placed the manuscript of this book before me to read, practically all that I knew about the Emperor consisted of legends of dubious veracity. We who live in San Francisco know those legends well, but Drury's biography really opened my eyes.

It does not surprise me in the least that the author had more than a passing interest in the Emperor of the United States. Bill had been a daily columnist for the old *Call-Bulletin,* an amalgamation of the *Morning Call* that had employed Mark Twain as a reporter in the Emperor's day and the *Evening Bulletin* that first printed His Imperial Majesty's "royal proclamations" and started him on the road to fame. Everybody I knew read Drury's column until the *Call-Bulletin* finally succumbed to the perils of publishing after more than a hundred years. He wrote about the city's screwballs, people who lived in a world of their own, most of them in the gutter. Bill dragged them out of the gutter and gave them a place in the sun. So it seems inevitable that he would one day write about the man of substance and wealth—Norton once owned land where skyscrapers now stand—who became the best-known guttersnipe of all. *Life* magazine once acclaimed me "The King of Torts," which proves that almost anyone can aspire to be royalty in this delightfully crazy city of ours, but Emperor Norton—well, he was something special.

William Drury, like Norton the First, was born in England, lived in South Africa in his youth and came to San Francisco when he was roughly the same age as the Emperor (though there all similarity ends). But the English seem to understand eccentricity better than anyone else—that island breeds tolerant men—and perhaps that is why he was able to lay bare the Emperor's soul to show us, quite clearly, that he was not nearly the clown everyone has always supposed.

Laughter abounds in this book, but it is not aimed at the remarkable ragamuffin who strolls through its pages in a shabby uniform. Instead, Drury has fun with those who made sport of the Emperor. In those unenlightened times any reporter who held the "Emp" up to ridicule in the public prints was considered a wit, and his newspaper's circulation increased in proportion to his reputation as a humorist, which often depended upon how many tales about Emperor Norton he could tell, even if he had to make them up. And Drury shows us here, the newspapermen invented many a tall tale. Some of their stories became the legends that still make us chuckle. The author demolishes the fables, however, and gives us a story that I suppose will unsettle the reader who would rather cling to the myths. I sincerely hope not, because the facts about Emperor Norton seem stranger than the fiction.

This biography holds many surprises. Mark Twain, who knew His Majesty, said in a letter to William Dean Howells, a major novelist and Twain's good friend, that he felt there was a lot more to Norton's story than had ever been told. Well, here at last is a really marvelous book that tells us more than even the Emperor's next-door neighbor, Mark Twain himself, ever knew. Few of us living today could have imagined just how much of His Majesty's strange life has been forgotten since he left us for a kindlier world.

It took Bill Drury, a diligent researcher, to dig up a multitude of facts about the Emperor that posterity has never heard of, facts he found in archives that nobody else had explored.

One thing this book reveals is the astonishing extent of the Emperor's former fame. Those who visit San Francisco today may stay at the Emperor Norton Inn, lunch in the Emperor Norton Room at the Sheraton-Palace Hotel, cruise the bay in the *Harbor Emperor* with its figurehead of Norton I, dine in restaurants that display his portrait, or munch Emperor Norton Sourdough Snacks if lunch is not enough, but very few tourists seem to have any idea who he was. His face on the bow of a boat or a packet of snacks means nothing to visitors now. Yet in the 1870s his name was known to travelers even before they boarded the train that brought them to California; they had read about him in their hometown papers and fully expected to see him when they arrived. Indeed, as the author points out, when he died on a street corner, the story was carried in newspapers all over the land.

Many people, mainly newspaperfolk, have written about Norton the First, but Bill Drury is the only writer who has recognized the Emperor's value to the tourist industry of his time—which may be the real reason he was so popular with San Francisco's business community—and he feels that the city should honor him for that. Bill may be right. It would not come amiss if we were to remember His Late Majesty with an official state plaque on some place connected with the Emperor, much like the plaque that adorns Caesar's Annex, the building that is part of mine, and the one on the wall of William T. Sherman's bank (which is there to commemorate the soldier-banker who built it but says nothing about the Englishman who dreamed an impossible dream in the adobe cottage that stood there first).

But read this enjoyable book. You, too, may think that the Emperor of the United States deserves to be remembered for all time.

Acknowledgments

My search for the Emperor proved fruitless in London, where most Californian newspapers of his day had said he was born, and it was not until I rummaged in South Africa's files that I struck gold, thanks to a clue in the San Francisco *Chronicle,* which claimed that he was born at the Cape of Good Hope in 1817 and spoke fluent Dutch (meaning what is now called Afrikaans). A wealth of information existed there about the settlers who sailed from Britain in 1820. The efficient colonial government of that time had carefully kept track of the family fathered by John Norton, whose name is still honored by Jews at the Cape for his role in bringing Judaism to that land. Dr. A. M. Lewin Robinson of the South African Public Library in Cape Town and Ms. Joan Davies of the Cape Archives supplied me with so many details that I was able to reconstruct much of Joshua Norton's life that had always been a riddle to Californians. It is worth noting that he was thirty-one when he left the Cape and sixty-two when he died, so that half of his years had been shrouded in mystery until these two South African archivists ferreted out the facts.

Those who helped me most in California were: Judy Sheldon, California Historical Society, San Francisco; Grace Baker, Society of California Pioneers, San Francisco; Gladys Hansen, San Francisco Public Library; and Irene Moran, Bancroft Library at the University of California in Berkeley. Foremost among those repositories that provided evidence of his widening fame in the 1870s were the public libraries of New York, Boston, Cincinnati, Philadelphia, Cleveland, Portland, Seattle, Los Angeles, and Denver.

xiv *Acknowledgments*

Yet no matter how deeply I dug in San Francisco's archives, it was impossible to learn everything about the Emperor because the fire of 1906 had destroyed so many old newspaper files, leaving gaps in his story that probably may never be filled. Any biographer who hopes to describe the last few years of his life, for instance, must rely chiefly on copies of the *Pacific Appeal* in the California Historical Society's collection. Fortunately, this was the weekly that His Majesty trusted enough to make it his "imperial gazette," so that the proclamations found within its pages are numerous and likely to be genuine. As for the decrees published in other papers that still exist, notably the *Alta* and the *Bulletin*, most of them try so hard to be comical that they cannot be anything but pranks. A comparison of those spurious edicts with several of the Emperor's handwritten letters, preserved in the Bancroft Library (including one to General William T. Sherman's brother, Senator John Sherman, penned on the engraved stationery of the Mechanics' Institute), quickly reveals that his own style was superior to that of any joker and his messages only unconsciously funny; after all, they were meant to be serious. I am quite convinced that Emperor Norton owed his fame rather more to proclamations he did not write than to those that he did.

I must express my appreciation to Judge Malcolm M. Champlin of Oakland for the stories he heard from his grandfather, Asa Champlin, who was in his teens when the Emperor came calling at the Champlin Ranch in the Sonoma Valley, bound for Petaluma to "straighten" a creek that had too many bends. Judge Champlin still owns the ranch, though the house in which His Majesty slept and supped has gone, leaving only the memories of those evenings when Asa and his parents sat under an oil lamp in the parlor, listening to the Emperor's plans for bridging the bay. Those memories, passed from one generation to the next, are too firmly embedded in family lore ever to perish. Nor should I forget Dr. Charles A. Shumate, ex–Sublime Noble Grand Humbug of E Clampus Vitus and a former president of the California Historical Society, who is inclined to see some merit in my theory that His Majesty became a Clamper one day without knowing it.*

My gratitude also goes to Jean Wilson for her skill with a word

---

*See Appendix A

Prologue

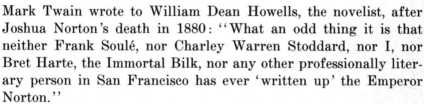

Mark Twain wrote to William Dean Howells, the novelist, after Joshua Norton's death in 1880: "What an odd thing it is that neither Frank Soulé, nor Charley Warren Stoddard, nor I, nor Bret Harte, the Immortal Bilk, nor any other professionally literary person in San Francisco has ever 'written up' the Emperor Norton."

What sort of a "write-up" did he have in mind? An article for *The Atlantic Monthly*? Howells was editor of the *Monthly,* and Twain usually sought his opinion of a story he wanted to offer the magazine before tackling the task of writing it. His letter had all the earmarks of a fishing expedition for approval of a biographical sketch about the famous guttersnipe who imagined he was the Emperor of the United States. Knowing that Howells, an exacting editor, would expect something more substantial than a whimsical tale about a king of shreds and patches, Twain made it clear that there was a lot more to the royal ragamuffin than had ever been told.

"Nobody," he pointed out, "has ever written him up who was able to see anything but his grotesque side, but I think that with all of his dirt and unsavoriness there was a pathetic side to him."

Sixteen years earlier, in San Francisco, no writer had been closer to Joshua Norton than Twain, Harte, and Franklin Soulé. Twain and Soulé had shared a newspaper office adjoining the Emperor's fleapit lodgings; Bret Harte, the "Immortal Bilk" (Twain had come to despise him), worked in the room below them, editing a new literary weekly, *The Californian*. Any one of them could have interviewed Norton "in depth"—as reporters say today—simply by climbing the stairs next door. If they didn't do it then, when they had the chance, presumably it was because the "Emp" was a relatively minor celebrity in those days, known in California and Nevada but practically nowhere else. Twain himself was no better known in 1864; he was still Sam Clemens of the *Morning Call,* and the pen name he had begun to use as a contributor to Harte's *Californian* never appeared in the "Morning Squeak." Sometimes, to enliven a dull local item, he would drag in His Imperial Majesty, whose name guaranteed a chuckle, but it could never have entered his head that the guttersnipe next door might one day be worth a lot more than a squib in the Squeak.

Who could have guessed that, in good time, Norton would actually become something of an American legend, a living folk hero, known the length and breadth of the land? Certainly the Emperor was enough of a celebrity to merit the attention of newspapers far from the Golden West (which should explain how Twain came to read of his death in Elmira, New York, probably in *The New York Times*).

Norton fascinated Twain. Having told Howells that the Emperor deserved to be immortalized by the best of pens, he went ahead and did it—in his own fashion. He put aside the novel he was writing, *The Prince and the Pauper,* and unearthed from a drawer the bothersome manuscript he had been struggling with, off and on, for longer than he cared to remember. Then, freshly inspired, he began a lively new chapter, introducing a princely pauper who would turn out to be the funniest of all the characters in *The Adventures of Huckleberry Finn.*

Twain said he drew his fictional characters from real life. Scholarly sleuths who have studied his works, hoping to pinpoint a prototype, are satisfied that no less than three characters—Captain Stormfield of *Captain Stormfield's Visit to Heaven,* Captain Hurricane Jones of *Some Rambling Notes of an Idle Excursion,* and Captain Ned Blakely of *Roughing It*—were all based upon that swashbuckling old mariner, Captain Ned Wakeman of San Francisco, who also has a part to play in the story of Emperor Norton. Naturally, scholars have also searched for a flesh-and-blood counterpart of the "King" in *Huckleberry Finn,* although no one has yet thought to look at another acquaintance of Twain's in his newspaper days, his eccentric next-door neighbor.*

---

* See Appendix B

Still, that's who he is, as you will discover if you stay the course.

Long after a disguised Norton appeared in Twain's most popular novel, Robert Louis Stevenson put him in one of his own, wearing no disguise at all. In Stevenson's *The Wrecker* the Emperor is allowed to be his unmajestically scruffy self.

Now, by all the rules of fiction writing, Norton I really has no business being in that novel at all. He plays no part in its plot, merely wanders into the story, utters a few lines, accepts a snifter of brandy, and then wanders out with a nod of his plumed head, leaving a modern reader to wonder just who the devil he was. Few readers in Stevenson's day would have wondered, however. Indeed, they would have expected to find Norton in the book and might even have felt cheated if he was not. *The Wrecker* begins in San Francisco in 1879, by which time San Francisco and Emperor Norton had become so inseparable in American minds that to write about one without mentioning the other would have been rather like describing the city today without mentioning its cable cars or its Golden Gate Bridge. And that is obviously why RLS put him in the novel undisguised; it would have been utterly pointless to give him a fictitious name, since the only purpose he could possibly serve in that book was to be himself, the Emperor everyone had heard about.

Perhaps the best proof of Joshua Norton's fame lies in the fact that he had been dead and buried for all of twelve years when *The Wrecker* was published in 1892. One would think that the public's interest in him should have waned considerably by then, which would have been excuse enough for any publisher to delete him from the manuscript. But no, Charles Scribner's Sons left him in the story intact, making no effort to explain him either by footnote or foreword, which suggests to me that he was still too well remembered to require an explanation, even though a dozen years had passed since his death on the other side of the continent.

To test that possibility, I wrote to cities all over the country, asking librarians whether they had anything in their archives about the Emperor of the United States. Back came the replies: *many* of them had found mention of him in local nineteenth-century newspapers, enough to justify my theory.

From other clues that began to emerge as I dug deeper, I learned why the Emperor had been so widely known: San Francisco's boosters had little else to talk about when they sought to lure tourists west in the early days of the transcontinental railroad. There was no bridge to brag about in the 1870s, and the cable cars of that time, unlike those now featured in every television show about San Francisco, were rattletrap contrivances that apparently nobody thought deserved a paragraph in another city's papers. The sheer audacity of San Francisco's claim that a ragamuffin was a tourist attraction worth seeing actually got the city all the publicity it needed.

Emperor Norton exists in a dozen books of that bygone day, besides Twain's and Robert Louis Stevenson's. And yet, except in the West, where his fame still lingers, very few Americans today may have heard of the Charlie Chaplinesque tramp (the comparison is inescapable) who kept their great-grandparents laughing for twenty incredible years. The passage of a century has finally dimmed the nation's memory of one of America's most colorful eccentrics.

It's time he was resurrected.

Californians may complain, with some justification, that I have omitted a great deal of the Emperor's story in this biography. I can only plead that it would have taken another volume, possibly thicker than this one, to tell all that is known about him as well as everything I discovered in archives hitherto unexplored.

Something had to go to make room for this new material, so I decided not to rehash what is already familiar to those who love the Emperor (except when it is just too good to ignore), but confine myself to things that will add to their knowledge. Much of what you will read here, therefore, will be new even to California's historians (for example, that Joshua Norton was an inventor, a gifted man whose only idiosyncrasy was that he imagined himself to be the nation's ruler).

To those who have never heard of His Imperial Majesty, this book must read like a work of fiction. But it should be remembered that Norton the First himself lived a life of fiction (although he never suspected it), believing until the end of his days that he was the Emperor of the United States and Protector of Mexico.

William Drury
San Francisco, 1986

NORTON I
Emperor of the United States

Chapter 1
Death of a Guttersnipe

———◆◇◆———

> *O, dear, it was always a painful thing for me to see the Emperor begging, for although nobody else believed he was an Emperor, he believed it.*
>
> —Mark Twain

The Emperor of the United States died in the street on the night of January 8, 1880, in the rain that streamed through the gleam of a gas lamp. His uniform was soiled and sodden and the plumes on his hat wilted in the downpour. He died oblivious to the throng gathering about him in the dusk, his breath slipping away in the bubbles of froth that dribbled down his damp gray beard. A clattering cable car, clanging its bell as it breasted the crest of San Francisco's steepest street on its way from the bay to Nob Hill, drowned the sigh that signaled the end of an extraordinary era and the flight of an uncommon soul.

The police arrived with a wagon and carted his corpse to the morgue, where His Imperial Majesty was laid on a marble slab and stripped of his dignity. Some telegrams were discovered in his bedraggled blue tunic. One, bearing the exalted name of Alexander II of Russia, complimented the American sovereign upon his impending marriage to Queen Victoria. Another cable beseeched him to consider the political consequences of such a union. "No good will come from it," warned the President of France, ever ready to distrust the motives of monarchs.

An old purse, removed from his rain-soaked trousers, yielded unexpected treasures: a gold piece worth two and a half dollars, three dollars in silver, and a French franc dated 1828. It was rather more than the mortuary workers usually found on a body brought in from the streets. Had this been an ordinary stiff, they might have pocketed the coins and glibly declared him penniless, but word of the Emperor's death had swiftly reached the newspaper offices, and reporters had already assembled to witness and record every detail, even to the date on a franc.

A bundle of papers found in his tattered uniform coat was unfolded and examined. They proved to be his Imperial Government bonds, each valued at fifty cents but really worth no more than the telegrams that wags had sent him in jest. The newspapermen read the fraudulent messages, making note of their contents, stole a few of the Emperor's bonds to keep as souvenirs, and then went off to break the sad news to the nation.

All night the sky wept. So did the papers next day.

"On the reeking pavement, in the darkness of a moonless night, under the dripping rain, and surrounded by wondering strangers," the *Morning Call* told a waking city, "Norton the First, by the grace of God Emperor of the United States and Protector of Mexico, departed this life."

"Le Roi Est Mort," mourned the *Chronicle*.

Many columns were squandered that weekend on Joshua Abraham Norton, the bedlam beggar who thought he was royalty. The story was splashed on every front page. Nothing else seemed to matter. California's new governor, George C. Perkins, searching the newspapers in Sacramento for some word about his inauguration the day before, must have been humiliated to discover that the death of a guttersnipe was considered much more important. One paper he had thought he could count on, the influential *Alta California*, his stoutest supporter during the election campaign, had actually dismissed his Inaugural Address in thirty-eight words, a mere four and a half lines, insultingly squeezed into a column of bad jokes and other trivia under the heading "Brevities." It gave the guttersnipe thirty-four inches.

But the beggar's name, unlike the governor's, was known the length and breadth of the land. "His eccentricities made him almost world-famous," the *Alta* said, with little exaggeration. Editors in cities that did not care a hoot who governed California would pick up this story and print it. Cincinnati's *Enquirer*, Cleveland's *Plain Dealer*, Seattle's *Intelligencer*, Denver's *Rocky Mountain News*, Philadelphia's *Public Record*, Portland's *Oregonian*, and *The New York Times* had already plucked it from the telegraph wires and sent it to their compositors.

In Cincinnati the *Enquirer* devoted sixteen inches to the Emperor's passing under what must have been the longest-winded headline in the history of American journalism:

LAID LOW

Emperor Norton Gives Up the Ghost and Surrenders His Scepter to the Man on the Pale Horse. The City by the Golden Gate Mourns Her Illustrious Dead. An Emperor Without Enemies, a King Without a Kingdom, Gone to Kingdom Come. Supported in Life by the Willing Tribute of a Free People, He Drops Dead at a Street Corner and Now Knows What Lies Beyond.

Mark Twain read of the Emperor's death in Elmira, New York, and it brought back memories. Long before, when he was a reporter in San Francisco, he had scribbled news items about Norton I for the *Morning Call*. The reporter and the Emperor had come a long way since then.

For twenty years Joshua Norton had trudged the city's sloping streets in broken boots and comic-opera uniform, a sword at his belt and a ridiculous hackle of peacock feathers and rooster quills in his hat, God's fool in tatters and tinsel, utterly convinced that he was destiny's choice to rule an American empire.

He was San Francisco's most popular tourist attraction. Those who came West on the transcontinental railroad knew all about the mad monarch from the travel books they had read. They bought picture postcards of Norton the First, Emperor Norton dolls in feathered hats, Emperor Norton Brand cigars with his portrait on the label, and colored lithographs of the Emperor to display beside the Currier prints in Victorian parlors. Plays and operettas were written about him, cartoonists caricatured him for the magazines, and tradesmen with a covetous eye on a wayfarer's wallet hung signs in their windows to boast that they enjoyed his royal patronage, even when they did not. "Fine Wines and Spirituous Liquors by Appointment to His Majesty, Norton I" lent a touch of distinction to a tavern that no East Coast hostelry could hope to match with a simple "George Washington Slept Here." The tourists chuckled and slapped their thighs, then went home with their souvenirs to add their own embroideries to the story that San Francisco's boosters were spreading far and wide.

They told how the city paid the Emperor homage, how fawning bankers bowed and scraped before him, how the politicians groveled for his favors, how the magnates and millionaires humbly bent the knee, how even the surly policeman on his beat respectfully saluted as he passed. He dined in the best of restaurants, they said, and never paid a bill; attended the theaters without a ticket; traveled his realm as an honored guest of the railroads; and entrusted his wardrobe to tailors and haberdashers who charged him not a penny. Ambrose Bierce could not resist a cynical parting shot in his weekly *Argonaut* when he heard that Norton had died of sanguineous apoplexy (in a gutter, as guttersnipes are supposed to die):

> In his own opinion he had a divine right to be maintained at the expense of others; to lead a useless, vagabond life, like other imperial mendicants; to get money and be supported like other kings out of a place. And who shall say that the Emperor was not right? Who shall presume to question the sanity of a mind that for twenty-three years enabled its body to live in luxury and idleness without physical or mental toil?

Despite his reputation as the city's gadfly, quick to prick her fibbers and fools, even "Bitter" Bierce was not above embellishing a bedtime story upon which her tourist trade thrived, though he must have raised a few eyebrows when he declared that the vagabond king lived in luxury, since it was common knowledge that he lived in a flophouse.

Robert Louis Stevenson gilded the lily, too, in the book he wrote years later with his Californian stepson, Lloyd Osbourne, who grew up in a time when children saw Emperor Norton as a fairy-tale character they could actually talk to and touch (which gave him a decided edge over Mother Goose and Jack Horner). But fairy-tale characters belong in fairy tales, so bear in mind that *The Wrecker*— published when Stevenson was at the height of his fame and could afford to share a title page with a young relative itching to see his own name in print—was a novel only very loosely based upon what the Scot saw and heard.

> Of all our visitors, I believe I preferred Emperor Norton; the very mention of whose name reminds me I am doing scant justice to the folks of San Francisco. In what other city would a harmless madman who supposed himself emperor of the two Americas [the United States and Mexico] have been so fostered and encouraged? Where else would even the people of the streets have respected the poor soul's illusion? Where else would bankers and merchants have received his visits, cashed his cheques, and submitted to his small assessments? Where else would he have been suffered to attend and address the exhibition days of schools and colleges? where else, in God's green earth, have taken his pick of restaurants, ransacked the bill of fare and departed scathless? They tell me he was even an exacting patron, threatening to withdraw his custom when dissatisfied; and I can believe it, for his face wore an expression distinctly gastronomical.

The novelist, who had arrived in San Francisco just two weeks before the Emperor's demise (in pursuit of Osbourne's mother, whom he married) knew only the fable, not the facts, and had to rely heavily on the stories he heard from Harry Biggelow of the *Examiner* and little Jimmy Bowman of the *Chronicle,* who showed him the town, two of the very boosters who had created the legend of a great-souled metropolis that so loved a pauper it treated him like a prince.

Stevenson's stepdaughter, Isobel Field, added to that legend with a book of her own. "He was a gentle, kindly man," she remembered in *This Life I've Loved,* "and fortunately found himself in the friendliest, most sentimental city in the world, the idea being 'let him be emperor if he wants to.' San Francisco played the game with him."

San Francisco did play the game, not merely because it was friendly and sentimental (no one could quarrel with that), but because it had a good head for business. Those who bent the knee, addressing him as "Your Majesty" without a wisp of a grin, were not entirely altruistic. The politicians courted him, in public if not in private, because he was the people's mascot, and to have shown him disrespect would have cost them votes. Editors willingly published the "royal proclamations" that flowed from his pen because his name sold newspapers. Theater managers gave him free seats because no opening night was considered complete without the Emperor's presence; he was part of the show. Leland Stanford, the president of the Central Pacific Railroad (and founder of Stanford University), gave Norton a pass to travel because the press was accusing the railroad magnate of avarice and he hoped to offset this villainous image by posing as a benefactor to the needy. No other deadhead could repay a small boon with a profusion of favorable publicity.

Not all of them played the game. When Biggelow and Bowman showed Stevenson the shops that advertised they were "Gentleman's Outfitters to His Imperial Majesty," did the marveling visitor think to ask why the Emperor was such a scarecrow? Had he dared to enter a fashionable restaurant in "all his dirt and unsavoriness"—Mark Twain's words—a fastidious maitre d'hotel would have quickly shown him the door. That yarn was pure Biggelow.

In what other city would a harmless madman have been so fostered and encouraged? Well, perhaps almost any city that yearned for a tourist attraction as effective as Emperor Norton. Other cities, in fact, had tried to lure him away. What else but a bribe was the famous Serpent Scepter, an elaborately carved walking-stick presented by "his faithful web-footed subjects" in Portland, Oregon? And what but the fear of losing him prompted San Francisco's leading daily paper to remind His Majesty that to forsake California for web-footed Oregon would be to swap sunshine for rain? Walking-sticks were favorite gifts; the reporters who searched the Emperor's lodgings, within an hour of his death, found more than a dozen from cities anxious to have him.

He had his imitators, of course. One, King Stellifer the First, turned up in New York City and briefly captured the nation's attention, but lacking the Emperor's flair for publicity, failed to win the support of the business community and was exiled to a lunatic asylum. New York did not believe in fairy-tale characters who could not promise a pot of gold at *both* ends of the rainbow.

Once the Emperor was wealthy. That was back in the Gold Rush years, when the world was mad and he was presumed to be sane. Twain's old paper, the *Morning Call*, which had been digging into city and county records, revealed that he was "one of the largest land speculators in those early times." Some of the tallest buildings in the financial district now stood on land that used to be his.

Jimmy Bowman went to the Pacific Club, an exclusive haunt of the rich, to interview its president, Joseph G. Eastland, who had been a business associate of Norton's in palmier days. Eastland told the man from the *Chronicle* that the ragamuffin had then been worth at least a quarter of a million dollars.

"What brought him down so low?" Bowman asked.

A rice deal, Eastland said. The Emperor had tried to corner the rice market, a disastrous venture in which he lost everything—lost his real estate, lost his riches, lost his reason.

Eastland, a founding partner in the San Francisco Gas Lighting Company, should have known the exact location of one valuable piece of land that had once belonged to the pauper. His own gasworks stood on it, his company having purchased the property in the hour of Norton's ruin from the banker who held the mortgage, William T. Sherman, the Sherman who nine years later would march a plundering Union army through Georgia to humiliate the South. A bankrupted Joshua Norton might have understood why his land was seized to settle a debt, but a "gentle, kindly man" like the Emperor would never have understood why the banker had burned Atlanta to settle a conflict already won.

That was insane.

Ten thousand came, the newspapers said, to see him lying in state. They came from the suburbs in streetcars pulled by plodding horses, in the crowded cable cars that swooped down the city's hills, in drays from the wharves and the markets, on foot from the slums, in carriages from the palaces of the rich. A platoon of police, struggling to clear a passage for vehicles trapped in the crush, coaxed and prodded the multitude into a ragged queue, four abreast and two blocks long.

The peddlers were busy, selling souvenirs.

"Picture postcards of the Emp! Every one a living likeness!"

"Emperor Norton dolls!"

"Cigars! Emperor Norton cigars!"

Policemen stationed at the door of the morgue marshaled the mourners into a single line, admitting them one by one.

"The visitors included all classes," Jimmy Bowman wrote, "from the capitalist to the pauper, the clergyman and the pickpocket, well-dressed ladies, the bowed with age, and the prattling child." For hours they filed past the casket, covering it with wreaths and bouquets. "Some of the choicest floral tributes came from childish hands, for the kindhearted old man had ever a cheerful smile for children, with whom he was a favorite."

But the fairy-tale character they could talk to and touch had no smile for the children who came to him now. Somehow he looked different. Without his funny old uniform and his funny old hat with its feathers, all the magic had gone.

"Mama, why won't he speak to me?"

"Hush, child, the Emperor is sleeping."

One day they would tell his story to wide-eyed children of their own, proudly saying that they really knew him, that he used to shepherd them into candy shops and command the people behind the counter to give them bonbons that nobody ever had to pay for, because the shops all had signs in their windows to say that they were Confectioners by Appointment to His Imperial Majesty, Norton I. And then there would come a time when no parent could boast of things like that, because there was no one living who had known him, and children would hear only fables about Mother Goose and Jack Horner.

Chapter 2
The Tailor's Tale

Careful now,
We are dealing here with an illusion.

—Ambrose Bierce

Who was he? Where did he come from? Nobody seemed to know. Joshua Norton had been maddeningly mysterious about his origin. His accent was decidedly English, his diction precise and refined, his bearing ponderously dignified, his face that "of a gentleman" in Robert Louis Stevenson's opinion. And to the Bowmans and Biggelows who made up fairy tales, no better evidence was needed to sustain a rumor that he was a secret child of William IV of England by the Irish actress Dorothea Jordan. According to the *Morning Call*:

> It is related that an English visitor who saw Norton, being informed of the story that he was a son of William IV, exclaimed, "Yes, yes, I thought I had seen that face before. Why, he's so much like His Majesty that forty years ago he would have been taken for the King. Just his figure, just his walk, and just about as shabby; just as I have seen him come to the theatre to draw Mrs. Jordan's salary before he became King.

The English visitor, if he really existed outside of a journalist's imagination, must have been incredibly old to remember a royal love affair that had withered seventy years before. He was an unreliable witness, in any event. William Henry, Duke of Clarence, who had ten children by Mrs. Jordan before he became William

IV, was certainly no dandy, but he could hardly have been "just about as shabby" as a tatterdemalion whose dirt and unsavoriness were enough to wrinkle Mark Twain's nose. Nor could he have ever been so short of a shilling that he had to beg for his mistress's wages at a stage door in Drury Lane. One could always send a footman for that.

The *Call* changed its tune, in fact, when its reporter saw Norton in his casket after the undertakers had cleaned him up, suggesting that he might have been an illegitimate son of Napoleon III of France: "There was the same lofty forehead, aquiline nose, and short imperial [beard]." But Jimmy Bowman quickly scotched that, pointing out in the *Chronicle* that Norton was much too old to be a son of the late Emperor of the French, if the age inscribed on the silver plate attached to his coffin lid was correct: "Louis Napoleon, who was born at the palace of the Tuileries on April 20, 1808, if still living, would be his senior by only six years."

The age on the coffin lid, however, was merely a guess. At the inquest, Eva Hutchinson, the landlady of Eureka Lodgings, the cheap hotel that was the Emperor's home for seventeen years, had testified that to the best of her belief he was "a Jew of London birth." And his age? Oh, about sixty-five. The coroner, lacking a birth certificate or any other material evidence, had simply accepted her word. And so the plate on his casket had been inscribed:

JOSHUA A. NORTON
DIED JANUARY 8, 1880
AGED 65 YEARS

But a Jew? Surely not. For the Reverend William Githens of the Episcopal Church of the Advent, who had conducted the funeral service at the morgue, had sent him on his way to a Christian's reward with an Episcopalian prayer and a children's choir singing "Jesus, Savior of my Soul."

In the little town of Vallejo, north of San Francisco Bay, lived a man who knew the truth. Or thought he did.

Nathan Peiser was a tailor, an Englishman aged about sixty. After reading all the wild theories about the Emperor's birth in the metropolitan newspapers, he went to see the editor of the Vallejo *Chronicle* and told him a tale he had sworn never to tell. And here is the tale he told that paper:

In 1842 I was one of the crew of the English transport ship *Waterloo,* on our way from London to Australia with 300 persons on board, consisting of officers, sailors, soldiers and transports [convicts bound for Botany Bay]. Becoming short of water, the ship put into Cape Town on the coast of Africa on the 25th day of August of that same year. While riding at anchor in Table Bay, three days later, a terrific north-easter swept over the water and caused the anchors to drag until the ship ran upon a reef of rocks and was dashed to pieces. A hundred and ninety-seven were drowned and many severely injured. Some of the men managed to save themselves by being taken ashore in lifeboats. I was among the unfortunate ones who received severe injuries and was taken to the English hospital on the outskirts of the town.

In Cape Town there was a number of merchants of Jewish extraction, and fearing that some of their friends might be among the injured at the hospital, a party called one day; among the number was a Mr. Norton, an Englishman, who was keeping a ship chandlery store in Cape Town. I, being a Jew, attracted his attention and we formed an acquaintance, and as luck would have it, I chanced to know his brother and several of his friends in London. Mr. Norton immediately had me taken to his residence and introduced me to his wife and children. The eldest of the children was Joshua Norton, the late "Emperor" Norton, then a young man between twenty-five and thirty years old. I was two or three years younger. At that time he talked freely of his birthplace as being in London.

While enjoying the hospitality of Mr. Norton, Jewish prayers were frequently said, which was always a source of amusement to Joshua. One day he provoked the father to such an extent that, old as he was, he received a castigation. While at Cape Town we were both very intimate, and Joshua assisted his father in the ship-chandlery store as a clerk, and had a keen, business-like air, and was much admired by the young as well as the old people in the settlement.

Peiser remained in Cape Town eleven months, living with the Nortons, then shipped out in a German vessel bound for Hamburg, eventually making his way to the United States, where he enlisted in a New York regiment and fought in the Civil War. When the war ended he sailed for San Francisco, where he wandered into a lodging house, looking for a place to stay. As he was talking to the landlord, he heard a heavy tread on the stairs and the thump of a walking-stick.

> In a moment in walked a man wearing a faded uniform with tarnished epaulets, a Kossuth hat with gold cord and an ostrich's plume on his head, and a twisted, knotted stick under his arm. As he entered the room, he raised the hat and, taking a red silk handkerchief from his pocket, wiped the perspiration from his brow. As he raised the hat from his head, it flashed across my mind that the man before me was my old friend, Joshua Norton, for there was the same stout figure, though bent with age, and the same striking countenance I had seen so often in the ship chandler's store on the African coast.

The landlord, David Hutchinson, introduced an astonished Peiser to His Imperial Majesty, Norton I.

> He at first did not seem to recollect me, until I called to his mind the wreck of the *Waterloo* and my being at his father's house. All at once he said, "Why, yes, Nathan, I distinctly remember you, and the correction I received for raising a disturbance at a Jewish prayer meeting."

A strange way to greet a friend one has not seen for about a quarter of a century. To remind Nathan, immediately upon meeting him, of a reprimand that he himself had once received, fully twenty-five years before, seems oddly out of place in a salutation. Most people would have said, "Why, yes, I remember you. It's been such a long time! How are you? I'm very glad to see you," or words to that effect, and not even thought of mentioning a scolding from an angry parent until much later, when sitting down to discuss old times together at leisure. But Joshua was not like others, and he must have been momentarily stunned to encounter the one man in America who knew all about his past life as a chandler's son in Cape Town and might very well reveal it.

It's possible, of course, that Joshua did mention the incident of the prayer meeting in later conversation and that Peiser actually quoted him out of sequence when he talked to the editor in Vallejo. But let it pass, because *what* His Majesty said counts more than *when* he said it. And we shall return to this later, for it happens to be more significant than at first appears. Meanwhile, Nathan still has the floor and is about to be flabbergasted further.

> I was then invited up another flight of stairs to his room, and we had a long conversation about his father, mother and sisters. I asked him, on the score of old friendship, to tell me how it was that he came by the title of Emperor, and why he wore the uniform he then had on. For some cause or other, the demeanor of the old man changed all of a sudden and he raised himself from the edge of his single bed and went to the door and turned the key, then stepped to where I was sitting in amazement at his strange proceedings, and stooping down almost whispered that before he would tell me he would first impose a silence upon my lips never to reveal to anyone about his folks at Cape Town. I thought it strange but, being interested, readily gave the promise.
>
> My old friend then told me that he was not the son of Mr. Norton of Cape Town, but a crown prince to the throne of France; that he had been sent to Cape Town to save himself from being assassinated; that he was adopted by Mr. Norton and had retained his name for the love he had for him, and taken the title "Emperor," which he was rightly entitled to bear; that the uniform was presented to him by Queen Victoria; and all the people, here and in Mexico, were his subjects.
>
> I looked at the man a moment and then told him I thought he was crazy; to which he replied, "And so do a good many others."

Shortly after His Majesty's encounter with Nathan Peiser, the sailor turned tailor, a Jewish newspaper in Cincinnati got wind of the story. The *American Israelite,* published by the famous Reverend Isaac Mayer Wise, the founder of Reform Judaism, asked the Emperor if it was true he was a Jew.

"How can I be a Jew," he had answered, "seeing I am so nearly related to the Bourbons?"

Odd that no one noticed the significance of the 1828 franc found in his purse at the morgue. It bore the face of Charles X, the last of the Bourbons, a King of France whose portrait any man might have been proud to keep if he believed himself to be a Bourbon.

Chapter 3

Boy on a Broomstick Horse

"Yes, my friend, it is true—your eyes is lookin' at this very moment on the pore disappeared Dauphin, Looy the Seventeen, son of Looy the Sixteen and Marry Antonette . . . you see before you, in blue jeans and misery, the wanderin', exiled, trampled-on, and sufferin' rightful King of France."

—*The Adventures of Huckleberry Finn*

Joshua Norton was born in the London borough of Deptford on a day lost to mortal memory. No trace of a birthdate can be found in England's incomplete files, but there is one broad hint in the archives of a land far from England. On May 2, 1820, when John and Sarah Norton arrived at the Cape of Good Hope with three small children, one a babe in Sarah's arms, John told an immigration clerk that the boy they called Joshua Abraham—that one there, clutching his mother's skirts and gaping fearfully at the Hottentots who handled their baggage—was two years old. So there you have it from a father's lips; he was born in 1818. No one can say more than that. If the circumstances of his birth are obscure, it was surely not because there was a French prince to hide, as he told Nathan Peiser. Britain was brimming with misplaced Bourbon princes in 1818, the children and grandchildren of royal refugees from the guillotines of the French Revolution, but there is no factual, historical reason to suppose that he was one of them.

Still, Joshua himself thought there was good reason to believe it, as we shall see in this chapter.

John Norton was twenty-five, Sarah twenty-two, when they disembarked from the vessel *La Belle Alliance*. Their eldest child, Louis, was four years old, and the infant, Philip, born at sea, was quite possibly the youngest of all the five thousand immigrants who swarmed ashore from a score of ships anchored in Algoa Bay. South Africa knows them as the 1820 Settlers, the Cape's first British colonists. Among them were eighteen Jews, the only Jews in that historic exodus from a Britain impoverished by war to the promised land called Good Hope, a Dutch possession until it was wrenched from Napoleon Bonaparte's grasp. The land that London had promised John Norton proved to be a hundred barren acres on the Great Fish River in Albany, a wilderness long known to the Dutch as Die Zuurveld, the sour field. Across the river lay Kaffraria, the hostile land of the Xhosa.

The Boers of the Zuurveld nicknamed the 1820 Settlers "Cockney gardeners." When flood, drought, and blight, one after the other, destroyed their crops during the first three years, many settlers turned to occupations for which they were better suited. One Jewish couple, Morris and Phyllis Sloman, farming on the Fish near the Nortons, moved to Cape Town after losing their son, Mark, age eight, to a Xhosa spear while the boy was tending cattle. John kept a wary eye on the border river for clay-daubed raiders who might harm his own family, which now included a teething daughter named Esther. He must have envied a young friend from Deptford, Benjamin Norden, who had prospered rapidly as a businessman in the growing settlement of Graham's Town, where he was now Commissioner of the Municipality (town council member). If a sympathetic Norden had not advanced John the capital to open a general store in Graham's Town the son called Joshua Abraham might have lived out his days on the Fish with a plough, and no one would ever have heard of him.

Madness was waiting in Graham's Town.

Psychiatrists today generally agree that schizophrenia, a mental disorder characterized by private fantasy and unrealistic behavior, germinates in the springtime years between puberty and early adulthood. If that is so, then Joshua Norton did not go mad in

California because of business losses, as everyone said, but was already half-mad when he got there.

It all began in Graham's Town when he was a boy.

In the beginning his grasp on reality was probably no weaker than any other small boy's, no weaker and no stronger. Children play games in their heads, indulging in delightful daydreams that can easily transform a wooden sword into Excalibur and a broomstick into a prancing steed. Such illusions normally vanish with the approach of adolescence, but for Joshua that would be the time when the seeds of more peculiar notions would start to sprout.

To explain why he later thought he was royalty, some curious facts about his childhood must be brought to light.

When Jewish historians pay tribute to the pioneers who carried the sacred Torah from England to the Cape and built the first synagogue there, they speak of Benjamin Norden and John Norton. But these two did something that endeared them to Gentiles, too. An Anglican bishop's plea for funds to give the settlement a church, to be known as St. George's, touched these men of another faith and both responded at once, passing the hat to every Jew in Albany. So it can be said that, long before they built a Hebrew temple, they helped to build the first Christian church on the frontier. (It stands there still, as St. George's Cathedral, a time-honored monument to the brotherhood of men of different faiths who joined hands to make a holy place for the God that both revered, though some would never pray there because their way of worship was not the minister's.)

John's store flourished to such an extent that soon he could afford to send his oldest son to college. When the South African College—now the University of Cape Town—opened its doors in 1829, Louis was enrolled among its first students. Eleven-year-old Joshua watched his brother's ox-wagon disappear in dust across the veld, then went back to his desk in the crude little schoolhouse called Grubb's Academy, where he received the rudiments of an education from a Cockney gardener who had decided it might be more rewarding to plant ideas in fertile young minds than crops in a sour field.

C. C. Grubb was his name. The early chroniclers, who found him worthy of mention because he was the only teacher on the frontier, neglected to say whether he was tall or short, stern or mild, or even whether he was christened with anything more than two initials. But they did leave an example of his thriftiness. To save money on pencils and paper, he made his pupils write and do their sums with their forefingers in boxes of sand. Precious little expense was wasted on the education of a future emperor.

That Mr. Grubb attended St. George's goes without saying. He could never have mustered enough pupils to open an academy in that solidly Anglican community if he had not demonstrated his allegiance to the Church of England, for he was expected to follow the practice of schoolteachers in the mother country, beginning each day with a passage from the Bible—Authorized Version— and a recitation from the Book of Common Prayer.

This daily instruction in Christianity would have a telling effect on a boy who had to chant prayers in Hebrew at home, a language he did not understand. There was no rabbi to teach him the ancient lessons of his people, none in all of South Africa. John would have to fill that role as best he could. He was doomed to fail, though. Joshua was growing up in a society completely dominated by Christians. The Nortons and the Nordens were the only Jews in Graham's Town, the only Jews he knew, and the only house of worship was a church with a Protestant clergyman whose stipend was paid by the government (to ensure that the King's religion would reign supreme in his African colony). Joshua's immature mind was bound to bend under the combined weight of church and state. Soon he would begin to question his father's faith. Then he would reject it.

His given names may have embarrassed him. A boy called Joshua Abraham, in a town of Georges and Jameses, must have seemed a bit of an oddity to his playmates, and they, as children will, would have been quick to poke fun. Why was he, and he alone of John Norton's three sons, chosen to bear such obvious Old Testament names? Why were his parents so anxious to emphasize *his* Hebrew heritage more than that of his brothers?

Actually, the greater mystery lay in John and Sarah's choice of names for their first child and their third. Louis and Philip were Bourbon names, royal Catholic names. And that's a mystery worth exploring.

In September 1792, when the first aristocratic refugees came streaming out of France with the staggering news that Louis XVI and Marie Antoinette had been imprisoned with their two children, they were coldly received in England, where there was little sympathy for a Catholic king whose aid to the rebels in America had cost a Protestant king thirteen colonies. Fanny Burney, the novelist, who was Mistress of the Robes to George III's queen, caustically described the boorish treatment accorded a daughter-in-law of the Duke of Broglie. Madame de Broglie and her small son, after a stormy Channel crossing in a cockleshell boat, had tried to rent a house in an English village but were rebuffed "upon the Christian-like supposition that, being nothing but French papishes, they would never pay."

France's declaration of war on England, following the execution of Louis XVI, did much to change that attitude. Twenty-one years later, with Napoleon's defeat at Leipzig and the capitulation of Paris, Miss Burney was happy to report the vastly different feelings of those who crowded London's streets to cheer the brother of the guillotined king when he returned to France as Louis XVIII. In his farewell speech he delighted the British by praising them for the part they had played in the Bourbon restoration:

"It is to this glorious country, and to the confidence of its citizens, along with Providence, that I attribute the re-establishment of our house upon the throne of our ancestors."

After that encomium the entire island kingdom of an aged and insane George III broke out in a veritable rash of British babies named Louis. No one could have guessed that, in less than a year, Louis XVIII would again be in exile, at least for a hundred days, until British and Prussian armies at Waterloo thrashed Bonaparte for the last time and shipped him off to St. Helena. That was in 1815, the year that John Norton married Sarah Simmonds, who gave him the son they named Louis.

It probably pained the young couple's parents that John and Sarah did not observe the Jewish custom of naming their child after a deceased relative or friend. Family disapproval may have prompted them to make up for it by naming their second son Joshua Abraham. But what about their third? All one can say is that in 1820, when Philip was born in *La Belle Alliance,* the Nortons were far at sea with no one to object if they gave him a Bourbon name, too.

For one so deeply concerned about the preservation of his own religion in a colony with so few Jews that it was not yet possible to build a synagogue or support a rabbi, it must be admitted that John Norton's interest in perpetuating the memory of a Catholic royal family did seem strange. Even the newest infant at Sarah's breast was named Louisa, a feminine version of Louis. It was enough to puzzle any son named Joshua Abraham.

Perhaps it was now that Joshua began to toy with the notion that he might be of exalted birth. At first it would be no more than a schoolboy's idle fancy, the sort of fantasy that fits in nicely with wooden swords and broomstick horses, but as he matured his imagination would build it into a tower of truth.

Meanwhile, when he was twelve, hovering on the very brink of that dangerous season when schizophrenia begins to bud unnoticed in an unwary young mind, a dramatic event occurred that was the talk of Graham's Town. The crown of France was again snatched from a Bourbon head.

England had made it a condition of the Bourbon restoration that Louis XVIII must rule under the terms of a charter, such as the Magna Carta, which restricted the powers and privileges of her own royal sovereigns. This appalled the new king's brother, Charles, Count of Artois, who had seen Britain's constitutional monarchy at work during his years of exile and wanted no part of a system that dared to clip the wings of a king.

"I would rather saw wood than be King of France under the conditions imposed upon the Kings of England," he had scoffed.

Charles sincerely believed that Bourbons were chosen to rule by God and so could do as they pleased. When he succeeded the childless Louis, as Charles X, he commanded France to march backward to the absolute monarchy of the past. Hostility grew with every step. In July 1830, he dismissed the Chamber of Deputies and sent police to smash the presses of those newspaper editors who most vigorously opposed him. That did it. Up went the barricades, out came the pistols and pikes. Within a week Paris was in the hands of the insurgents and the King's guards were on the run.

Charles offered to abdicate in favor of a grandson, the Count of Chambord, age ten, but the French would have nothing further to do with Bourbons, great or small. They offered the crown to his more liberal cousin, Louis Philippe, Duke of Orleans, proclaiming him "King of the French by the Grace of God and the Will of the

People," as if to remind him that in modern France the people did the choosing and God merely rubber-stamped their choice. That, to the departing Charles, was heresy. Wearily he crossed the Channel again to England, where he had spent so many years, banished by the first Revolution, and where he would now end his days (which would not be many, for he was seventy-three). So passed the Bourbon king whose coin would be found in a pauper's purse in California fifty years later.

One day, when he is old and gray, Joshua will tell a man who had known his parents that he was not the son of John Norton but a crown prince of France who had been sent to the Cape "to save himself from being assassinated."

"I think you are crazy," Nathan Peiser would say.

"And so do a good many others," the Emperor would calmly reply, as if to imply that he knew something about French history that the historians would never know.

For where better to hide a French prince, Joshua must have "reasoned," than in the home of English Jews who had already shown their devotion to the Bourbon cause by giving their firstborn a Bourbon name? John and Sarah, having perhaps thoroughly displeased their kinfolk by naming a Jewish child after a Bourbon king, had placated them—and fooled them—by naming a Bourbon child Joshua Abraham.

A bit farfetched? Oh, absolutely. But it might have been the only sort of explanation likely to satisfy a mind that could build an empire out of nothing but dreams.

Royal changelings were not a bit uncommon when Joshua was growing up. Cape Colony's newspapers seemed to be filled with stories about people who claimed to have been robbed of a crown. Kaspar Hauser astounded Europe in 1828 when he limped into history by way of Nuremberg, a stumbling, mumbling, bumbling young vagrant with an incoherent yarn about his being kept in a dungeon for all of his sixteen years. Many thought his imprisonment pretty strong evidence that he was really the Grand Duke Stefan of Baden, who was kidnapped from his cradle when hardly more than a fortnight old. (His mysterious murder in 1833 caused even the staid London *Times* to look askance at the reigning Grand Duke Leopold, whose right to rule had been in serious dispute while the boy was alive). Then there was Maria Stella, Countess Newborough, the Italian widow of an English peer, whose autobiography in 1830 declared Louis Philippe, the new King of the French, to be the humble son of a village constable in Tuscany, supposedly swapped at birth for a daughter inconveniently born to the wife of that Duke of Orleans known as Philippe Egalité, who needed a male child to carry on his line (the unwanted daughter being Lady Newborough).

But, without any doubt, the most famous of all was the Prussian clockmaker who professed to be the long-lost son of Louis XVI and Queen Marie Antoinette, the crown prince who should have been Louis XVII.

The clockmaker, Karl Wilhelm Naundorff, arrived in Paris shortly after the July Revolution that unseated Charles X and elevated Louis Philippe, insisting that the crown was his. Naundorff claimed to be none other than Louis Charles de Bourbon, Duke of Normandy, the Dauphin of France, who at the age of eight became king in the eyes of all French royalists the instant the guillotine blade kissed his father's neck.

Louis Charles, caged alone in the ancient Temple, was supposed to have perished in prison of a wasting disease, but there was mystery surrounding that death. No one who could identify the Dauphin was permitted to see the body, which was buried at night in a hidden grave, thus lending an air of credibility to Naundorff's story that he was spirited out of the Temple by his jailer, who had locked a deaf mute in his room, a child who could not protest. To prove he was Louis Charles he produced a variety of witnesses who had served the royal family in happier days at Versailles, all of whom swore that he was the Dauphin. When he sued the government of Louis Philippe for the return of the Dauphin's estate, he was expelled from the country. In London he turned inventor and published his memoirs, the sale of which must have been helped enormously by newspaper accounts of several attempts made on his life. His workshop was set ablaze and he was badly burned. A second fire destroyed his home, but he escaped the flames. And once, in the backyard lavatory behind his house, where he was literally a sitting target, he was shot in the breast with a bullet fired through the door.

Naundorff was possibly the most plausible of some thirty "lost Dauphins" who plagued Louis XVIII, Charles X, and Louis Philippe. The press reports of their escapades, arriving at the Cape with every ship, kept English and Dutch Afrikaner tongues wagging from Table Bay to the Fish. In a frontier town like Graham's Town, where the only diversion after sundown was to sit on the stoop and swap stories, many an evening must have been spent discussing the claims of Karl Naundorff, Kasper Hauser, and Lady Newborough. And all of this gossip about royal infants abducted and reared as commoners was sure to impress a country shopkeeper's son already dreaming an impossible dream.

Six of Sarah's nine children were born on the border. After Esther and Louisa came Selina, Mary Ann, Henry, and Benjamin John, all named for friends or relatives long gone. No more Bourbon names for small English Jews. There were no more Bourbon kings.

And far too few Jews in Albany for growing Nortons to marry; almost all would marry Gentiles. When Louis and Philip took Scottish brides, John made Louis a partner in the store and bought Philip a farm. He was also generous to a son who would never marry. In 1839, when Joshua was twenty-one, his father gave him the capital to open a ship chandlery on the coast in partnership with Henry Kirch, a young Afrikaner who had just married seventeen-year-old Esther, and a happy Mrs. Kirch bounced off in a stagecoach to Algoa Bay with her Gentile husband and the brother who was no longer certain what he was.

Benjamin Norden, just twenty-two when he disembarked from *La Belle Alliance* with the Nortons in 1820, had built a wharf at Algoa Bay on the site where the settlers had landed. Now a fine harbor flourished there, Port Elizabeth. Joshua rented a warehouse, close to Norden's Wharf, and over its door painted the sign "Joshua Norton & Company." It was April the first, hardly an auspicious date. Within eighteen months he was bankrupt.

And that, too, may have helped unhinge him.

Norden was now Commissioner of the Municipality in Cape Town. On September 27, 1841, the eve of the Day of Atonement, seventeen men met in his home to read the Kol Nidre service. It was the first meeting of Jews for public worship in South Africa. A week later he founded Tikvath Israel, the Jewish Community Society of Cape Town. John and Sarah Norton moved to the capital with Joshua and their five youngest children, John to open a ship chandlery, Joshua to be his clerk, John to build a synagogue, Joshua to renounce Judaism.

Joshua's growing apostasy may have troubled John for some time, but he could hardly have guessed the awful extent of it. It came to light at a prayer meeting in their home on Bree Street and a shocked Nathan Peiser was there to witness it. This young sailor, hurled out of the sea on the wind to be a guest of the Nortons for almost a year, has already told the story but it now becomes important to reiterate:

"While enjoying the hospitality of Mr. Norton, Jewish prayers were frequently said, which was always a source of amusement to Joshua. One day he provoked the father to such an extent that, old as he was, he received a castigation." And, according to Peiser, the very first thing Joshua said to him when they met again in San Francisco, twenty-five years later, was: "Why, yes, Nathan, I distinctly remember you, and the correction I received for raising a disturbance at a Jewish prayer meeting."

What a whale of a correction that must have been to have remained in his memory a quarter of a century!

Peiser probably thought Joshua richly deserved it, but the sailor did not know the whole story, and neither did good John Norton, for both were quite unaware of the real reason for Joshua's impious behavior at family worship and the cause of his disgraceful disruption. *What they saw and heard that day was almost certainly the first outward sign of the madness that had been festering in his brain since childhood.* By 1842, at the age of twenty-four, after a decade of doubt about his identity, he had traveled too far along a twisted path to follow a faith to which he had never really felt he was born.

Cape Town was theatrically beautiful; the sun-splashed face of Table Mountain towered over the town like a painted backdrop while the picturesque castle on the beach, facing the harbor, might almost have been a stage prop, placed there by early Dutch settlers merely to enhance the decor. Indeed, the Castle of Good Hope looked much too civilized to be a fortress, a reputation it had managed to preserve for the better part of two hundred years by never firing a cannon except to salute a ship. Officially, it was the home of the Governor of Cape Colony. Unofficially, and to His Excellency's own continual amazement, it served as the home of Old Moses.

Isaac Moses was one of the sights of Cape Town. Joshua must often have seen him grumpily stomping through the Heerengracht in his wide-brimmed hat, his faded army uniform, and his cloak of camel hair and silk, puffing on his Meerschaum pipe and glaring balefully at the shopkeepers who called "Good day, mijnheer" as he passed. The cantankerous old German, a former captain of the 60th Regiment, now living on an army pension, still occupied a room in the castle barracks and dined in the officers' mess. When he was retired from duty, so long ago that nobody could remember, he had simply refused to move out. A succession of British governors had closed their eyes to his unauthorized presence, not knowing quite what to do with him. Despite his disposition, which was as foul as his pipe, he became the castle's mascot, regarded with affection and treated with respect. The sentries at the gates presented arms when he approached—"Gawd! Here comes his bloomin' lordship!"—and any soldier who failed to salute could expect a tongue-lashing. Old Moses would accept no excuse for insubordination.

"Homboggery!" he would growl. "Alles flaussen and homboggery!" It became Cape Town's favorite catchphrase. Everybody used it to express disbelief.

Years later, in a city that never knew Old Moses, Joshua would parade the streets in a faded army uniform, demanding respect for a wholly imaginary rank. Whether he borrowed the idea from the crotchety old man in Cape Town no one will ever know, but it does seem worth considering. Of course, he thoroughly upstaged Old Moses when he called himself Emperor of the United States. Captain Isaac Moses would have thought that sheer homboggery.

Sarah died shortly after Nathan sailed away, and soon after that Louis was killed by a fall from his horse in Graham's Town, in Church Square, before the door of the Christian church his father had helped to build. Then, a year later, a sad letter from a Scottish daughter-in-law on a farm in Albany told John that Philip had succumbed to an illness. John himself was failing in health when he returned to England in 1848 to find a rabbi for Tikvath Israel; ten days after his ship docked in the Thames, he died in Deptford, leaving the bulk of his estate to his oldest surviving son, the one who believed he was *not* the child of John and Sarah Norton (though that did not deter Joshua from accepting a princely inheritance).

In the spring of 1849 the Reverend Isaac Pulver sailed from Deptford to be the colony's first rabbi, arriving twenty years too late to stop a boy on a broomstick horse from a mad ride down a road that a frontier schoolmaster had shown him in the sincere belief that there was no other way to reach the kingdom of glory but the Christian way.

At the Cape of Good Hope there's a legendary bird called the Oof Bird. Its eggs are nuggets of purest gold, and those who hope to rob its nest must listen for its song and follow it. In 1849 Joshua heard the Oof Bird's song, and it came from out of the West. He followed it across the South Atlantic to Rio de Janeiro, and from there to California.

Chapter 4

The Oof Bird's Nest

―――◆―――

*There's a divinity that shapes our ends,
Rough-hew them how we will.*

—*Hamlet,* Act V, Scene ii

Late in the afternoon of November 23, 1849, a tall German ship appeared at the entrance to San Francisco Bay. Her spars creaked and her canvas shuddered, smacked by the buffeting wind, as she turned her stern to the sullen Pacific and ploughed through the Golden Gate. Captain Nicholas Deach gazed with dismay upon the great bay that now stretched before him. For more than three months, since Rio de Janeiro, he had battled gales and misfortune; yet even now, safe inside the sound, his troubles were far from over. The ships in the bay told him that. More than four hundred rusted at anchor, abandoned by crews gone in search of gold. His own men could not be trusted. Most, perhaps all, would probably desert.

The seven passengers he carried were all on deck with their baggage, eager to land, the perils of the voyage almost forgotten as they scanned the sand and scrub on shore for some sign of a port not yet in sight, hidden by a distant headland from which a mirror flashed.

"What ship?" asked the heliograph.

The incoming German winked a reply.

"*Franzeska,* Deach, Hamburg."

Some boats came out to guide the creeping vessel through the forsaken fleet of brigs and barks. As she rounded the headland

San Francisco suddenly appeared, a dense cluster of wooden buildings on the edge of a cove surrounded by hills, its muddy streets climbing steeply from the water to the sky.

The mirror on Telegraph Hill blinked a last message, reflecting the glint of a setting sun. For Joshua Norton the golden gleam signaled the end of an odyssey. He had found the Oof Bird's nest.

Peter Robertson, a young shipping clerk from Baltimore with money to invest, agreed to join him as the junior partner of Joshua Norton & Company, General Merchants. They searched the teeming town for an office and found one on the waterfront, a room in a cottage made of adobe bricks beside a busy wharf. It wasn't much of a place, but the commission agents and auctioneers who leased its mud-walled chambers probably would have paid an exorbitant rent to the skinflint who owned it.

James Lick has gone down in history as California's most eccentric millionaire. He ate frugally, dressed in rags, and drove about in a creaking cart, collecting bones from butcher shops, which he ground into dust to enrich his orchards in the Santa Clara Valley, south of the bay. A visiting nephew confirmed all this after Lick's death, complaining bitterly that he was made to sleep on top of an old piano. But others had good reason to remember the miser more fondly, for he sleeps today high on a mountain overlooking his valley, entombed beneath the splendid Lick Observatory that was only a part of his generous bequest to the University of California, whose regents never had to lie on his piano and so bore him no malice.

Lick, a Pennsylvanian, arrived in San Francisco when it was still a sleepy trading village of less than five hundred people—before the Gold Rush increased that handful to more than thirty thousand within a single year and the price of land soared beyond all reason. His offer of three thousand dollars for a lot beside the cove, therefore, seemed fair enough to Alfred J. Ellis, who had built the cottage on it. When Norton and Robertson came to its door, seeking a room, it's possible that neither partner had yet heard the macabre story told about that cottage when it was a tavern called The Points.

Alfred Ellis had named it because of the view. From its windows could be seen the headlands, Clark's Point and Rincon Point, between which lay the crescent cove. Both points were probably lost on Ellis's customers, roistering seamen more interested in liquor than landscape. Apparently they never suspected the innkeeper of diluting his whiskey, although after a while they did notice a marked change in its flavor. Some said it tasted abominable; others commended it highly, declaring that it improved as it aged. In time its taste became so strong that only a true connoisseur would drink it. Ellis himself was greatly puzzled until he explored the well in his yard and fished out the remains of a Russian sailor.

San Francisco had no water system in 1849, which suggests that Ellis's well would have still been there, serving James Lick's tenants. If Norton ever learned its history—and there were many who'd have been delighted to tell it—he must have thought twice before lowering a bucket.

The town, enclosed on three sides by hills and needing space to grow, was crawling into the bay on soil dumped into the cove. When this "made-ground" was offered at public auction, Norton bought three lots, and in choosing them showed considerable foresight, for he now owned three of the four corners of Sansome and Jackson Streets, soon to be one of the busiest intersections in San Francisco. He also bought two water lots near Rincon Point. These, marked off by stakes driven into the mud, possessed one asset of immediate value. An abandoned brig, the *Genesee,* had been fenced in by the surveyor's stakes. She was an ugly old derelict, rusted and scarred, but her holds were sound, so Norton removed her masts, roofed her deck like the biblical ark, and used her as a storeship. No longer would he have to pay excessive charges to warehouse the cargoes he bought.

He lived at the Jones Hotel, a four-story "portable" on Sansome Street, built in Boston or Baltimore and shipped in sections around the Horn, as were many of San Francisco's wooden buildings. From a balcony that skirted the top floor it was possible to see, across the roofs slanting up the hill on which the town was built, the frame hotels and gambling hells around the plaza, Portsmouth Square, and it's not unreasonable to suppose that on May 4, 1851, at four o'clock in the morning, Norton would have been on that balcony with other half-clad residents who had been aroused from sleep by the clanging of firebells. An orange glow above the plaza meant that a gaming house was ablaze.

The flames spread swiftly, fanned by a Pacific wind, eastward toward the waterfront and north to Telegraph Hill. It was the fifth great fire in eighteen months, and by far the worst. The *Alta California* performed a heroic feat to describe it; its compositors, snatching up the pages of copy that poured from the editor's pen, were feverishly setting type as block after block burned and tumbled about them. Almost the last words written concerned Norton's lodgings:

> All of the buildings about the Jones Hotel had been consumed when we went to press, and it is thought the hotel itself will burn, although the firemen were making extraordinary exertions.

The firemen, furiously pumping water from the cove, succeeded in saving the hotel, but when an anxious Norton stumbled through smoking ruins to find out what had become of his office, there was no sign of Lick's adobe.

"Little doubt, if any, remains that this city was set on fire by some fiend for the purpose of robbery," declared the *Alta*, ignoring the fact that a town constructed almost entirely of timber—a tinderbox town with no water system—was likely to burn without an arsonist's help.

The press knew where to point the finger. Immediately behind the blackened rubble of Lick's cottage, on the lower slope of Telegraph Hill, was the thoroughly disreputable quarter called Sydney Town, believed to be infested with escaped convicts and ticket-of-leave men from Britain's penal settlements in Australia. These rogues rejoiced in such florid nicknames as Bungaraby Jack, Jemmy-from-Town, Big Brummy, Billy Sweet Cheese, and Tommy Round Head, and were known collectively as the Sydney Ducks.

The *Daily Herald* wanted to stretch their necks. "If two or three were caught and treated to Lynch Law," the paper thundered, "their fellows would be more careful about future depredations." And it counseled those "who are interested in the welfare of this community" to do just that. Thus the San Francisco Committee of Vigilance was born, a fraternity devoted exclusively to the sport of Duck hunting.

On the night of June 10, a hundred merchants met in a storeroom on Sansome Street to draft a constitution and elect officers. It was not the best hour to commit a burglary, but John Jenkins was not the brightest of Sydney Ducks. He stole a safe from a shipping agent's office on Long Wharf and was surprised in the act. Some watermen, alerted by the agent's cry, pursued the skiff in which the thief was making his escape. After overtaking him, they towed him to shore, thrashed him soundly, and bundled him off to face a kangaroo court. Sentenced to hang that same night, he was marched in shackles through crowded streets to meet his doom on the moonlit plaza. A flagpole, some forty yards in front of an old adobe customhouse, was chosen for a gallows. The noose was dropped over his head and a man began to climb the pole, intending to slip the rope through the tackle block, when someone suggested it might be in poor taste to hang a thief from a staff dedicated to the nobler purpose of flying the nation's flag, whereupon an impatient executioner snatched up the loose end of the rope, ran to the customhouse, tossed the line over a beam, and shouted, "Haul away!" Two score of hands instantly seized the rope and pulled, jerking the manacled Jenkins off his feet. Then they dragged him by the neck to the portico of the adobe, heaved him off the ground, and hoisted him up to the beam.

The man who slung the rope over the beam was Captain Edgar Wakeman, the "burly, hairy, sunburned, stormy-voiced old salt" so extravagantly admired by Mark Twain, as much for his colorful cussing as anything else.

In 1851 the stormy-voiced "old salt" was thirty-three years old and had yet to meet the author who would immortalize him as Captain Stormfield in *Captain Stormfield's Visit to Heaven*. He was "profoundly and sincerely religious," according to Twain, though his chances of entering Heaven must have been somewhat slim if one can believe his own boastful book, *The Log of an Ancient Mariner*. When he strung up John Jenkins he already had a record of piracy and barratry that made the Duck's theft of a little safe—which the owner got back intact—seem a trifling offense. At that moment, as a matter of fact, a glowering sheriff in New York was asking every skipper who sailed into port where he might find the master of the *New World*. The sheriff, it seems, had gone aboard the steamer with a writ of attachment, forbidding her to sail until a certain large debt was paid. Ned Wakeman's reply was to kidnap the lawman, leaving him marooned on a sandbank in the East River before sailing on to California.

The *New World* was now the fastest side-wheeler on the Sacramento River, and her captain was the Vigilance Committee's lawless chief of police.

Norton was in a dilemma. The vigilantes were urging "all men of good moral character" to join them. He had no stomach for violence, but a refusal to enlist would have angered those who knew that he had suffered little in the fire. His goods were in the *Genesee*, beyond the reach of the flames, and he may even have profited from the misfortunes of his competitors by renting space in the storeship to those whose warehouses had been destroyed. The loss of his office was only a temporary inconvenience; a single line in the *Alta California*—"Joshua Norton & Co., Box 612, Post Office"—told customers where to pay their bills during the two weeks it took James Lick to erect a portable on the site of his burned cottage. The leaders of the Vigilance Committee were powerful men who enjoyed the support of a lickspittle press; any merchant who remained unmoved by their call for recruits—especially an English merchant, a compatriot of the Sydney Ducks—ran a grave risk of being ostracized by the entire business community. And ostracism meant financial ruin. He had no choice but to join.

At the Committee's headquarters on Battery Street, where Norton was sworn to secrecy and enrolled in the Book of Names, his photograph was taken so that his face might be kept on file. An old daguerreotype still in existence may have been the one provided. It shows a bald, broad-shouldered Norton with a mustache and thick muttonchop sideburns, fashionably attired in the black broadcloth suit and studded shirt of a prosperous businessman. There is a strange, faraway look in his eyes, perhaps the hint of a glint of madness, though it may only have been due to the strain of gazing stiffly into a primitive camera for the length of time needed to capture an image on a copper plate.

Norton's true opinion of vigilante justice was clearly revealed in the affair of James Stuart, alias English Jim, wanted for murder in Marysville, for robbery with violence in San Francisco, and for roadside banditry all over the map. Only an unusually generous heart would have tried to obtain a fair trial for that unmitigated scoundrel.

Norton was dismayed to learn that even the right to plead guilty or innocent was denied a prisoner of the Committee, who was also not permitted to be present when he was tried. Under such circumstances, no defense was possible. At a general meeting he pointed this out and moved that the rules be amended so that the accused might be heard. This did not suit some hard-liners, but he stood his ground until he got a majority vote on at least a diluted version of his proposal. The resolution, as it was written by the Committee's secretary, Isaac Bluxome, plainly showed what *he* thought of it:

> On motion of Mr. Norton. Resolved: that no criminal shall be sentenced until he or she shall have an opportunity of pleading guilty or not guilty and assigning his or her reasons why judgement should not be passed.

The word "she" may be safely ignored, since there is no evidence that a Duck of tender gender ever nested in Sydney Town (at least, none was arrested by the Committee), but the rest of that paragraph deserves to be studied under a microscope; any student of jurisprudence would have thrown up his hands in horror upon reading it. That "no *criminal* shall be sentenced" until after he had pleaded could only mean that in Bluxome's mind the accused was guilty no matter what his plea; he would be sentenced anyway. It was a pitifully small victory for Norton and of little comfort to Stuart, whose plea of innocence was heard by a stony-faced court that had reached a verdict without the disturbing influence of his presence before bringing him in to spout the few words that would have no bearing anyway on those uttered by the "judge." On July 11 the tolling of a firebell beckoned the town to a hanging, and at two o'clock in the afternoon, on the Market Street Wharf, Captain Edgar Wakeman dangled English Jim from a derrick.

There was more to come. Two of Stuart's accomplices, Sam Whittaker and Bob McKenzie, were already serving time for their crimes in the County Jail on Broadway, but that did not satisfy the Committee. One sunny Sunday, while the Reverend Albert Williams was preaching to the prisoners in the jail yard, a raiding party burst through the gates, plucked the Ducks from the captive congregation, hustled them into a carriage, and galloped off to Battery Street, where a "profoundly and sincerely religious" man was waiting with his rope.

The Committee's headquarters was a long room above a store. Two windows, wide and tall, looked down upon the street, a stout beam projecting from each, equipped with iron pulleys for hauling goods in and out of the storeroom, ideal for hanging men in a hurry. All the church bells that chimed in the city that Sunday could not attract the vast crowd that one firebell could summon. Several thousand jeering, cheering spectators watched Whittaker and McKenzie take the single faltering step that carried them straight to hell.

It was more fun than going to church.

The Committee never formally disbanded; it simply petered out. A printer marked its passing by producing a certificate of membership, an ornate diploma that any vigilante might purchase to frame and hang in his home. Norton may have been too ashamed to buy one; though the contents of his lodgings would be amply described by visitors in years to come, even to the pictures on his walls, nothing would ever be said about a certificate of membership in the Committee of Vigilance.

Ned Wakeman received a handsome reward for performing his grisly duties. At a banquet given in his honor, he recalled in his *Log of an Ancient Mariner*, "nine large diamonds, elegantly set, were pinned to my breast, a large and heavy silver speaking trumpet, appropriately inscribed, was tucked under my arm, and a full-chronometer watch of solid gold with double cases was placed about my neck by a heavy chain, seven feet four inches long, to which were attached a massive anchor and large ring of California gold."

Then, because he was such a fine fellow, he was given command of a side-wheeler bound for Sydney, Australia, where he ran full tilt into a squall much heavier than any he might have encountered during the crossing.

"Captain Edgar Wakeman of the American steamer, lately arrived, assisted in murdering some of Australia's finest citizens, is a most dangerous person, and will have but twenty-four hours in which to leave the country," the Sydney *Herald* warned.

A mob went down to the docks, intent upon avenging the deaths of Australia's finest, but failed to receive any response from the American ship to their reasonable request that the captain come out and be hanged like a man. They contented themselves with swearing mightily at the armed seamen posted about her decks to repel boarders. Good thing nobody knew that a heavy chain seven feet long, with golden anchor attached, now reposed in Wakeman's sea chest, or he might have wound up in Sydney Harbor with San Francisco's gift around his neck as a sinker.

Chapter 5

Perchance to Dream

"If I were Emperor of the United States . . ."
—Joshua A. Norton

A new San Francisco rose from the ashes of a timber town, a city of brick and stone, with water piped from a distant lake to cisterns under the streets. Joshua Norton moved from James Lick's portable to No. 110 Battery Street, a substantial granite building that housed the offices of some of the most influential men in the state, men of the stamp of Sir William Lane Booker, the British consul, whose immense wealth came from his New Almaden quicksilver mine near San Jose. Norton was on familiar terms with this tall, distinguished Englishman, recently knighted by Queen Victoria for his services to the Crown; both were Freemasons, charter members of Occidental Lodge No. 22.

On his made-ground at the southwest corner of Jackson and Sansome Streets, Norton opened a cigar factory. On the southeast corner he put up a large frame building, renting its rooms to businessmen. Then, on the northwest corner, he built a rice mill. It was crude—a mule provided the power, plodding endlessly around a ship's wheel—but it was the first on the Pacific coast. He did nothing to improve his water lots at Rincon Point. There was no need; their value increased immediately when the Pacific Mail Steamship Company built a passenger terminal and a warehouse alongside. When a big side-wheeler from Panama berthed beside the *Genesee*, the warehouse was crammed with cargo and so was his storeship.

The steamers brought wealthier immigrants, and a society of sorts began to emerge; men who had "made their pile" sent home for their wives, who had their own ideas as to how the rich should live. The Jones Hotel was no longer socially acceptable, so Norton moved to the newer, more prestigious Rassette House. A good address was important these days, for he was walking with gods. That is to say, he knew the McAllisters.

Hall McAllister, an urbane lawyer from Georgia who would reign over San Francisco's fashionable set for more than thirty years, lived in a cottage on Pike Street with a younger brother who was about to return East. A day would come when New York's aristocrats would gladly surrender an eyetooth for a nod of recognition from the arrogant Ward McAllister, who created the privileged order known as "The Four Hundred" by pruning Mrs. William B. Astor's guest lists of names he considered unworthy to associate with the crème de la crème. In the San Francisco of the 1850s, this social arbiter would have found it immensely trying to think of even forty names he would have dared recommend to an Astor. He had to be content with the company of merchants like Norton, who came to Pike Street to discuss business ventures with Hall over brandy and cigars. Dinner with the brothers was something to brag about, particularly when their witty cousin, Sam Ward, was on hand to supervise the menu and select the wines.

Sam Ward is remembered in half a dozen books as the short, slight, irrepressibly cheerful bon vivant who taught America how to dine; the "King of the Lobby" whose political string-pulling saved President Andrew Johnson from impeachment by a single vote; a patron of poets and publishers, whose very least claim to fame was that he happened to be the brother of that Julia Ward Howe who wrote "The Battle Hymn of the Republic." In 1852 much of that still lay ahead, though he was already far better known among the literati than his sister; Henry Wadsworth Longfellow called him "the best of Sams," and Ward called the bard "Longo." Even the Astors had found him eligible enough to be admitted into the family; some fifteen years before, when he was a banker in New York, he had won the heart and hand of William B. Astor's lovely daughter, Emily, only to lose her in childbirth. Now he was married to Medora Grymes, a pampered beauty whose wifely devotion, sad to say, had proved too fragile to survive the failure of his Wall Street bank. Promising to do better in future, he had sailed with Hall and Ward McAllister to California, jauntily convinced that he would return with gold enough to satisfy even the spoiled Medora.

Ward had just returned from the Merced River, where he had staked out a gold-bearing quartz mine, and was lodging with his McAllister kinsmen while he rounded up the capital to work his claim.

"Hall," he said to his cousin when he moved into the cottage, "give me the run of the kitchen and you shall have the feast of your life."

Hall McAllister was never one to stifle genius.

"Go to it, old fellow," he said, "and hang the expense."

Sam took him at his word. Dismissing the cook for the day, he brought in some workmen and tore down the entire kitchen. Then he built one more to his liking.

Among the guests were two rough diamonds who probably would never have been invited if Ward McAllister had been the host. William Sim and Alexander Sibley had been on the Merced with Sam and had some gold to invest. Hence the dinner party; Sam needed some of that gold for his quartz mine. But Bill Sim, an amiable giant from Glasgow, was tired of mining and not much interested in Sam Ward's quartz. He wanted to go into the mercantile business, and Hall McAllister knew just the thing. Joshua Norton happened to be in need of a partner; Peter Robertson, after two years of fires and lynch mobs, was yearning for quieter parts. A meeting was arranged and a deal was made. Robertson relinquished his interest in Joshua Norton & Company to the burly Scot and sailed away.

That Sim and Sibley lacked the polish that might have endeared them to the younger McAllister is obvious from Sam Ward's account of their adventures on the Merced in a New York weekly, *Porter's Spirit of the Times.* It contained an anecdote that neatly captured Sim's rich Glaswegian accent and made Sibley sound like a tobacco-chewing prairie scout in a dime novel by Ned Buntline.

Bill Sim was not accustomed to roughing it. After an evening's drinking and yarning with miners in a small hotel near Quartzburg, he viewed with dismay the hard bunks provided by the innkeeper and hurried outside to appropriate the only comfortable couch available, a hammock slung between two trees. Alex Sibley, who coveted the hammock himself, decided to get it by fair means or foul. Arousing the drowsing tenderfoot, he inquired whether his pistol was loaded.

Sim, who was unarmed, asked why.

"Thar's b'ars about," said Sibley. "Couple of nights ago, they stole a mutton that was hung out to cool."

The trick didn't work. Sim, saying only that he would be tickled to meet his first grizzly, borrowed a revolver from the hotelier and settled down again. Refusing to give up, Sibley hid in a thicket and waited for the Scot to fall asleep. Inside the crude hotel, Sam Ward and his bunkmates listened gleefully for the next move. Suddenly they heard a growl outside, then a great roar and a tremendous crashing in the bushes. A moment later came a sharp rap at the door.

"Halloo," called Ward, trying to smother his laughter. "Is that you, Sim?"

"Aye," came the reply. "I find it ower caud [a bit cold] oot here in the dew. I think I'll sleep in the hoose after all."

So much for Norton's new partner.

One thing about Americans amused Norton. During those Gold Rush years, following the acquisition of California and other Mexican provinces by conquest, they described their greatly expanded land as an "empire" just as a Briton might speak of Victoria's far-flung possessions. Newspapers used the word constantly in editorials, poets in patriotic verse, authors in books (the most successful best-seller in 1852 was Bayard Taylor's *El Dorado, or Adventures in the Path of Empire*). Almost every town and mining camp in the Far West boasted an Empire House hotel. San Francisco had an Empire House, an Empire Saloon, an Empire Brewery, an Empire Oil Works, and a volunteer fire company called Empire Engine Company No. 1. Norton thought all this foolish. Empires, he pointed out, were ruled by emperors, not elected politicians.

One member of the McAllister coterie, Joseph Eastland, would remember this years later, telling the *Alta California:*

> Norton was a strong anti-Republican, advocating England's system of government, and insisting that that of the United States was infamously crude and should be reconstructed. What it wanted was an emperor, and he would add: "If I were Emperor of the United States, you would see great changes effected."

He must have become a bit of a bore about this, because the Pike Street crowd gave him a nickname; they called him "Emperor." But what Eastland did not know, what nobody knew in those days, was that Norton had already crossed the fine line dividing sanity from madness—and was perfectly serious.

On the sandy shore of North Beach, facing the stark rock of Alcatraz, a city alderman named Henry Meiggs built a wharf, thrusting it far into the bay where a captain in search of a berth needed no spyglass to see it as he sailed through the Golden Gate. To develop the property surrounding his wharf, he borrowed heavily, confidently predicting that San Francisco must soon stop creeping into a cove already choked with landfill and start crawling north, where there was more room to expand. One could easily believe a man whom the newspapers called "Honest Harry," and there was a rush to buy the beach lots he offered for sale in the area now known to every tourist as Fisherman's Wharf. Norton bought eight, four in his own name and four in partnership with Judge Lansing Bond Mizner.

The books that have been written about the Mizners have largely been concerned with the madcap antics of two of Judge Mizner's tall sons. Wilson Mizner, the artful dodger who staggered Ward McAllister's privileged Four Hundred when he married the widow of Charles Tyson Yerkes—"the second richest woman in the world"—began his gaudy career selling Dr. Slocum's Sweet Vermifuge Mastodon Medicine at a tent show in Spokane. He went on to be a Klondike gold miner, a gambler, a prizefighter's manager, a Broadway playwright, a screenwriter, and finally the well-known restaurateur whose Brown Derby was the favorite haunt of movie stars in the 1940s. His brother, Addison, the architect who put Palm Beach on the map of Florida and kept New York in stitches with epigrams that Oscar Wilde might have envied, was unconventional enough to go shopping in his dressing gown and sometimes in his pajamas.

"And I thought they were going to be at least bishops or ambassadors," their mother sighed before she died. Ella Watson Mizner had good reason to expect better things of children whose father had been the United States Minister to Guatemala and Envoy Extraordinary to Costa Rica, Nicaragua, El Salvador, and Honduras.

Lansing Bond Mizner was twenty-seven, still unmarried, and an

Associate Justice of the First Court of Sessions in Solano County, across the bay, when he went into partnership with Joshua Norton. But Franklin Pierce had just been elected President and was about to push Judge Mizner one step further up the political ladder by appointing him Collector of Customs for the Northern District of California. It would do Norton no harm to be associated with a customs chief whose jurisdiction extended from the Bay of San Francisco to the Oregon border.

Mizner's uncle was Dr. Robert Semple, the lanky dentist from Illinois who rode into Alta California with John Charles Fremont, the Pathfinder, to play a cloak-and-dagger role in the revolt by American settlers that raised the curtain on the conquest of Mexico's least prepared province. It was Semple, a conspicuous conspirator in buckskin, seven feet seven inches tall from his moccasins to his Davey Crockett cap, who had imprisoned the local Mexican commandante, General Mariano Vallejo, leaving an unguarded Golden Gate wide open to invading U.S. marines.

General Vallejo, a practical man, accepting defeat with a shrug, had gone into partnership with his former captor in a scheme to build a new town on a corner of his estate beside the Carquinez Strait, the channel through which the riverboats passed on their way to Sacramento, the gateway to the goldfields. They had proposed to call the settlement Francesca, after the general's lady, Donna Francesca Benicia Vallejo, but decided to honor her by calling it Benicia, thinking her first name too closely resembled that of San Francisco, which might confuse visiting ship captains and cause them to deposit their cargoes in entirely the wrong spot. When Semple's nephew Lansing arrived, in 1849, they set out to make the little port the busiest on the bay.

Judge Mizner was in a jubilant mood when he crossed the water to buy land with Norton that autumn. For two years, since the new territory was granted statehood, while its legislators hemmed and hawed about where the state capital should be, wandering from one idyllic town to another, finding fault with each, Dr. Semple had lobbied ceaselessly to have the seat of government transferred to Benicia. Now he had just learned that the Legislature had voted to move there in February. Benicia's future was assured. The United States Arsenal was already located there and Pacific Mail was even now building docks and machine shops for the maintenance of its steamships. There was little doubt in Mizner's mind that a capital city with a harbor that could accommodate steamers, strategically placed to capture the traffic of both river and bay, must soon dislodge San Francisco as the center of trade.

He was due for a shock. The legislators would move to Benicia in February, only to move out again at the end of the year, having decided that Sacramento would make a much better capital.

"Papa Mizner was the best wrong guesser the world had probably ever produced," Addison Mizner wrote in his book, *The Many Mizners*.

The world's best wrong guesser certainly proved his right to that title when he threw in his lot with Joshua Norton.

Disaster struck almost at once. China, which supplied the rice that California consumed, suffered a terrible famine and banned the export of grain. Norton's mule ceased to plod, the ship's wheel ceased to turn, and the price of rice climbed from four cents a pound to thirty-six. That would mean a windfall for the trader who could supply it, but there was none to be bought. At the Merchant's Exchange, where Norton went daily to bid for cargoes, he anxiously watched the board for news of a shipment. Then, one day, a shipping agent took him aside to whisper the word that would dramatically change his life.

The German firm of Godeffroy & Sillem was the largest mercantile banking house in the city. Alfred Godeffroy and Willy Sillem were members of the McAllister set and not at all averse to doing a friend a favor that would also benefit themselves.

Sillem showed Norton some rice.

"That's from Peru, and there are two hundred thousand pounds of it in the *Glyde*."

Capital news! Where was the *Glyde*?

"In the bay. She cannot discharge because of the weather, but you may have the whole of her cargo if you buy it before anyone else gets wind of it."

And the price?

"Twelve and a half cents a pound."

Twenty-five thousand dollars was an enormous amount to risk on a venture in those days, but the rice would be worth seventy-two thousand at the current retail price (and to arrive at a better understanding of today's value, simply multiply by ten).

Sillem, acting for the consignors, Ruiz Brothers of Lima, Peru, agreed to accept two thousand dollars as a down payment with this proviso written into the contract: "Payment to be made cash before delivery of any portion, and the whole to be taken away and paid for within thirty days." The date was December 22, 1852. Norton signed the agreement, paid the deposit, and told his stockman in the *Genesee* to clear the decks for rice.

And then the blow fell.

Next day, the *Syren* sailed into port with 218 barrels of Peruvian rice. And the day after that, Christmas Eve, the *Merceditas* arrived with two hundred thousand pounds. Then came the *Dragon* with two hundred and fifty thousand, followed by ship after ship with barrel upon barrel until the market was glutted and the price just three cents a pound.

When Norton tried to nullify the contract, claiming that the grain in the *Glyde* was inferior to the sample that Sillem had shown him, Ruiz Brothers took him to court, seeking to attach his property. It was all too much for Bill Sim. The embarrassed Scot threw up his hands and went off to join Sam Ward on the Merced. He would rather face a hundred bears than one sheriff armed with a writ.

The same sheriff, it so happened, was looking for little Sam Ward. A banker named William T. Sherman had set the law on him for issuing bad checks.

Chapter 6

The Edge of Hell

"Ay, but thou talk'st as if thou wert a king."
"Why, so I am—in mind; and that's enough."

—*King Henry the Sixth*, Part Three

Captain William Tecumseh Sherman, who had soldiered in California before the Forty-Niners came, had returned as a civilian to build a bank for Lucas, Turner & Company of St. Louis, in which he was a partner. Searching for a suitable location, his eyes fell on James Lick's property at Montgomery and Jackson. The miserly millionaire, who had bought the lot from a saloonkeeper for three thousand dollars, was perfectly willing to sell half of it for thirty-one thousand. Lick's portable was demolished and a fine brick building, three stories tall, rose on the site of Norton's old office.

So much had changed in the six years since Sherman's last visit in 1848. Montgomery Street, once a wisp of a track fronting a muddy beach, was now a busy thoroughfare of banking houses, shipping companies and brokerage firms, throbbing with traffic. Streetlamps had just been installed along its sidewalks by the San Francisco Gas Lighting Company. Sherman's new Lucas-Turner Building was one of the first in the city to be lighted with gas,

Sherman's bank was founded on faith in San Francisco's economic stability, which was ironic considering that when he lighted his gas mantles and opened his door, in 1854, the city was already teetering on the brink of a severe depression. This would not be known until Alderman Henry Meiggs—Honest Harry—secretly chartered a ship and sailed for Peru, leaving his stunned investors to discover that he had financed his wharf and the entire North Beach development with forged city warrants. Banks and reputations toppled together in '55. San Francisco, almost two million dollars in debt, managed to avoid bankruptcy only by repudiating the warrants. In a letter to his partners in St. Louis, Sherman noted the plight of Godeffroy & Sillem: "The German house, which was humbugged, were heavy losers and failed." One asset they sold before they crumbled was the mortgage on Norton's land at North Beach. The title deeds were now Sherman's.

Norton had trouble making the payments. His legal battle with Ruiz Brothers was swallowing up too much of his capital. Time and time he faced the rice shippers in court as first one side and then the other appealed a ruling. The final judgment, in May 1855, awarded the plaintiffs twenty thousand dollars and costs. When Norton failed to meet his obligations to Lucas, Turner & Company, Sherman foreclosed and the beach lots were lost. That same month he was suspended from his Masonic lodge for failing to pay his dues.

The depression finished him. Cargoes, going begging for buyers, were left on the wharves to rot. Unable to recover his losses through trading, he ventured into stock brokerage with Isaac Thorne, an attorney and state assemblyman. Norton & Thorne, Stock & Gold Dust Brokers, 120 Montgomery Street, lasted only three months. Norton opened a real estate office at the same address, but money was scarce and buyers interested only in bargains. His property at Sansome and Jackson went at a loss—land, mill, mule, and cigars.

Worse, he was accused of embezzlement.

In '52, when he was still in McAllister's good graces, a Pike Street architect, Norman Bugbee, who was planning a protracted visit to the East, had given him power of attorney to manage his financial affairs while he was gone. Now, three years later, Bugbee was back and wanted an accounting. Norton made excuses, stalling for time, possibly hoping to turn a profit on some transaction to rescue him from his predicament, but the architect became convinced that he had misappropriated his money, using it and losing it in that foolish venture with Thorne.

Embezzlement, now a felony, was then a civil offense. Bugbee engaged a lawyer and sued. Norton must have been horrified when the newspapers reported it. He went to see Captain Sherman, offering his water lots at Rincon Point as security for a loan, but the banker would not lend more than would satisfy Bugbee. At least it would stave off another embarrassing court appearance, one that would surely have destroyed his reputation, which had already been called into question by press accounts of his attempts to wriggle out of a contract by accusing Willy Sillem of deceiving him with a handful of rice. Bugbee was paid, the suit was dropped, and the papers said no more about it. But Norton was no longer welcome in Pike Street. When Lansing Mizner married Ella Watson, an event that ranked high on the social calendar of 1855, it's unlikely he was invited.

Hall McAllister married too, and moved into a mansion on fashionable Stockton Street. Pike Street was no place to take a bride, having become the resort of prostitutes. The notorious Belle Ryan had her bagnio there, next to Ah Toy's and Irene McCready's. The papers, ever alert for a scandal, were telling an improbable story about a house on that street.

Judge Edward McGowan, a walrus-mustached Justice of the Court of Quarter Sessions, had deeded his own Pike Street cottage to a French courtesan, Fanny Perriere, on the reckless understanding that she would share her favors with no one else. One evening, dropping in without thinking to knock, he found the lady entertaining a more attractive visitor, Alfred Godeffroy, who dived for the door when he heard the judge roar and was speeding for cover like a startled gazelle by the time McGowan drew his five-barreled Colt and fired. Godeffroy escaped unhurt, but any suggestion that McGowan must have missed him was quickly corrected by the judge, who rather prided himself on his marksmanship. Not at all, said he, Godeffroy moved so fast that he almost outpaced the bullet; so swift was his sprint that the leaden ball was spent when it reached its target and merely flattened itself against his bottom without penetrating. McGowan swore to the truth of this and for proof pointed to the fact that the German could still sit down. Thereafter, Willy Sillem's partner would always be known in the less polite sections of the press as "Old Cast Iron Posterior."

Norton wrote to Ned McGowan, seeking his help. The judge was County Chairman of the Democratic Party, and on May 20 the Democrats would hold a convention to choose their candidates for city and county elective positions. This year's election would be a milestone in San Francisco's history; under the terms of a new charter the city and the county would become one, incorporated as the City and County of San Francisco, administered by a mayor and a Board of Supervisors. In his letter, as cool as you please, the monarchist who deplored republican politics asked the chairman to nominate him for the post of County Tax Collector!

Since an alien would not have been eligible for public office—indeed, could not even vote—Norton's request would seem to suggest that he had recently become a United States citizen (a possibility that cannot now be determined, all Immigration and Naturalization records for the San Francisco area having disappeared in the fire and earthquake of 1906). Federal law required then, as it does today, that an applicant for citizenship must have resided in the States not less than five years. He could have applied in December 1854, five months before the Democratic convention, but his own country would still have considered him British, since Britain did not yet recognize the American naturalization of British-born subjects. There is the chance that he sought election without bothering to apply for citizenship, in which case his letter to McGowan could be a clue that his mental processes were not functioning properly. However, the fact that he was not considered as a candidate does not necessarily mean that the Democrats dismissed him as a crank. Actually, he hadn't a chance of getting on the public payroll as long as David C. Broderick was running the city.

Broderick, a burly, redheaded New York Irishman, was president of the State Senate. It was said that he "looked upon the state as an oyster." If California was his oyster, San Francisco was the pearl. And that precious gem was in his hands before he became a state senator, thanks to the shipload of Tammany Hall henchmen he had imported from New York. Even his most ardent admirer, Jeremiah Lynch, had to admit in his biography of Broderick, *A Senator of the Fifties,* that his methods were hardly in keeping with the golden rules:

> At a forthcoming election a number of offices were to be filled. Several of these positions were very lucrative, notably that of sheriff, tax-collector, and assessor. The incumbents received no specified salary, but were entitled to all or a portion of the fees. These fees occasionally exceeded $50,000 per annum. Broderick

would say to the most popular or the most desirable aspirant: "This office is worth $50,000 a year. Keep half and give me the other half, which I require to keep up our organization in the state."

A tax collector's lucrative post might have solved all of Norton's problems, but he was not the sort of candidate Senator Broderick was inclined to favor, the Irishman's idea of "the most desirable aspirant" being another Irishman. Ned McGowan was certainly what the press called "one of the B'hoys." David Scannell, Broderick's choice for sheriff, and Billy Mulligan, his nominee for Keeper of the County Jail, were both Irish. Empire Engine Company No. 1, the volunteer fire brigade founded by Broderick, supplied the muscle that kept the city under his control; its red-shirted heroes bore names that smacked strongly of their Hibernian origin: Tom Mulloy, Billy Mulligan, Jim Henessey, Rube Maloney, Jack McGuire, Marty Gallagher, Francis Sullivan. An Englishman would have been about as welcome in the Broderick camp as a teetotaler at a wake.

It was about this time that William T. Sherman had occasion to speak sharply to a tenant of his Lucas-Turner Building. James P. Casey, a Broderick man newly elected to the Board of Supervisors, edited the *Sunday Times* in a room on the top floor. An article he had published, accusing the banking fraternity of collusion in the Meiggs fraud, angered Sherman, who stormed upstairs and "told him plainly that I could not tolerate his attempts to print and circulate slanders in our building, and if he repeated it, I would cause him and his press to be thrown out of the window."

The politician wisely vacated the premises.

Casey's wayward pen aroused the ire of another editor, the oddly named James King of William, a banker himself until the crash of 1855, now owner of the *Evening Bulletin,* a lively new daily that specialized in exposing the sins of Broderick's B'hoy's. Casey's attack on the banks sparked an explosion in the *Bulletin,* which accused the new Supervisor of political fraud. One thing led to another, with accusations flying back and forth. When the *Bulletin* alleged that the politician had once served time in Sing Sing for stealing a prostitute's furniture, Casey went to King's office on Montgomery Street to demand a retraction, only to be advised that he could expect further revelations in the next issue. At five o'clock that evening, when King left his desk in the Montgomery Block to go home, Casey was waiting on the sidewalk with a Derringer.

The shot that rang through Montgomery Street echoed next day in the newspapers, and within hours a second Committee of Vigilance was born. Casey, who had sought sanctuary from a sympathetic Irish sheriff, heard the news in prison. His victim, shot in the breast, was still breathing four days later when three thousand vigilantes wheeled a fieldpiece up Broadway, aimed it at the door of the County Jail, and ordered Sheriff Scannell and Keeper Billy Mulligan to surrender the prisoner.

That Sunday noon, May 18, 1856, William T. Sherman was on the roof of the International Hotel with the Governor of California, who had just appointed him major-general commanding the San Francisco division of the California Militia. From this position he could see the jail and the rooftops surrounding it. "All of the houses commanding a view were covered with people," he wrote some two hours later to his partners in St. Louis. "Telegraph Hill was black with them."

Norton was on that hill. His bank balance having dictated a move to humbler lodgings, he now lived in the boardinghouse of a Mrs. Rutledge on Montgomery Street, overlooking the County Jail. Here, where the street crossed Broadway and suddenly climbed like a roller coaster, the shoulder of Telegraph Hill had been excavated to make room for the jail, leaving the Rutledge house perched on a man-made cliff thirty feet above the prison yard. Few could have had a better view than Norton. If his room was on the south side of the house, he had no need to climb to the roof with the other lodgers; he had only to step to his window.

Sherman knew all about the view from Mrs. Rutledge's windows. He had already reconnoitered the area and seen for himself "how utterly indefensible the jail-yard was, open to the rear, overlooked on all sides by brick houses with parapet walls, no part of the interior safe from shots."

But there was no need of snipers in Norton's lodgings. The Vigilance Committee had promised there would be no violence if the sheriff would give up Casey, and Scannell had no choice, being helpless against three thousand men with a cannon. In his letter to St. Louis, Sherman described exactly what Norton would have seen from his window. Casey was taken from the jail and put into a waiting carriage, which bore him away "with two files of armed men on each side, followed by a promiscuous crowd."

Then another carriage was brought to the jail and a second prisoner was removed—Charles Cora, a gambler who had shot and killed a drunken U. S. marshal for insulting his mistress, Belle Ryan, the parlor-house madam of Pike Street. James King of William had been demanding his execution for months.

Cora and Casey were taken to the Committee's headquarters, a warehouse known as Fort Gunnybags because of the barricade of sandbags the vigilantes had put up to protect it from attack. Sherman would have stormed that redoubt if the Governor had not stayed his arm, but lacking the order—and the bullets—all he could do was knock on the door and ask that the captives be fairly tried, a futile request as Norton had discovered five years earlier. Word of the editor's death sealed the fate of both. As James King's funeral cortege crawled through the streets to Lone Mountain Cemetery, Casey and Cora stepped from the windows of Fort Gunnybags with rope about their necks.

Norton soon moved from Mrs. Rutledge's boardinghouse on Montgomery Street. He was earning a living as a commission agent, and an advertisement in the *Herald* showed he was able to afford slightly better quarters:

"100,000 pounds China rice; 2,000 gallons Boiled Linseed Oil in tins. For sale by Joshua Norton, Tehama House."

The *Morning Call* would later say: "Some businessmen tried to help him by entrusting him with the sale of a quantity of goods on commission. The result was disastrous and unsatisfactory to all concerned and Norton was censured for bad faith with both sellers and purchasers. He is reported to have cleared considerable money in the transaction and left his lodging-house, taking a room at the International Hotel, one of the leading hotels at the time."

Well, it wasn't the International but the Tehama House, as Norton's own advertisements indicated, and he would not have needed "considerable money" to live there, since the Tehama House was merely the old Jones Hotel under new ownership and possibly a new coat of paint, hardly "one of the leading hotels."

But few would remember this period of his life. There were more pressing matters to think about in 1856. Guns were blazing in Kansas and there was scarcely a soul in San Francisco who did not think that the fighting there might suddenly erupt into a full-scale revolution that could dismember the empire state by state.

Chapter 7

Over the Edge

*"But if thou be a king, where is thy crown?"
"My crown is in my heart, not on my head;
not deck'd with diamonds and Indian stones,
nor to be seen. My crown is call'd content;
and a crown it is that seldom kings enjoy."*

—*King Henry the Sixth*, Part Three

For thirty-five years, since the admission of Missouri into the Union as a slave state in 1821, it had been the custom to admit slave states and free states in pairs to maintain the balance of political power between North and South. This had worked well enough until California was admitted as a free state at a time when there happened to be no slave territory that could be granted statehood, and the South was greatly perturbed by the prospect of two anti-slavery senators taking their seats in Washington with no new pro-slavery senators to offset their influence. To placate the South, Congress passed the Fugitive Slave Law, which held that a slave who escaped to free soil must be returned to his master and commanded all citizens to assist in his capture, providing heavy penalties for those who helped him. That law infuriated the North, for it meant that the sovereignty of the states had been superseded by a federal government dominated by Southerners. To many the burning issue now was not the plight of the slave so much as the inviolability of states' rights.

The Fugitive Slave Law split the Democratic Party, many joining with Whigs and Free-Soilers to found the Republican Party, which gained immediate strength when President Pierce, a proslavery Democrat, angered the North still further by signing the Kansas-Nebraska Act, which permitted the settlers of Kansas and Nebraska to decide by ballot whether they wished their territories to be slave states or free. Republicans saw this as a Southern trick, protesting that it would be an easy matter for the slave state of Missouri to fill neighboring Kansas with enough voters to bring it into the proslavery fold. Abolitionist societies provided funds to send settlers into Kansas who would vote to keep its soil free, while the South sent settlers to enslave it. Guerrilla bands on both sides, Border Ruffians from Missouri and Jayhawkers from the North, rode from farm to farm, terrorizing the homesteaders into voting their way. With ballot and bullet the Missourians filled every public office in the territory and established a government in Lecompton that outlawed the Abolitionist movement and made it an offense worth five years in prison even to voice an opinion against slavery. When rebellious Free-Soilers formed their own legislature, in Lawrence, an army of Border Ruffians attacked and sacked the town.

"The Rape of Lawrence" reaped a terrible revenge. An aging religious fanatic named John Brown, riding at night with four of his sons along the banks of the Pottawatamie, aroused from their beds five settlers known to have voted for slavery—though too poor to own a slave—and butchered them with broadswords for the greater glory of God. Then he carried his holy war into Missouri.

"Should desperate men bring about civil war, an awful calamity, you in St. Louis will be the first to feel the blow," Sherman warned his partners in Missouri.

He was already thinking that perhaps he ought to be back in uniform, with the Army in Kansas. Which reminded him: "We are under the government of the *Evening Bulletin*, edited by my old clerk, Thomas King, whom I hope some Casey will dispatch." James King of William's brother, who had inherited the *Bulletin*, had soldiered in Kansas with Sherman, chiefly by writing his letters.

Thomas Sim King called the vigilantes "San Francisco's Purest and Best" and urged them on to further excesses. Two more men were lynched, others marched aboard ship and deported. But the

Purest and Best went much too far when they arrested the Chief Justice of the California Supreme Court.

Judge David S. Terry, trying to rescue a friend from a posse of vigilantes, had stabbed their leader in the neck with a Bowie knife. The wounded man, Sterling Hopkins, had assumed the role that would surely have been Ned Wakeman's if the captain of the *New World* had not grown tired of riverboating and gone back to sea. It was Hopkins who knocked out the pegs supporting the hinged platforms on which Casey and Cora had stood to be hanged. The *Bulletin* called him the "sheriff" of the Vigilance Committee, possibly hoping to justify the arrest of the Chief Justice on the grounds that his victim was also a man of importance, but the comparison was patently ridiculous because everyone knew that he was a pimp for his prostitute sister.

The Committee announced that Judge Terry would hang if Hopkins should die of his wound. This was a crass mistake, for though the press might applaud the lynching of a gambler and an unpopular Irish politician, no paper other than the *Bulletin* was prepared to condone the murder of the state's chief justice. Some editors found the courage to urge restraint, and the tide of public opinion began to turn. Fortunately, Hopkins was in no great danger, though he made a brave show of clinging desperately to life and prolonged the performance for a month until even the Committee tired of his acting and ordered him to get well. His miraculous recovery released the judge from Fort Gunnybags and the Committee from an embarrassing situation.

On August 25 the *Bulletin* wistfully reported that the Committee had disbanded. In the same issue, tucked away in an inside page, was this brief notice:

> Joshua Norton filed a petition for the benefit of the Insolvency Law. Liabilities, $55,811; assets stated at $15,000, uncertain in value.

Norton's only remaining assets, the water lots at Rincon Point, were by no means uncertain in value. Sherman listed their worth in a report to St. Louis: "Two fifty-vara lots near the Pacific Mail Steamship Company's site on First Street, valued in 1853 at $12,000 but standing the bank $3,000." (The vara, a Spanish standard of measurement, was then still in use in California.)

The San Francisco Gas Lighting Company acquired the lots from

Sherman. Gas lamps, until now a novelty enjoyed by only a few favored buildings on Montgomery Street, were beginning to sprout all over the city, and the gas company, which owned the land adjoining the water lots at First and Howard Streets, needed to expand its plant. Norton's lots were quickly filled in with soil and sand and the broken bones of the *Genesee*.

From time to time in '57 and '58, a line or two in the *Alta California* offered coffee for sale by Joshua Norton, or beans, or boots, or barley, for it seemed that some still trusted him to sell their goods on commission. But as the months went by the advertisements appeared less frequently and then ceased altogether, while a change of address in the city directory indicated the depths to which he had sunk.

No. 255 Kearny Street was a lodging house of the cheaper sort, a working-class home kept by a Mrs. Carswell, and there Norton must have felt like a fish out of water. The laborers who lodged with Mrs. Carswell would not have taken kindly to a tenant whose clothes were better than their own, who spoke with a "fancy" accent, and compared their republic unfavorably with a monarchy they had been raised from birth to distrust. Any "lime-juicer" who scorned republican ideals would have been wise to keep his thoughts to himself. They were strange thoughts, anyway.

Everyone talked of secession. The Democrats had made it the chief issue of their national election campaign. A strong new voice had been heard in the land, the Republican voice of Abraham Lincoln demanding an end to slavery, which the Democrats warned would leave the southern states no choice but to secede from the Union to protect a cotton trade that thrived on slave labor.

California was populated by Northerners and Southerners in almost equal proportions, and its newspapers reflected the political bias of editors and publishers from both sides of the Mason-Dixon Line. The views on slavery held by Mrs. Carswell's boarders would have depended largely upon where they were born and which paper they read. Only one man in that household, in fact, would have had any practical experience of slavery—the Englishman who kept his mouth shut.

Norton's parents had owned slaves. There had been one on their farm beside the Great Fish—a "male slave under the age of sixteen," according to an 1824 census that listed John Norton's property—and a slave must have cooked and cleaned for Sarah in their home in Graham's Town, for every white housewife in that frontier settlement had a "Kaffir" to do her bidding. Even when Britain abolished slavery in her colonies, in 1833, a fifteen-year-old Joshua would have noticed no difference whatever in a paid servant who still called him "Master." Having grown up with Africans who did not know when they were slaves and when they were free, only that they now got paid to do what they had always done, he had no strong feelings about the "peculiar institution" one way or another, and may have been genuinely puzzled by the fierce arguments that sometimes broke out at Mrs. Carswell's breakfast table between men from the North who subscribed to the *Alta* and men from the South who swore by the *Herald*.

The question of states' rights was quite another matter. That troubled Norton deeply. He thought it simply disgraceful that any state could threaten to secede to safeguard its economy, placing its own welfare before that of the nation. It could only happen in a land divided by the political interests of thirty-one sovereign states, never in one whose provinces were united under a single sovereign. He had been saying that for years.

One morning he came down to breakfast to hear startling news. Sacramento was talking treason. California's new governor, John B. Weller, had declared: "If the wild spirit of fanaticism which now pervades the land should destroy the magnificent confederation, California will not go with North or South, but here on the shores of the Pacific will form a mighty republic, which in the end may prove the greatest of them all." But that was not enough for Congressman John Burch, who demanded immediate separation, calling upon "the enlightened nations of the earth to acknowledge our independence."

The *Alta* announced that a leading banker, Captain William T. Sherman, had closed his bank and gone back east to rejoin the Army.

The empire was falling apart.

Tom King was not dispatched by a Casey, as Sherman had hoped. He was tumbled by a writer's pen and humbled by a strumpet's scorn. The writer was Ned McGowan, the harlot Belle Ryan, now

Belle Cora, a wife for less than an hour, having been married in the shadow of a gallows by a priest who had thought he was there only to speed an errant soul on its way with a prayer.

McGowan had founded a weekly paper in Sacramento, *The Phoenix*. Its first issue carried a story headlined "The Life of Thomas S. King, alias Slippery Sim! The Fratricide! The Bawd's Pimp! Who Lives on the Bones of His Brother and the Flesh of His Wife!" Readers were titillated to learn that Slippery Sim's divorced wife was flourishing as a whore in Washington, D.C. The gambler's widow enjoyed a sweet revenge by publicly offering Mrs. King ten thousand dollars to come to San Francisco and be the main attraction of her brothel on Pike Street. When Judge McGowan printed his own sly fib that she had accepted, Tom King did not wait to see if it was true. He sold the *Bulletin* and fled.

The editorial chair was filled by George Kenyon Fitch, a decent man who completely reversed the paper's anti-Irish policy by hailing the election of David Colbreth Broderick to the United States Senate.

At the end of August 1859, Horace Greeley, the editor and publisher of the New York *Tribune,* arrived covered with boils, having spent three months in jolting stagecoaches traveling from St. Joseph, Missouri, which was as far west as he could go by train. Not too surprisingly, he urged the building of a railroad across the continent. He returned to New York by steamship on September 5, barely missing the drama that would make headlines in his *Tribune*.

At sunrise on September 13, beside a misty lake an hour's drive from town and prying eyes, Chief Justice David S. Terry faced United States Senator David C. Broderick with a pistol. The judge, a Southerner, favored slavery; the senator, a Northerner, opposed it. Their dispute was quickly settled. Broderick fired into the ground; Terry fired into Broderick.

Saturday, September 17, was a day of mourning. Every building of importance in the city was draped with crepe, every flag at half-mast, when Joshua Abraham Norton climbed the stairs of No. 517 Clay Street to George K. Fitch's office, the fervor and fever of madness bright as the light in his eyes.

Chapter 8

Fitch the Kingmaker

> *Take the example of a man who says, again and again, "I am a King, I am a King." By concentrating on being a King, he could eventually produce within himself a state of mind in which . . . even if he has to beg on the street, he feels within himself that he is a King.*
>
> —Maharishi Mahesh Yogi,
> *The Science of Being and the Art of Living*

When Ella Sterling Cummins called upon George Fitch to interview him for a book, she found him in a "tiny place lighted only by a skylight with the rain dripping through and making a wet spot on the floor." George Kenyon Fitch was a church deacon, and apparently looked like one to the author of *The Story of the Files*, who described him as "a clerical gentleman, neat and prim."

> Not a hair was out of place, not a button-hole unmatched to its button, his Prince Albert coat severely neat and irreproachable. His manner was pleasant but cautiously reserved. Conservatism reigned in this little room.

But that was in 1892, when the editor of the *Bulletin* was sixty-six. He could not have been much like the Deacon Fitch who had sat in that same cubbyhole thirty-three years earlier, composing an obituary for David C. Broderick, when a man with a very strange gleam in his eye came to his door with a very strange message. In

1859, a dash of deviltry must have been lurking behind that prim and proper facade, for only a clerical gentleman with an imp in his soul could have thought that a newspaper mourning a fallen senator, its pages bordered black, needed a touch of comic relief.

"Have We an Emperor Among Us?" asked a headline in that evening's issue. And under it Fitch explained:

> This forenoon a well-dressed and serious-looking man entered our office and quietly left the following document, which he respectfully requested we would examine and insert in the *Bulletin*. Promising him to look at it, he politely retired without saying anything further. Here is the paper:
>
>> At the peremptory request of a large majority of the citizens of these United States, I, Joshua Norton, formerly of Algoa Bay, Cape of Good Hope, and now for the past nine years and ten months of San Francisco, California, declare and proclaim myself Emperor of these U. S., and in virtue of the authority thereby in me vested, do hereby order and direct the representatives of the different States of the Union to assemble in the Musical Hall of this city on the 1st day of February next, then and there to make such alterations in the existing laws of the Union as may ameliorate the evils under which the country is laboring, and thereby cause confidence to exist, both at home and abroad, in our stability and integrity.
>>
>> NORTON I,
>> Emperor of the United States.

Now, something about that announcement should intrigue us. Why on earth would he profess to be "formerly of Algoa Bay," where he had lived only eighteen months as a young man, when his last eight years in the colony had actually been spent in Cape Town? We can only guess. Those years in Cape Town, like his boyhood years in Graham's Town and on the Fish River, had been lived under his father's roof, eating his father's bread, subject to his father's will, always the shopkeeper's son, never anything more. That would hardly sit well with one who believed he was a prince. And so Cape Town had been banished from mind with the farm on the Fish and the frontier store, leaving only the memory of those few months with Henry Kirch in Port Elizabeth, where he was king of his own castle, never mind that the castle was quick to topple.

Another odd thing was his signature. He was Norton I, not Joshua I, the only monarch in history ever to be known by his last name instead of his first, a remarkable departure from tradition for one better versed in the ways of royalty than the average American (as Britons usually are, having had to put up with them so much longer). How he must have hated the name that John and Sarah had given him; it appears here for the last time—"I, Joshua Norton"—and was never to be used again.

All that year, on the other side of the Sierra Nevada, in a desolate district of Utah called Washoe, a prospector by the name of James Fennimore, though better known as Old Virginny because he hailed from there, had been digging gold from a mountain claim abandoned by one Henry Comstock.

"Oh, the color is there all right," Comstock had said when asked why he was quitting, "but it's all mixed up with that infernal blue stuff and not worth the trouble."

"What's the blue stuff? Pyrites, you reckon?"

"Damned if I know," said the disgruntled miner.

And he wandered off to seek gold easier to extract from Mount Davidson's cracks and crevices, leaving Old Virginny in full possession.

Henry Comstock was right. It seemed to take forever to chisel a grain of gold from rock heavily streaked with that gray-blue metal. Then one day in October, before the first winter snow came to blanket the bare brown breast of that bleak peak, an inquisitive visitor picked up some of the blue stuff and carried it across the Sierras to Grass Valley in California, where it was assayed. Some two weeks later, the visitor returned in a stagecoach with astonishing news: for every ounce of gold Old Virginny had scraped from his mountain, he had thrown away three ounces of silver. From that day on, the vein of wealth was known as the Comstock Lode. Old Virginny himself, drunk as a lord, broke a bottle of whiskey on the side of his cabin to name the town that mushroomed around it Virginia City. And Congress, in its wisdom, took that godless corner of Utah from the Mormons, gave it to the Gentiles, and called it Nevada.

George Fitch's *Bulletin* was full of Washoe's wonders that October, but there was still room to announce "Another Ukase from Czar Norton." The headline beggared belief:

CONGRESS ABOLISHED! TAKE NOTICE, THE WORLD!

His Imperial Majesty, Norton I, has issued the following edict, which he desires the *Bulletin* to spread before the world. Let her rip!

It is represented to us that the universal suffrage, as now existing throughout the Union, is abused; that fraud and corruption prevent a fair and proper expression of the public voice; that open violation of the laws are constantly occurring, caused by mobs, parties, factions and undue influence of political sects; that the citizen has not that protection of person and property which he is entitled to by paying his *pro rata* of the expense of Government—in consequence of which, WE do hereby abolish Congress, and it is therefore abolished; and WE order and desire the representatives of all parties interested to appear at the Musical Hall of this city on the first of February next, and then and there take *the most effective steps* to remedy the evil complained of.

NORTON I,
Emperor of the United States of America.

Two weeks later, in the same paper, another proclamation abolished California's Supreme Court. Judge Terry, who had fled the city after his illegal duel with Senator Broderick, was arrested near the state border, on his way to Washoe, and brought back to be tried for murder. His acquittal would have been reason enough for Norton to dismiss a Supreme Court that knew how to take care of its own. But, about then, an incident occurred in the East that, when it became known in San Francisco, would elbow all other news aside, leaving no space for whimsical items that might have lessened the shock.

Old John Brown was in Virginia with his broadsword and his Bible, obsessed with a desperate scheme. He planned to recruit a black army, hiding slaves in the mountains as he freed them and giving them rifles to free others. To get the weapons he had crossed the Potomac in the dead of night with seventeen men and captured the United States Arsenal at Harper's Ferry. A company of marines, rushed to the town, surrounded the arsenal and demanded surrender, which the zealot scorned to do. In the battle that ensued he was wounded and ten of his men killed. Utterly certain that he had God on his side, as always, he was led off in chains, unrepentent, calling upon the Lord to witness the fitness of his deed.

Cities in the East, linked by telegraph to Harper's Ferry, had the story within hours. Those in the West would have to wait until the Overland stagecoach arrived with dispatches from St. Louis, where the wires ended. John Brown's trial was avidly followed in California, where "sesesh" newspapers called him a fiend, abolitionist papers a saint, and editors who straddled the fence, mindful of readers from both North and South, somehow managed to give the impression that he was either a saintly fiend, a fiendish saint, or possibly neither, or both. Norton I at least had the sense to see that he was simply demented and therefore not responsible for his actions (doubtless prompting some to say that it takes one to know one). When the stage from St. Louis brought news in December that "General" Brown had been hanged for his crime, Norton's indignation blazed in the *Bulletin* like a beacon:

>DISAPPROVING of the act of Gov. Wise of Virginia in hanging Gen. Brown at Charlestown, Va., on 2nd December;
>
>AND CONSIDERING that the said Brown was insane and that he ought to have been sent to the Insane Asylum for capturing the State of Virginia with seventeen men;
>
>NOW KNOW ALL MEN that I do hereby discharge him, Henry A. Wise, from said office, and appoint John C. Breckenridge, of Kentucky, to said office of Governor of our Province of Virginia.
>
>>NORTON I,
>>Emperor of the United States of America.

George Fitch knew by now that he had stumbled onto a good thing; the "royal proclamations" were immensely popular and his paper's circulation had increased. He hoped they would continue and that Norton I—whoever he was—would give them to no other editor.

Congress convened in January, defying Norton's order to disband. He decided to send in troops.

PROCLAMATION

WHEREAS, a body of men calling themselves the National Congress are now in session in Washington City, in violation of our Imperial edict of the 12th of October last, declaring the said Congress abolished;

WHEREAS, it is necessary for the repose of our Empire that the said decree should be strictly complied with;

NOW, THEREFORE, we do hereby Order and Direct Major-General Scott, the Commander-in-Chief of our Armies, immediately upon receipt of this, our Decree, to proceed with a suitable force and clear the Halls of Congress.

NORTON I,
Emperor of the United States.

General Winfield Scott, the hero of Mexico, still active at seventy-four, would rout the rascals just as surely as he had routed Santa Anna at Churubusco and Chapultepec. But "Old Fuss and Feathers" was in Washington Territory, trying to settle an international dispute over whether some islands on the Canadian border belonged to Britain or the United States.

Congress was safe.

Two snarling lions, made of cast iron, guarded the doors of the Musical Hall. In the past, each had stood with a forepaw raised, as though poised for attack, but the paws had been broken off by rowdies on a spree and the beasts now looked rather pathetic. That January, covered with ash, they were all that remained of the Musical Hall when a fire consumed the building. Norton immediately issued another ukase, changing the date and place of his national convention. The states' delegates were now to meet at the Assembly Hall at Post and Kearny on Wednesday, February 5, and the public was invited to attend. George Fitch, eager to exploit the fictitious gathering to promote his newspaper's sales, published an editorial warning readers to expect a crush at the door and urging them to go early to be certain of a seat.

Fitch the Kingmaker 63

"Perhaps it would be advisable," Fitch wrote, "to take a chair, a blanket or two, an umbrella (if need be), a pile of sandwiches, a bottle of something, and just make a night of it, as close to the doors as possible, so as to be ready, when the time comes, for the squeeze. Wednesday is going to be a great day for California."

Despite that fanfare, the *Bulletin* said nothing on February 6 about California's great day. Nor did any other paper mention a convention; after all, it was the Deacon's joke and up to him to explain why the doors of the Assembly Hall were locked tight the previous night. Nobody, presumably, had had the heart to tell Norton there would be no meeting. Seeing the hall in darkness, with no one waiting outside, he must have turned away in dismay and walked sadly back to his lodgings.

There can be little doubt that he was deeply hurt. For five months the *Bulletin* heard nothing from him, much to the regret of those who bought the paper just to read what he had to say. The best that Fitch could do was publish the text of the speech he would have delivered at the Assembly Hall if any of the delegates had been present to hear it. It briefly reviewed the problems besetting the Union, and ended with these words: "Taking all of these circumstances into consideration, and the internal dissensions on Slavery, we are certain that nothing will save the nation from utter ruin except an Absolute Monarchy under the supervision and authority of an independent Emperor."

An absolute monarchy, ruled by divine right, was exactly what Charles X had tried so hard to impose upon an obstinate France.

Chapter 9

Thunder in the East

I want to be a soldier and go to Dixie's land,
A knapsack on my shoulder and a gun in my hand;
Then I will shoot Jeff Davis and Beauregard will hang,
And make all Rebels tremble throughout our glorious land.

—Union song

I want to be a soldier and with the soldiers stand,
A knapsack on my shoulder and musket in my hand;
And there beside Jeff Davis, so glorious and brave,
I'll whip the cussed Yankee and drive him to his grave.

—Confederate song

In April the Pony Express arrived. Thousands turned out to cheer the lithe animal that trotted ashore from a riverboat at one o'clock in the morning with mail that had traveled nearly two thousand miles from St. Joseph, Missouri, in just a week and a half. The

Bulletin, more accustomed to publishing dispatches that were almost a month old after crossing the plains in a stagecoach, hailed the achievement as the wonder of the age: "It took 75 ponies to make the trip from Missouri to California in 10½ days, but the last one—the little fellow who came down in the Sacramento boat this morning—had the glory of them all."

The pony got all the glory, the rider none. George Fitch forgot to mention his name: "The California Band traveled up and down the streets, waking all the echoes and making the night melodious. Bonfires were kindled here and there—on the Plaza, on the wharves, wherever there was an old tar-barrel to steal, a gathering of shavings, or a dry-goods box to burn. A stranger would have thought the bay was on fire."

A jubilant crowd escorted the animal to the Pony Express office on Montgomery Street, where the mail was distributed and the Mayor tried to make a speech but was howled down by the merrymakers. When he asked if he might have silence to continue, he was told it was up to "the Hippogriff." But that poor beast, the *Bulletin* reported, had suffered enough; he "considered for a moment, eyed the ribbons about his neck, looked a bit sleepy, thought of his oats, and uttered a loud *neigh.* So the speeches were corked down."

In May the pony brought word from Chicago that Abraham Lincoln had been nominated as the Republican Party's choice for President. That news infuriated the South, which seethed anew with threats to secede if "the gorilla" who had vowed to free the slaves should win the election. The hubbub in San Francisco's papers brought Norton out of his lodgings at last, determined to try once more to bring the nation to its senses. He called upon Fitch with another proclamation:

> WHEREAS, it is necessary for our Peace, Prosperity and Happiness, as also to the National Advancement of the people of the United States, that they should dissolve the Republican form of government and establish in its stead an Absolute Monarchy;
>
> NOW, THEREFORE, WE, Norton I, by the Grace of God Emperor of the Thirty-three States and the multitude of Territories of the United States of North America, do hereby *dissolve* the Republic of the United States, and it is hereby dissolved;

And all laws made from and after this date, either by the National Congress or any State Legislature, shall be null and of no effect.

All Governors, and all other persons in authority, shall maintain order by enforcing the heretofore existing laws and regulations until the necessary alterations can be effected.

Given under our hand and seal, at Headquarters, San Francisco, this 26th day of July, 1860.

NORTON I.

George III, the last mad English monarch of America, could not have said it better.

Norton no longer lived at 255 Kearny; either he was evicted for his bizarre behavior or had departed voluntarily, unable to endure the jeers and jibes at Mrs. Carswell's table when the *Bulletin* was passed around. His home now was a shabby hotel on Bush Street, the Metropolitan, whose proprietors apparently cared little about a tenant's idiosyncrasies so long as the rent was paid. How he paid it nobody knew for certain, though the press would later guess.

"Norton was a member of the Masonic Order, belonging to Occidental Lodge," one newspaper explained. "As he was in good standing up to the time of his malady, his brethren have since contributed a regular stipend to his support."

To some extent that was true, though he had not been a member in good standing for years, since his suspension in 1855. Still, a few of the brethren, it seemed, were willing to help him. Sir William Lane Booker was one, by all accounts, and Joseph Eastland was probably another. It would have to be done tactfully, of course, without hurting his pride, but Norton himself provided the solution to that. He simply "taxed" them, and did it with dignity, meticulously recording in a notebook he carried the precise amount each taxpayer owed.

"Poor old Norton," they would say when he had gone his way, the Imperial Treasury richer by fifty cents. And they would recall how he used to tell them: "If I were Emperor of the United States . . ."

Well, now he was.

*   *   *

Thunder in the East 67

Abraham Lincoln's election victory in November brought the South to a boil. On December 2, in the waning days of James Buchanan's presidency, South Carolina seceded and demanded the surrender of all federal property on its soil, aiming heavy artillery at two United States fortresses in Charleston's harbor to enforce that ultimatum. One bastion, Fort Moultrie, surrounded by dwellings, was indefensible, so its garrison withdrew to the safer walls of Fort Sumter.

With the dawn of 1861 a series of dramas unfolded. In January six more cotton states seceded, uniting in February to found a new nation under a new flag, and a Southern senator, Jefferson Davis of Mississippi, bade Congress a sad farewell and went off to be the President of the Confederate States of America. In March a departing President Buchanan handed President Lincoln the remnants of a shattered republic, which further disintegrated in April when Carolinian cannon roared, firing on Fort Sumter. Virginia, North Carolina, Tennessee, and Arkansas immediately joined South Carolina, Georgia, Mississippi, Alabama, Florida, Louisiana, and Texas under the Confederate banner.

All over the North, all over the South, men swapped suits and overalls for regimentals. So did Joshua Norton, who put on a blue military uniform with a private's kepi and strapped to his waist a cavalry saber, a relic of the Mexican war that might have had a keener edge at Chapultepec.

San Francisco's pawnshops had lots of blue uniforms for sale that summer when the guns of Bull Run thundered, Union tunics pledged by deserters who would never redeem them. They had torn up the tickets and gone off whistling "The Bonnie Blue Flag"—the battle hymn of a new republic—to don coats of gray for Dixie and Jeff Davis. All of these accoutrements—sword, tunic, and kepi—would have cost next to nothing, because nobody wanted a soldier's discarded trappings except the Emperor of the United States, who could not afford better regalia.

The Pony Express rider's moment of glory was brief; the wires of the magnetic telegraph, inching slowly across the plains, brought his gallop to a halt only eighteen months after it began. On January 24, 1861, the click of a key in New York was answered in an instant by a chattering key in San Francisco. Now the news from the East could be on George Fitch's desk in a day, brought by the speed of sound. But the words that came singing along the telegraph wires made depressing reading in the *Bulletin,* for they told of dreadful slaughter on blood-red battlefields. The only thing that brightened the Deacon's day was when a middle-aged man in a soldier's coat, rumpled and wrinkled, carelessly unbuttoned, politely tapped on his door and handed him another proclamation.

Edict followed edict. Fitch's circulation soared, and the rest of the press watched with envy. The influential *Daily Alta California,* the so-called "Mother of Newspapers," first in the state ever published and first on the Governor of California's desk every morning, decided it must have the Emperor.

Norton the First was on his way to fame, if not fortune.

Chapter 10

Colonel Moustache

All the physicians and authors in the world could not give a clear account of his madness. He is mad in patches, full of lucid intervals.

—Cervantes, *Don Quixote*

I am but mad north-north-west: when the wind is southerly I know a hawk from a handsaw.

—*Hamlet*

A local playwright whose name is unknown was the first to see Norton as a subject for the stage. On September 17, 1861, a new theater opened its doors with a comic opera titled *Norton the First*. The daily papers made no mention of it, but *The Golden Era,* a weekly literary journal, found space among its serialized romances, poetry, recipes, and execrable jokes for a paragraph of praise:

ACADEMY OF MUSIC—The new melodeon at Tucker's Hall is among the most popular places of resort in the city. An original burlesque entitled "Norton the First" or "An Emperor for a Day" is now being played nightly, creating roars of irrepressible laughter. Walter Bray enacts Norton I, making up his part very effectively and clothing the character with his inexhaustible fund of comicalities. The whole dramatic company is enlisted in this musical extravaganza.

The "extravaganza" occupied the second half of a program that began with an hour of song and banter with banjos by the soot-blackened cast of Monsieur and Madame Schwegerle's Terpsichorean and Negro Minstrel Troupe, whose most notable contribution to the evening's entertainment was a rousing new square dance called "The Turkey in the Straw."

The date is worth noticing. That September 17 happened to be the second anniversary of the day Norton proclaimed himself Emperor. This coincidence is so remarkable it is tempting to suppose that the manager might have chosen this particular play for the opening of his theater to induce His Majesty to attend. Perhaps he thought his presence would attract some attention in the press, though it is fairly safe to say that Norton would have declined any invitation to see a farce that merely made sport of him.

And yet, in a way, it was fortunate that the public saw him only as a figure of fun. Three weeks after the musical opened, another poor lunatic who imagined he was royalty, George Koenig, a shopkeeper of Austrian birth, was committed to the State Insane Asylum in Stockton for stoutly maintaining that he was the rightful King of Austria (as indeed he was, Koenig being German for "king").

A contributor to *Scribner's Monthly Magazine*, writing in Norton's day, described San Francisco as "the Elysium of bummers," where a worthless fellow "too lazy to work and too cowardly to steal" could get a meal for nothing if he had the price of a drink. He was alluding to that time-honored institution, the "free lunch counter." Every tavern had one. In a modest establishment like the Ivy Green or the Blue Wing, which charged only fifteen cents for a cocktail, the free lunch might consist of boiled eggs and cold mutton, but Barry & Patten's, Martin & Horton's, and the Bank Exchange, where a Brandy Smash cost as much as a quarter, provided a generous repast of "soup, boiled salmon, roast beef, bread and butter, potatoes, tomatoes, crackers and cheese."

Martin & Horton's was a favorite haunt of the press. Albert S. Evans of the *Alta California* and Frank Gross of the *Bulletin* must have eaten there often, if the frequency of their visits may be measured by the number of times they mentioned Clark Martin and Tom Horton's saloon in their columns. The whole town knew that Emperor Norton ate there, because Gross and Evans said so, which ought to dispose of the fiction that he dined like royalty in restaurants of quality that never presented a bill. He ate free where everyone else ate free, in taverns, shoulder to shoulder with bankers and brokers who called him a bummer for doing exactly what they did themselves.

The story that Norton could dine wherever he chose without payment was entirely unknown in his own lifetime and did not begin to surface until long after his death, twelve years after to be precise, when Robert Louis Stevenson gave birth to the fable in *The Wrecker,* the novel he wrote with Lloyd Osbourne. It first appeared as a serial in *Scribner's Magazine* in 1892 before it was reprinted in book form by Charles Scribner's Sons. You may remember the passage:

> . . . where else, in God's green earth, [could he] have taken his pick of restaurants, ransacked the bill of fare and departed scathless? They tell me he was even an exacting patron, threatening to withdraw his custom when dissatisfied; and I can believe it, for his face wore an expression distinctly gastronomical.

There was nothing like that in the books and newspapers when he was alive, no mention at all of restaurateurs who plied him with costly comestibles. If he did dine in style, it was a remarkably well-kept secret, unknown even to Gross and Evans.

The saloonkeepers welcomed him, since the mere sight of him in a taproom often inspired some reporter hard up for a snippet of news to unparalleled flights of fancy, especially when stimulated by a free cocktail offered by the landlord. The result was usually a puff in the press that boosted business and filled the till. So, you see, he really paid for his beef and salmon, not in coin but in priceless publicity, just as the journalists did.

There is a remarkable absence of alcohol in all of these tales about taverns told by his contemporaries. Many a glass or goblet must have been pressed upon him by the businessmen who browsed beside him at the luncheon table, but if he did down a drink with his meal it apparently was not considered worth noting. The only reference to liquor appears in Stevenson's fiction, where Norton the First samples a snifter of Thirteen Star, a homemade brandy of doubtful distinction offered by the merchant who made it ("I am always delighted to patronize native industries," he tells Jim Pinkerton). Stevenson, who arrived just before the emperor died, scarcely knew him, of course, and even the newspapermen who entertained the author with tall stories about His Majesty considered him abstemious.

"Emperor Norton never was a drinking man, despite the glowing splendor of his nose, the main attraction of a saloon being always its lunch counter," Jimmy Bowman, one of Stevenson's friends, wrote in the *Chronicle* on that dismal day in 1880 when the town learned to its dismay that His Majesty was no more.

And the *Morning Call* agreed: "He was temperate in his habits."

As for the glowing splendor of his nose—well, that should not be taken too literally, for this was the nose that the *Call* thought "aquiline" and much like Napoleon III's, the glow being no more than a journalist's jest, a feeble attempt at humor to color a column that was as gray as the day that he died.

His barroom conversation was equally sober. Benjamin E. Lloyd testified to that in his *Lights and Shades in San Francisco,* a booster book published in 1876 and the first to tell tourists about Norton while he was alive.

> He will talk very readily upon any subject, and his opinions are usually very correct, except when relating to himself. He is more familiar with history than the ordinary citizen, and his scientific knowledge, though sometimes mixed, is considerable.

Paranoid schizophrenia, Norton's affliction, often leaves the intelligence unimpaired. Dr. Alexander R.K. Mitchell, a British psychiatrist of our own day, explains in his treatise, *Schizophrenia: the Meaning of Madness*: "He [the schizophrenic] is rarely hallucinated and may appear quite normal until someone touches upon a sensitive subject which releases all of his paranoia." So it was with Norton; only when discussing matters "relating to himself" was he inclined to be irrational. Anyone who called him "Mr. Norton" was gently reminded of his imperial rank and admonished to address him with proper respect.

The banker and the broker who joined him for lunch soon learned to call him "Your Majesty."

There were those who suspected that Norton was not nearly so demented as was popularly believed. Albert Evans was one. "The Emperor is supposed, by the ignorant, to be touched in the upper story," he told his readers, "but we think his head is perfectly clear. In taking a passing glance at His Majesty, one would imagine that he was a fit subject for [the insane asylum in] Stockton, but such is not the case."

Evans may have heard His Majesty in Martin & Horton's airing his scientific knowledge or his familiarity with history, as did Benjamin Lloyd, and concluded that, because he seemed to be perfectly lucid when discussing matters *not* relating to himself, his madness must be simulated for some dark reason he would not disclose.

General William Tecumseh Sherman, then in command of the Army of the Cumberland in Kentucky, might have supplied an answer to that, if anyone had asked. In 1858, when he was trying to wind up his bank's affairs before returning east, Sherman had written to explain to his partners in St. Louis why he had not been able to collect several thousand dollars owed by a lawyer in Downieville. The debtor had feigned insanity, pretending to know nothing about the matter. Such knavery was really quite common after the bank crash of '55, Sherman told James Lucas and Henry Turner. "The city and every man in San Francisco will avoid a debt created before 1855 on the ground that everybody there was *non compos mentis*—about true."

But Norton had not escaped his debts; Sherman himself had taken his last pound of flesh. His madness was authentic.

The days were long gone when a Bourbon prince had to be hidden from Louis Philippe's assassins, the King, crowned by the will of the people and precipitously uncrowned when the people discovered their mistake, having fled in disguise to England. A Bonaparte now reigned in France, Napoleon III, nephew of the conquering Bonaparte and an empire builder like his uncle. In the fall of 1861, after adding Cochin China to his domains, Louis Napoleon invaded Mexico upon the pretext of collecting a debt, whereupon the Emperor of the United States proclaimed himself Protector of Mexico.

The Emperor had known a Bonaparte once, in Pike Street, Sam Ward's brother-in-law.

Bonaparte blood certainly flowed in the veins of Adolphe Mailliard; his father, Louis Mailliard, was a natural son of Napoleon Bonaparte's brother Joseph, King of Naples and later of Spain in the days of Napoleonic glory. After Waterloo, when King Joseph fled to America, the faithful Louis went with him, accompanied by his pregnant wife. He was majordomo of the exiled monarch's estate near Bordentown, New Jersey, when Adolphe was born.

Adolphe Mailliard was enough of a Bonaparte to risk his life and liberty in that family's cause. When he first met Sam Ward, Mailliard had just returned from Tuscany, where he had been put in prison for plotting to seat another Bonaparte upon an Italian throne, and having assumed the stewardship of the Bordentown estate after his father's death had gone to Wall Street to confer with Sam about the disposition of some Bonaparte funds in Ward's bank. Sam was so captivated by this gallant adventurer that he took him home to meet his youngest sister, Annie, who had no objection at all to being wooed by a handsome grandson of the former King of Spain. Adolphe's and Annie's marriage, in 1846, was the highlight of New York's social season.

Mailliard joined the Gold Rush to California, to try his luck with Sam, and stayed with the McAllister brothers in Pike Street whenever he was in San Francisco, later sending for Annie and their small son (christened Louis Napoleon, after Napoleon III, but called Poley). Their home now was a sprawling ranch in Marin County, across the Golden Gate. Sam had been a welcome visitor there, pampering their palates with delectable dishes, but he had returned to his Medora on Long Island (having made enough of a fortune to wake her up on the morning of his arrival in his own grand manner—by peppering her windows with pebbles which proved to be nuggets of gold).

The Mailliards often crossed the bay to attend a ball or a banquet at the McAllister mansion on Stockton Street.

"They gave the merriest parties at the Stockton Street house," Amelia Ransome Neville, a frequent guest, remembered. "One evening we had charades, with 'The Seasons' represented by men of the party. Hall McAllister was Spring with a wreath of artificial flowers on his head. . . . Autumn was presented by Arthur Godeffroy, who carried a pumpkin." (Mrs. Neville may have thought that Alfred Godeffroy's first name was Arthur, but that sheltered young lady could not have known Old Cast Iron Posterior nearly as well as Fanny Perriere had known him.)

In her book *The Fantastic City* (completed when she was ninety and still in love with a town younger than herself), she explained what Willy Sillem had done when he heard that Henry Meiggs had become a millionaire by building railroads in Chile and Peru. He took a steamer to Lima, returning with a chest full of gold and a bride on his arm, Honest Harry having repaid Godeffroy and Sillem every cent that they had lost when he absconded and tossed in a bonus—his niece.

Amelia Neville, a Connecticut beauty married at sixteen to a dashing army captain during a visit to Ireland, arrived in San Francisco with her English husband in 1856 and stayed for fifty years. She was rather proud of the fact that in London, when hardly more than a child, she had danced with dukes, dined with earls, and been presented at the Court of St. James. And yet, although she greatly admired the British queen whose plump little hand she had kissed, she devoted quite as much space in her memoirs to Norton Imperator as to Victoria Regina. "During shopping hours," she wrote, "one saw him in Kearny or Montgomery Street, walking toward some destination which I fancy was never reached, his old army uniform and military cap with its rakish feather worn with an air. A sword hung from his sword-belt and he sometimes carried a short, knotted stick which might have been a scepter. The whole town knew him."

And, like a true San Franciscan, Amelia Neville clung faithfully to the legend that the city loved:

> "Emperor" Norton was a favored ward of the town who could dine in any restaurant and imperially ignore the cost, buy theatre tickets in any box office with no more than an imperial nod of thanks, and draw checks on San Francisco banks, although he owned not a dollar on earth.

But Mrs. Neville, who dwelt in splendor, viewed the Emperor from heights too lofty to be able to distinguish clearly how much of that was true and how much of it merely myth. In the 1860s, when she dined in Stockton Street, she was still in her twenties and full of wonder. The bankers she met at the McAllister house may have told her that they cashed the checks of a madman who owned not a dollar on earth, and did it right willingly, but middle-aged men are often inclined to wear haloes when they dine in the presence of angels. Did Sillem or Godeffroy, bankers both, ever tell her of the part they had played in a former friend's ruin? It's unlikely. Better to bask in the glow of a pretty woman's smile than risk her profound displeasure. So if, in her book, she stretched the truth a trifle (well, really more than a trifle), she did it in all innocence, trusting the tales she had heard from a guest blessed with her company at dinner, who sought only to amuse a lovely lady and make her dark eyes twinkle.

The charades they played in a parlor with pumpkins must have seemed rather dull compared to the charade they played at the table.

Like so many other San Franciscans of her time, Amelia Neville collected the Emperor's proclamations in a scrapbook. Here is one she treasured enough to put in her autobiography:

> Know ye whom it may concern that We, Norton I, Emperor of the United States and Protector of Mexico, have heard serious complaints that our wardrobe is a national disgrace and even His Majesty, the King of Pain, has had his sympathy excited so far as to offer us a suit of clothing, which we have a delicacy in accepting. Therefore we warn those whose duty it is to attend to these affairs that their scalps are in danger if our said need is unheeded.

That decree, unfortunately, has all the earmarks of a forgery, a joke perpetrated by Albert Evans to amuse his readers, who must have roared with glee when they read it in the *Alta* (although Mrs. Neville herself evidently missed the point if she pasted it in her scrapbook in the belief that it was genuine). The joke was that the King of Pain had no clothes to offer. None at all. At least, he wore none himself. The King of Pain was a health faddist who peddled liniment outside the Pacific Clinical Infirmary to anyone who emerged with a muscular ache and a doctor's advice to apply salve. He was an astonishing sight in his red union suit and bare feet, the threadbare blanket around his thin shoulders his only protection against wind and rain, for it was his proud boast that he needed no garments so long as his body was smeared with the ointment he sold.

The Emperor's wardrobe must have been in sad disrepair after a year of hard service, however. The story goes that he visited a tailoring establishment, Walter & Tompkins, and commanded the clothiers to provide suitable raiment. Now, it could be true that they measured him for a new uniform, as Evans said, making note of the breadth of his back and the length of his legs—he was about five feet, nine inches—before bowing him out of the door with an empty promise. But we have only the word of a reporter who may have made up the whole thing, possibly to secure a bargain on clothes for himself, for he kept the town laughing for a month with "royal proclamations" purporting to come from His Majesty's pen (which might have been worth a free suit to a tailor).

One such decree, addressed to Major Leonard, the officer in charge of the old Presidio beside the Golden Gate, ordered him to compel Walter & Tompkins to deliver the garments or the clothiers would face a unique form of punishment:

> WHEREAS, avaricious persons and others are conspiring against our person, right and dignity by refusing to supply us with suitable clothing, although repeatedly requested to do so; and
>
> WHEREAS, the national dignity and rights are thereby injured;
>
> NOW, THEREFORE, we command that you proceed on receipt of this our decree forthwith to the tailors, Walter & Tompkins, on Montgomery Street of this city, and then and there proceed to take the rivets out of their shears and prohibit any person from repairing them or furnish them with new ones until they shall furnish us with our clothing, which they have long ago been requested to do.
>
> Given under our hand this 11th day of September, 1862.
>
> NORTON I.

The decree did little good when published, though. Walter & Tompkins could not make him even a handkerchief without rivets in their shears.

But the tailors did get some publicity out of it. And it slowly began to dawn on San Francisco's business community that, to get a puff in the *Alta,* all one had to do was slip Albert Evans a bribe—promise him a suit, invite him to dinner, or simply ply him with liquor—and he would publish a fake proclamation, linking one's name with the Emperor's.

The gentle madman who made it all possible simply grew shabbier and shabbier. And dirtier. And thinner. All of the many photographs taken at this time of his life, in the early 1860s, show a pitifully undernourished Emperor, a mere bag of bones, nothing like the "portly, rather flabby man" Robert Louis Stevenson would see nearly two decades later. Quite obviously, the bankers were not cashing his checks as willingly as they told Mrs. Neville they were.

To make his uniform look a little more impressive the Emperor added epaulets about the size of saucers, with gilded fringes, after the fashion of Louis Napoleon's imperial shoulder ornaments (except that Norton's tassels were old and discolored).

Albert S. Evans syndicated the items he wrote, mailing copies to editors all over California, across the mountains to Washoe, and even as far as Chicago, changing only the pen name he used in each paper. His columns in the *Alta* appeared under the byline "Fitz Smythe" but he was "Amigo" in the Gold Hill *Evening News* on the Comstock Lode and "Altamonte" in the Chicago *Tribune.* He also had a name that he may not have known about, since it was conferred upon him by the newspaper fraternity when his back was turned and probably never uttered within earshot. Because of his British tweeds and his absurd mustache—a truly monstrous appendage, waxed and twisted into long spikes like the garbels of a catfish—he looked more like a pompous colonel of Her Britannic Majesty's Brigade of Guards than a reporter, so his colleagues called him "Colonel Moustache."

Evans had appointed himself official biographer to San Francisco's crackpots; the colorful characters who infested its streets were all grist to his mill.

"Probably no town of the same size in the world has so many public individuals who have become noted for their peculiarities," he bragged with pardonable civic pride, all unaware that the hirsute peculiarity adorning his own upper lip had earned him the reputation of being something of a character himself. "Among some of its leading notorieties we may claim as first on the list the Emperor, Norton I.''

So, it was Colonel Moustache who raised Norton the First high above the rank and file of the great unwashed and made him Emperor of the West long before *The New York Times* dubbed him Emperor of the World.

Chapter 11

The Bummers

WHEREAS, there is a class of low scum, degrading to humanity, in the habit of calling "Bummer" when we enter a theatre or hotel, who are evidently put up to it by some thieving scoundrels or proscriptive traitors;

NOW, THEREFORE, we do hereby decree that the Police have full Authority to place these rascals in the chain-gang to learn better manners.

—Norton I.

"Say, what's the name of this place?" the black-bearded young man asked the proprietor of the wayside inn.

"The Grizzly Bear," replied the hosteler.

"Grizzly Bear, you say? Well, my friend, you need a new sign. That one outside is faded so bad, you can't tell if there's a bear on it or a cross-eyed bedbug. Now, see here, I'm an artist and have my colors right here in my bundle. So give me a square meal and an agreeable fee and I'll paint you a grizzly you can be proud of."

They settled on a dinner and a dollar.

"How do you want this bear?" asked the artist, unpacking his paints and brushes. "Chained or unchained? Fast or loose?"

"Loose," said the boniface.

And that's what he got, a fearsome brute, unfettered.

The traveler ate his fill, pocketed his pay, shouldered his bedroll with a glance at the glowering sky, and hurried off down the trail before the innkeeper could discover that watercolors do not hold fast in the rain. That bear would come loose with the first heavy shower.

Edward E. Jump, a cartoonist down on his luck, was on his way from a dying camp on the well-plundered Mother Lode to the city beside the bay, where he would add a flourish of his own to the legend of Emperor Norton.

San Francisco tolerated eccentricity to a degree that strangers, transplanted from harsher soil, found difficult to fathom.

"So many quaint gentlemen, who in a modern city would face the indignity of being 'run in,' passed unmolested in Montgomery Street," wrote Amelia Neville, whose carriage frequently traveled that avenue of banks and cranks. She recognized them because the press had so often described them. In a day when newspapers were pitifully slim, rarely more than four pages, editors like Deacon Fitch and Frederick MacCrellish of the *Alta California* would always try to find room for some comical item brought in from the streets about the King of Pain, the Money King, Bummer and Lazarus, Norton the First, or George Washington the Second.

The Money King, a loan shark, conducted his curbside business in front of the Hall of Brokers. He was incredibly stingy, if the *Alta* can be believed, although the yarn that Albert Evans told about his gift to a loving niece is a bit hard to swallow. She had written from New York to ask for some small token of remembrance, so he sent her his toenail clippings.

George Washington II, a corpulent copy of the first, was "Professor" Freddie Coombs, a phrenologist who analyzed bumps on the heads of the gullible in Montgomery Street's saloons, discovering matchless intelligence in this bulge and the wisdom of Solomon in that, qualities not readily apparent to the bartenders who kept those same heads addled with alcohol. He wore a three-cornered hat, knee breeches, and a powdered periwig, the costume of colonial days, and carried a banner emblazoned with the stirring device: "The Spirit of Washington Still Lives!" (though it cut no ice with Colonel Moustache, who irreverently called him "Wash"). Perhaps it was to attract a wealthy widow that he advertised himself on posters all over town as "The Great Matrimonial Candidate." If so, the hint went unheeded; nobody, it seems, wanted to be Martha Washington II.

Bummer and Lazarus were two vagrant dogs whose ancestry baffled every reporter who tried to describe them. The best that one can say is that Lazarus was a puny yellow cur and Bummer black and shaggy. The term "publicity hound" must have originated with these two, for no one—not even Norton the First in those days—could charm a paragraph out of a newspaperman quite as easily as Bummer and Lazarus. Every day, without fail, they appeared at Martin & Horton's lunch counter to cadge tidbits from the reporters and get their names in the papers. But an astute reader would have noticed that any item about the dogs in the *Alta* or the *Bulletin* was invariably a thinly veiled excuse to publicize somebody's business. Markets seemed especially favored:

> In front of the Clay Street French Market we have seen two or three men for a day's sport tear up the sidewalk and begin to shovel out live rats, two to a spade; not one of them could strike the ground without meeting Bummer's fierce teeth. Occasionally, he would fall back and wait for Lazarus to go in, and then it was delightful to see how his bushy tail was affected with joy at his weak friend's enterprise. Between the two, no rat ever saw the light of their eyes and escaped alive.

Shortly after that piece appeared in the *Alta,* Frank Gross topped it in the *Bulletin:* "Gould & Martin cleared off a gallery in their fruit market, and during the process the two dogs, with the aid of some clubs wielded by earnest men, killed over 400 rats!"

What better way to persuade the public that the markets were now free from vermin and fit to satisfy even the most rigid Department of Health inspection? Other merchants, eager to see their own names in print, suddenly discovered rats on their premises and began calling in the dogs and reporters. Some of the merchants, however, would soon regret it. When a newsdealer locked Bummer in his depot overnight, ostensibly to rid the place of rodents, Lazarus came to the rescue, diving headlong at the window and shattering it beyond repair. A jeweler who locked up both dogs, hoping for an honorable mention, found his showcase wrecked next morning and diamonds all over the floor. So it went on, week after week, month after month, for more than two years, the town never tiring of the adventures of two mutts without a master.

And then, one day, Lazarus fell afoul of the law.

An ordinance had recently been passed, forbidding dogs to roam the streets without a muzzle. Any found unmuzzled would be taken to the city pound and put to death if not redeemed upon payment of a fine within forty-eight hours. When Clark Martin learned that Lazarus had been captured and was awaiting execution, he marched down to the pound, paid the five dollars demanded, and threatened to break the dogcatcher's head. Evans and Gross backed him foursquare in the papers, and somebody drew up a petition to the Mayor and the Board of Supervisors, praying that Bummer and Lazarus be consecrated as city property "whereby they may be exempted from taxation or destruction and suffered to wander unmolested in search of their daily food." More than a thousand signed the petition.

Both dogs were at City Hall, crouched at the door of the council chamber, when the Supervisors met to consider their fate. "If any man carried them there, it was a cute dodge to get favorable action on their petition," wrote Fitz Smythe, who might have done it himself.

The politicians, uncomfortably aware that the press was present in force, pencils poised to praise or condemn their decision, hastily voted to grant Bummer and Lazarus the freedom of the city.

And that's when Ed Jump came to town.

Joseph Roos examined, with growing excitement, the sketches that the stranger had left on his counter, for these were nothing like the pastoral prints that Currier & Ives shipped to his shop from New York. He showed them to his partner, Albert Wunderlich (the sign over the shop said "Snow & Roos" but Wunderlich was now his partner).

"Who's the artist?" asked Wunderlich, seeing only the initials "E.J." on the drawings.

"His name is Edward Jump."

"Well, he's a corker, whoever he is. These should sell quicker than darkies in Dixie."

He was right. The cartoons sold as fast as they could be printed. San Franciscans much preferred pictures of local scenes, filled with familiar faces, to Nathaniel Currier's hand-colored lithographs of hayrides in Connecticut and sleighrides in Vermont, which bore no relation at all to life in California. Parlors all over town were quickly decorated with Ed Jump's comical caricatures of Norton I, the Money King, the Great Unknown, the Guttersnipe, George Washington II in his knee breeches, the King of Pain in his drawers. But the print that everyone loved the best was the one that caused all the rumpus.

It showed Norton I at a lunch counter, about to swallow a morsel of meat, while at his feet, wistfully eyeing his fork, were Bummer and Lazarus. And the trouble began when Roos and Wunderlich put it in their windows at Montgomery and California streets.

The thump of a walking-stick on glass brought Joe Roos out of his shop on the double.

"Stop! Stop!" the print-seller cried.

"An insult, sir!" spluttered the Emperor, flailing away at the window, for the cartoon on display clearly implied that he was no better than the dogs, three bummers together.

Some wags who had stopped to watch, attracted by the uproar, gleefully shouted encouragement.

"Go to it, Emp!"

"Bully for you!"

"Lay on, Yer Majesty!"

But the pane proved stouter than the cane, which cracked.

"His Imperial Majesty stalked off with his usual dignity," Fitz Smythe told the town next morning, "his hand holding the balance of power in the shape of a broken cane."

The press made much of the incident, and Snow & Roos profited from the publicity. Customers flocked to the shop to buy "The Three Bummers." Several saloonkeepers purchased copies to hang in their taverns with signs that read:

HIS IMPERIAL MAJESTY, NORTON I,
EATS HERE WITH BUMMER AND LAZARUS

Even the Metropolitan Theater on Montgomery Street, the city's largest playhouse, sought to cash in on the cartoon's popularity by producing a burletta, *Life in San Francisco,* starring Bummer and Lazarus, whose roles consisted chiefly of being dragged onstage by two red-nosed comedians dressed as Norton I and George Washington II.

The Emperor profited, too, for soon he was seen with a handsome new cane, the gift of some unknown admirer. On its black knotted shaft was a miniature shield made of silver, which bore the inscription:

NORTON I
EMPEROR OF THE UNITED STATES
AND PROTECTOR OF MEXICO

Nothing concerning the "Emp" escaped the pen of Albert Evans, no matter how trivial, for he was greatly skilled in the art of embroidery and could make a purse from any pig's ear. When, for example, Heuston & Hastings ("Gentlemen's Clothing of Quality and Distinction"), a large department store with an eye for publicity, presented the Emperor with a splendid new hat, richly adorned with a plume of jet-black ostrich feathers, Colonel Moustache waxed lyrical in the *Alta* to the point of sheer absurdity, not only borrowing a snatch of verse to describe it but even tossing in a volcano:

> His Imperial Majesty, Norton I, appeared on Montgomery Street yesterday under a hat which could not be less than—hold! It is not for us to indulge in familiarities with royalty; we can therefore give no definite measurement of its height.
> "Know ye the height of the green-capped rush
> "Which grew in Fingal's garden?"
> Suffice it to say that it is as tall as you can remember, and towered aloft above his rugged royal brows as the fiery smoke-clad Vesuvius during an eruption.

Such a hat had not been seen since the early 1850s, when Louis Kossuth, the exiled Hungarian statesman, introduced it to America. Ten years earlier, every man in the East who thought himself a dandy had worn a Kossuth hat, though it had never been popular in the West, where its waving plume would have been a target too tempting for any rowdy armed with a slingshot or a brickbat. Thus, a hat that must have been gathering dust on a shopkeeper's shelf for a decade became a "crown fit for a king." And perhaps a card appeared in a window of the clothing store on the corner of Montgomery and Sutter to tell all who passed that Heuston & Hastings were now "Gentlemen's Outfitters by Appointment to His Imperial Majesty."

But urchins still called "Bummer!" as the Emperor walked down the street, proud as a peacock, his silver-knobbed hickory stick pacing his stride, his feathers aflutter in the morning breeze, his boots agape at the toes.

Chapter 12

Fifty Cents a Night

The nobility were represented by his Grace the Duke of Benicia, the Countess of San Jose, Lord Blessyou, Lord Geeminy, and many others whose titles and whose faces have passed from my memory. Owing to a pressure of imperial business, the Emperor Norton was unable to come.

—Mark Twain

Every Sunday the Emperor went to church and every Saturday to synagogue, taking a pew at St. Mary's one week and perhaps the First Unitarian Church the next, but always observing the Jewish Sabbath from a seat in the front row of the balcony at Temple Emanu-El. Catholic priests, Protestant ministers, and rabbis alike would remember that in their memoirs.

"I think it my duty to encourage religion and morality by showing myself at church," he explained to a Methodist minister, the Reverend O.P. Fitzgerald, "and to avoid jealousy I attend them all in turn."

He disapproved strongly of clergymen who used the pulpit to express political views, abolitionists who vented their wrath upon the South, and secessionists who railed at the North. "I will put a stop to it," he promised the Reverend Fitzgerald. "The preachers must stop preaching politics or they must all come into one State Church." The pastor of Minna Street Methodist Church South did not say whether he thought the Emperor meant that as a warning to himself, but possibly it was. A church that added "South" to its name did so to signify which side of the conflict it supported.

It troubled the Emperor deeply that he had never been crowned with God's blessing, as his "dear cousin" Victoria had been crowned by the Archbishop of Canterbury in Westminster Abbey. To correct that oversight he issued an edict:

> We do hereby command the Leaders of the Hebrew, Catholic and Protestant Churches to sanctify and have us crowned Emperor of the United States and Protector of Mexico.
>
> Given under our hand and Seal of State this 10th day of July, 1862.
>
> NORTON I.

His acknowledgment of Jewish leaders, like his attendance at synagogue, suggests that he sincerely regretted his disrespectful attitude toward John Norton's religion during family prayers in Cape Town, and that it bothered his conscience. Perhaps that's why the memory of that Sabbath scolding on Bree Street was uppermost in his mind when Nathan Peiser came out of the past to haunt him. It does not, however, imply that he now had doubts about his "Christian" birth, for he would believe in that to the end of his days.

On August 22, 1862, in a letter to the New York *Tribune*, President Lincoln publicly revealed that he would proclaim the emancipation of every slave in rebel territory on the first day of the coming year. This, to many of his cabinet ministers, was a tactical blunder that would simply encourage the South to fight harder to protect its cotton trade. Recent heavy casualties, often suffered in battles neither won nor lost, had dampened the ministers' enthusiasm for liberating slaves. Antietam alone had cost each side thirteen thousand dead.

Another dark day dawned for the Union in December when General Ambrose Burnside unwisely launched a massive frontal attack on a rebel army strongly entrenched at Fredericksburg, Virginia, under General Robert E. Lee. Thirteen thousand more were slaughtered by Confederate guns that day and Burnside withdrew, soundly beaten. Word of that disaster, wired to San Francisco, angered local Democrats, who blamed Lincoln's determined stand on slavery for the debacle. And this appeared in the *Alta:*

> We, Norton I, do hereby decree that the offices of President, Vice President, and Speaker of the House of Representatives are, from and after this date, abolished.
>
> We further decree that the Senate of the United States elect a prominent Democrat as their presiding officer, to act as President until the next election, and to reconstruct the Cabinet according to our wishes hereafter to be declared.
>
> Done at our palace this 21st day of December, A.D. 1862.

But this too may have been a hoax, perpetrated not by Albert Evans, who stoutly supported Lincoln, but by a Democrat—the wording prompts that suspicion—or by a Southerner who thought that a Democrat in the White House might be more sympathetic to the South's economic needs. In the days ahead there would be a lot of political skulduggery of that sort done without the Emperor's prior knowledge.

Frank Gross broke the news first: Lazarus was dead. He had bitten a boy and for that had been rewarded with a piece of meat well seasoned with ratsbane.

The town was shocked. Angry letters poured in to the *Bulletin,* demanding to know the poisoner's name. George Fitch begged his readers to be calm: "We do not want to so prejudice the community that when the slayer of Lazarus is found, it will be impossible to get a jury."

Clark Martin, in particular, thirsted for blood.

"The party that claimed to own Lazarus, because he once bailed him out of the Pound and got the Supervisors to ease his case over with a special ordinance, has offered a reward of $50 for the discovery of the man who threw the poison."

Albert Evans suggested in the *Alta* that, since the dog was a ward of the city, he ought to be buried with civic honors in Lone Mountain Cemetery beside such murdered martyrs as James King of William and David Broderick. That idea inspired another cartoon by Jump. In this print, "Funeral of Lazarus," the dogcatcher's wagon served as a hearse, attended by a long line of mourners led by the Mayor and the Board of Supervisors. Bummer was there, tail drooped in sorrow. The gravedigger, leaning on his spade in a shallow hole, mopping his brow with a handkerchief, was George Washington II. The "clergyman" reading the burial service, resplendent in a white surplice, was Norton I.

But there was life in the old dog yet. Or, rather, there was still some value in his miserable carcass. Clark Martin took Lazarus to a taxidermist, had him stuffed, and put him in a glass case behind his bar. But it was all that he had to advertise his lunch counter now (except for Bummer, who continued to call there alone), for His Majesty firmly refused to dignify with his presence any establishment that reminded him of that outrageous cartoon by Jump.

George Parker of the Bank Exchange enjoyed the Emperor's patronage instead.

Commercial Street was a remarkably narrow thoroughfare, a thin ribbon of unpretentious hotels, seedy lodging houses, inexpensive restaurants, oyster saloons, and pawnshops, stretching nine blocks from Long Wharf to Chinatown. Eureka Lodgings, at 624 Commercial, on the north side near Montgomery Street, was a small hotel of three stories, each floor having no more than five or six rooms. A sign above the door, black letters on a box of blue glass, illuminated from within by a gas jet at dusk, read:

ROOMS TO LET
25 & 50 CENTS A NIGHT

Alfred Babcock, the proprietor, may have wondered whether Norton could afford even those low rates, but the Emperor gave him fifty cents and asked for the best room available. Babcock, still wary, probably established the rule there and then that the rent must be paid daily in advance; all that is known for certain is that every morning for the next seventeen years, as long as His Majesty lived, he knocked on the landlord's door and paid him fifty cents. For that we have the word of David Hutchinson, who bought the hotel and ran it for ten of those seventeen years (and in all that time, apparently, never raised the rent, for the reporters who called there on the night that the Emperor died saw the same black-and-blue sign: "Rooms to Let, 25 and 50 cents").

Fifty cents entitled His Majesty to a room on the topmost floor, a tiny cubicle measuring no more than nine feet by six, one of Babcock's better chambers, a room with a view (its single grimy window overlooked the noisy street). The furniture consisted of an iron cot, a kitchen chair, a sagging couch, a washstand with a chipped pitcher and basin, and a small bedside table bearing the stump of a candle in a holder smothered with stalactites of white tallow. There was no space for a closet; the Emperor had to hang his Kossuth hat, his army caps, and his soiled uniform on tenpenny nails driven into the walls. On another nail, in a place of honor on the wall above his bed, he hung a colored lithograph of the recently widowed Queen Victoria, carefully clipped from *Leslie's Weekly Illustrated* and mounted in a cheap tin frame. She was then forty-three, a year younger than himself.

The Emperor's morning activities now followed a regular pattern. Rising before eight, he would put on his tunic and trousers, take his plumed hat from its nail, and go downstairs to pay his rent. Then he would enter the Empire House next door, a larger hotel kept by William Church, boasting a reading room where the daily papers were always available. There, he would while away an hour with the *Alta California* and the *Morning Call,* absorbing the latest dispatches from the East concerning the war, before venturing up Commercial Street toward Kearny, less than a block away.

Commercial Street was untidy. Empty barrels and boxes littered the sidewalks outside its cafes and saloons, while here and there a bored drayhorse, waiting in its shafts for an absent teamster, stamped and snorted and made the air reek with its droppings. The Emperor would turn right on Kearny Street, heading for Portsmouth Square.

The plaza, once a mud patch surrounded by gambling dens, had been transformed into a small park with gravel paths and neat lawns, enclosed by an iron fence. The gaming halls of Gold Rush days had vanished in flame long ago, except the Bella Union, which was now a music hall of low repute owned by Sam Tetlow, whose "pretty waiter girls" sometimes doubled as actresses but rather more often as prostitutes. One of Tetlow's leading ladies was Nellie Cole, sister of the Sterling Hopkins who had hanged Casey and Cora and almost Judge Terry as well. If a patron was willing to pay her price, she would bring a bottle of champagne to his booth at the back of the auditorium and entertain him herself, making him lose all interest in the buffoonery on the stage.

On the sidewalk in front of City Hall—formerly the Jenny Lind Theatre—stood a handcart filled with blossoms.

"Good morning, Your Majesty." Marcelin Aurignace, the flower seller from Alsace, waited for this moment every morning. He would pin a carnation to the Emperor's breast and clumsily kowtow, clowning for the benefit of the hackmen who waited with their cabs across the street, beside the park's fence. It would cost Aurignace nothing to give the Emperor a slightly wilted boutonniere left over from yesterday's trade, while his own reward was His Majesty's permission to display the message scrawled in pencil on a card nailed to his barrow: "By Appointment to Norton I."

The benches in the park were filled with bent and tired old men who spent their days trying to remember long-dead yesteryears and hometowns from which they had sailed to seek the gold they had never found (or, having found it, had quickly squandered). They were merely killing time, awaiting Norton's arrival. He might have been a bit odd, but he was a Forty-Niner like themselves and therefore an acceptable companion. They would soon be forgotten, these old ones. The name of only one has survived, Ah How, who would have been unusual in such a gathering because he was Chinese and might have expected more hostility than goodwill from whites in those unenlightened days. Albert Evans called Ah How the Emperor's "Grand Chamberlain" (whatever that meant).

His Majesty brought stirring news from the Empire House reading room one morning. All week long they had been hearing about Confederate successes. In Pennsylvania one rebel raider, General Jubal Early, had demanded a hundred thousand dollars in supplies from the crushed city of York. Another, Jeb Stuart, had crossed the Potomac below Washington and thrown that city into a panic, his cavalry "swarming about the very gates of the Capitol." But now there was word of a decisive Union victory at Gettysburg. The Army of the Potomac, forced back all along the line, had taken a stand on Cemetery Hill and there had turned the tide. It was a near thing; only the timely arrival of an ammunition train had saved the Union defenders. Rebel cavalry, attacking on foot, had smashed their way up the hill to the breastworks and beyond.

"They were upon the guns, bayoneting the gunners," one war

correspondent had written. "But they had penetrated to the fatal point. A storm of grape and canister tore its way from man to man and marked its track with corpses straight down the line."

The papers said the carnage was dreadful, more than forty thousand men lost, the worst disaster that either side had suffered in all the dark days of the war.

In the near distance the clock of St. Mary's chimed the hour for lunch. The Emperor rose from his bench and bade them all a good day. At the Bank Exchange, in the Montgomery Block, George Parker would be putting out the salmon and the beef. And there His Majesty was almost sure to find a taxpayer or two who had neglected to pay him fifty cents, the cost of his room.

The Lick House on Montgomery Street was San Francisco's newest and most splendid hotel, a monument to the miser who had built it. Samuel Langhorne Clemens checked in, tossed his carpetbag into his room, and sauntered down to the Turkish baths in the Montgomery Block to rid himself of the alkali dust that covered every stagecoach passenger from Washoe. (He always went there when he came to town, and later would remember another who frequented the steam room, a friendly fireman called Tom Sawyer, whose name he would one day use in a novel.)

This was Sam Clemens's third visit to the metropolis. The others had been idly spent, loafing in saloons with "Old Unreliable" Rice, another Comstock journalist. But Clemens could always claim to be working, since he was expected to tell the readers of Nevada's *Territorial Enterprise* everything he saw; Washoe liked to keep in touch with the city beside the Golden Gate. And now he had come on a mission of some importance. Adah Isaacs Menken was in San Francisco, appearing in *Mazeppa; or The Wild Horse of Tartary*. She wore pink tights in the play, and every manjack on the Comstock Lode wanted to know if it was true what they had heard: that when she made her sensational entrance in the third act, bound to the back of a horse, it was not pink tights that the audience saw but Miss Menken's own flesh! Albert Evans had given them that idea. "No pure youth could witness her performance and come away untainted," Evans had written in his dispatch to the *Evening News* in Gold Hill, the mining town next to Virginia City on the side of Mount Davidson, and Mark Twain—as Sam Clemens now called himself—had decided it was his bounden duty to look into the matter for his own readers, who had heard that after her engagement in San Francisco she would be coming to Virginia City.

From the baths to the Bank Exchange was but a step, and one he would have taken lightly, since it was a saloon that he esteemed most highly. George Parker's place was the last word in barroom elegance, with its marble pillars and marble floor, Wedgewood beer pumps imported from England, and ornately framed oil paintings that customers liked to believe were both artistic and valuable, a view not entirely shared by Twain, who had already pointed out in an article for the *Golden Era* a most remarkable anachronism in Parker's portrait of Samson and Delilah:

> Now, what is the first thing you see in looking at this picture down at the Bank Exchange? Is it the gleaming eyes and fine face of Samson? Or the muscular Philistine gazing furtively at the lovely Delilah? Or is it the rich drapery, or the truth to Nature of that pretty foot? No, sir! The first thing that catches the eye is the scissors on the floor at her feet. Them scissors is too modern—there warn't no scissors like them in them days by a d——d sight.

In the Bank Exchange Twain could swap newspaper yarns with Frank Gross of the *Bulletin*, R. H. McHenry of the *Democratic Press*, John McComb of the *Argus*, Tremenhere Lanyon Johns of the pictorial weekly *Puck*, and Jimmy Bowman of the *American Flag* (and later of the *Chronicle*). Ed Jump, the cartoonist who had made Emperor Norton famous (or was it the other way around?), would also be there. Twain might have seen the Emperor, too, grazing at the lunch counter, or standing at the bar in all of his seedy majesty, his sword at his belt, his cane under his arm, sipping a complimentary brandy with the banker who had bought it, or graciously declining the offer because he had already accepted one from Parker and so had reached his limit.

Twain had seen him before, of course. In a previous report to the *Enterprise* he had mentioned the Emperor, calling him a "lovable old humbug," that being the impression Colonel Moustache had given everyone on the Comstock Lode in the Gold Hill *News*. But now, as Twain heard him talk to those gathered around, without a twinkle in their eyes or a grin upon their faces, he realized that His Majesty was not the calculating sham that Evans had led Washoe to suppose. No sane man would be content to play a role that earned him nothing but ridicule in the *Alta*—or at best a free lunch that might have been his without putting on a feathered hat and pretending to be a monarch.

Twain put on a clawhammer coat and went to Maguire's Opera House to see *Mazeppa,* emerging some two hours later quite disappointingly unsullied. Despite what Evans had told Washoe, the pure youth who hoped to lose his innocence would have had to go to the Bella Union to see Sam Tetlow's burlesque of *The Wild Horse of Tartary,* in which a clown in very baggy "tights" was hauled all over the stage lashed to the back of a wheeled rocking horse (although if he were closeted in a booth with Mrs. Cole during the performance he would not have been able to describe much of the plot afterward).

In a sketch he wrote for the *Golden Era* about a ball at the Lick House, Twain gave James Lick's palatial hotel some free publicity. "The parlors," he wrote, satirizing the style of those who usually described such places for the *Era,* "were . . . covered with a rich white carpet of mauve domestique, imported from Massachusetts or the kingdom of New Jersey, I have forgotten which." Then, still mimicking the gossip writers, he spoofed the apparel worn by the ladies—"On the roof of her bonnet was a menagerie of rare and beautiful bugs and reptiles"—and invented a few blue-blooded guests to give the ball an additional touch of elegance. The Duke of Benicia was there, he said, with the Countess of San Jose, Lord Blessyou, and Lord Geeminy. But one of California's nobility was missing: "Owing to a pressure of imperial business, the Emperor Norton was unable to come."

And that was about as close as Mark Twain ever came to making fun of Joshua Norton. Thus began his lifelong fascination with the Emperor of the United States.

Chapter 13
Emperor of the West

>*His face is a free ticket for him to all places of amusement and public gatherings, and often times he makes quite extended journeys by rail and other public conveyances without expending a dollar. Sacramento is a favorite resort during the sessions of the Legislature, whither he goes to see that the legislators do not prostitute their privileges.*
>
>—Benjamin E. Lloyd

There can be little doubt that the Emperor visited theaters regularly as a guest of management, a fact fully confirmed by those few contemporaries who made no attempt to embroider his story, thinking the truth strange enough. The sensible theater manager, knowing that playgoers would be sorely disappointed if His Majesty did not attend an opening night and might think he had been refused admission, would reserve a seat for him and personally escort him to it when a burst of applause from the audience and a playful fanfare from the orchestra announced his arrival. New York or Baltimore might be content with Edwin Booth as Shakespeare's crook-backed king, but San Francisco expected to see Richard III on the stage and Norton I in the stalls.

It was the same with the horse-drawn streetcars and the ferry boats that plied the bay. No conductor would dare to ask the Emperor for the five-cent fare from Montgomery Street to the Market

Street Wharf, not because he feared a royal reprimand but because he dreaded what the company's directors would say if it ever got bruited about in the press that the city's mascot had been kicked off his car. That sort of publicity was certainly not wanted. Nor would the Emperor have been charged to board the side-wheeler that carried him across the bay to visit Camp Allen, the new training camp for Oakland's militia in the growing city among the oak groves on the opposite shore. The only embarrassment on that occasion occurred when he reached the camp.

On this grand opening day the citizen soldiers of the Oakland Guard were playing host to militia companies from counties all around the bay, including the Second Brigade from San Francisco, and hundreds of people, the Emperor among them, were ferried over the water that morning to see the great parade.

Oakland, unfortunately, did not regard the Emperor with quite the same degree of affection that San Francisco felt. This became obvious when, approaching a private of the Oakland Guard stationed beside the rope barrier that separated the parade ground from the viewing area, His Majesty asked the private to inform his commander that the Emperor was present and ready to review the troops, to which the saucy fellow reportedly replied, "Be off, you old rubbish."

Ignoring him, the Emperor passed through the opening in the rope that the man was guarding and set off across the field toward the paraded ranks of militiamen.

"Stand!" called the guardsman. "You cannot go further."

But he did go further.

The sentry at once sprang after him, seized his arm, and began to pull him back, calling to a watching comrade to help him. A mixed roar of cheers and groans suddenly split the air, groans from dismayed San Franciscans among the spectators behind the barrier, cheers and catcalls from delighted Oaklanders, whose loyalty to royalty would always be in doubt. The two militiamen hustled him off the field and took him to the guardhouse, where he was compelled to nurse his wounded dignity until the parade was over.

The San Franciscans who accompanied the Emperor home on the ferry were simply furious. The incident moved Albert Evans to publish a stinging rebuke in the *Alta*. For the Oakland Guard to lay hands upon His Imperial Majesty, he charged, was nothing short of high treason.

The real purpose of this outburst, however, actually had very little to do with Emperor Norton. Earlier that year, in Sacramento, Leland Stanford, the Governor of California, had turned the first spadeful of soil to symbolize the beginning of work on the transcontinental railroad. When the railroad was completed, passengers and goods would flow into Oakland from all parts of the country. That little town was the only possible terminus; no rails could span the wide bay to reach San Francisco, isolated on its peninsula and the city now saw itself in danger of losing most of its trade. Oakland's mayor was already boasting of a great new metropolis that would soon replace San Francisco as the chief entrepôt on the bay. So it's hardly surprising that in the fall of 1863, when the first metal tracks of the Central Pacific were laid in Sacramento, San Francisco's newspapers were doing everything they could to belittle Oakland's aspirations. And that included a rap on its provincial knuckles for its churlish treatment of San Francisco's favorite citizen.

Evans's attack on Oakland produced an unexpected result. Three cities immediately wrote to the *Alta,* pledging their allegiance to the Crown. Marysville, in distant Yuba County, invited His Majesty to attend the inauguration of a railroad to Oroville, thirty miles to the north. Oroville spoke for itself: "We wish to show that Oroville is the most progressive and the most loyal city in the Empire. If your Highness would but give the word, we would consider it an honor to whip the breeches of those proscriptive traitors in Oakland."

Petaluma, in Sonoma County, not to be outdone, pleaded for a visit, too, promising the Emperor a civic welcome if he came there. For by now it was abundantly clear to all that the surest way to get a paragraph of publicity in San Francisco's leading newspaper was to swear fealty to the Emperor of the United States.

He promised to visit them all.

In January 1864, the Emperor traveled aboard a river steamer to Sacramento, where he inspected the newly laid tracks of the transcontinental railroad, attended both houses of the Legislature, and addressed a proclamation to the President of the State Senate commanding the legislators to "pass an Act declaring our Decrees the law of California." Then, on February 14, some gentlemen from Marysville arrived in the capital to escort him to their own city in style. A fast six-horse stage carried them the forty miles to Marysville, where supper and accommodations awaited His Majesty at a "first-class hotel of one hundred rooms, well furnished." The local *Daily Californian Express* revealed his whereabouts next morning:

> Yesterday the renowned Emperor Norton I of San Francisco, with his huge epaulettes and a hickory knotted stick, arrived in this city, under escort, on the stage from Sacramento, and put up at the Western House. We believe it is the intention of His Majesty to visit Oroville today, and join in the railroad celebration.

Flags were flying that Sunday at Marysville's railroad depot, where a long line of people waited to buy tickets to board the gaily decorated train. Two of the twelve passenger cars were reserved for invited guests and two for the men of the Marysville Rifles and the Union Guard, who were to take part in a military display at Oroville. When the Emperor arrived with his entourage, the Marysville Rifles cheered and ushered him into their car. Departure was delayed while the less privileged scrambled for seats. Finally, when all were aboard and the stationmaster had dropped his flag, the tap of a telegraph key told Oroville that the train was on its way.

It was a pleasant journey. The Rifles sang to him all the way to Honcut and from Honcut to Oroville: "Old Bob Ridley" and "My Pretty Yaller Girls" and "O, Wrap the Flag Around Me, Boys" and "Weeping, Sad and Lonely." The Union Guard in the car behind said it was an awful cruel thing to do to a guest of honor.

Oroville was in a holiday mood. As noon approached, the whole town seemed to hold its breath, straining to hear the sound of the locomotive. Soon it came, faint at first, the wail of a whistle and the pant of a smokestack, growing louder. Everyone cheered when the train, bunting flying in the wind, came squealing into the station.

In front of the depot, the Oroville Guard was mustered in a hollow square around a cannon, which barked a salute. Then all the dignitaries piled into carriages and the militia lined up in marching order behind a brass band, which blasted the air with the jaunty strains of "Buffalo Gals" as the long procession began to crawl through the town to the plaza. In the last coach, flanked on each side by marching men in frock coats and chimney-pot hats, rode the Emperor.

The spectators lining the route cheered and held up children to give them a better view.

"See the Emperor!"

"Oh, what a sight!"

"Give him three of the best, boys. Hip-hip-hip!"

"Hoorah!"

His Majesty bowed graciously.

A local correspondent sent an account of the Emperor's activities in Oroville to the *Alta California*:

> He demonstrated his love for his people by eating a square meal [at the principal hotel], surrounded by an admiring throng. This unlooked-for and wonderful condescension on the part of the Head of the Nation so affected the people of Oroville that several acres of garden fence were washed away and one man was drowned in the tears. . . .

"Last evening," the Marysville *Express* reported next morning, "he was enlightening some of his subjects on the great issues of the day." They particularly wanted to know what he thought of greenbacks, the paper money introduced by Washington as a wartime measure to meet currency needs. Greenbacks were legal tender in the East and Congress was contemplating making them legal in the West, too, a touchy topic in the land of gold, where it was estimated that a hundred dollars in gold coin had the purchasing power of more than one hundred and fifty paper dollars. His Majesty had plenty to say about greenbacks:

> . . . he is of the opinion that Congress has no power to make them legal tender, for the reason that they could not compel the Bank of England to accept or receive them; that they were not issued on a proper basis; that there was no security for their redemption [by the government after the war], and that their value depended upon the uncertain mutation of future events [what, for example, if the North lost the war?]. Yet he thinks a proper national currency may be established, with sufficient safeguards thrown around it to protect the people from fraud.

"He returns to Sacramento today," the paper continued, "for the purpose of procuring passage of some important resolutions in relation to national affairs, which concluded [he will visit] Washington and in conjunction with the President will fulminate another proclamation, which will settle the war and establish his sway over the entire country. The Legislature will doubtless render him their valuable assistance, for the members are about as sane as the Emperor."

On March 17 the Petaluma *Argus* reported his presence in that city. "The mighty destinies of empires appear to rest upon his shoulders," it said, "judging from the number of telegraphic dispatches and letters he is constantly receiving."

The telegrams were from practical jokers bent on airing their wit. One, purportedly from Richmond, Virginia, and plainly composed by a Southerner, read:

> To His Excellency, Emperor Norton: it is with pain and regret that I learn you are in communication with that arch-traitor, Abe Lincoln, the so-called President of the United States. Is this true? If so, I cannot longer count you among my friends. The South has long looked to you as their guiding star to finally settle the present war. Please answer at once. With high consideration, I am,
>
> JEFFERSON DAVIS,
President, C.S.A.

The Emperor repaired at once to the telegraph office, where he scribbled two telegrams, one to Lincoln and one to Davis, commanding both to appear before him in San Francisco to resolve their dispute. The clerk who took them from him, promising to forward them at once to Washington and Richmond, sent them instead to the *Argus,* which concocted "replies" from Davis and Lincoln and published them. President Lincoln said he had no time to spare for a trip to California, "being very busy settling accounts with a seedy individual by the name of Jeff Davis," while President Davis apparently could not travel anywhere unless the Emperor provided him with a pair of trousers:

> To Emperor Norton I, Petaluma: If you wish me to appear before you in appropriate costume, you must send me at least five hundred dollars

($500), gold or greenbacks, as I have but one pair of breeches left, and they, I am sorry to say, are minus a seat. Yours, with great respect,

JEFFERSON DAVIS.

There was a third telegram, badly misspelled, from the manager of a new hotel in the nearby village of Sonoma, who must have been wracking his brains to find some way to publicize the ball he was planning to hold on the night that his hostelry opened:

Emperor Naughton: your royal Highness is envite to attend a ball giving in honor of you at the union Hall, sonoma. no Excuse will be taken on your part.

J.C. WEBSTOR, MANGER.

It is not known whether His Majesty attended this ball at the Union Hotel in Sonoma, possibly because the *Argus* reporter himself was not "envite" and so could not report it. The illiterate "manger" certainly slipped up in that oversight.

Chapter 14
The Feud

Our Emp is a model in every particular. Nobody in town has anything so nobby as his stick; nobody's hair curls like his; his manner of bowing to the humblest of his subjects brings tears to the eyes of all observers, and his cap is the tallest thing in town. Our Emperor forever!

—Albert S. Evans

The Emperor's lodging house was sandwiched between the Empire House on one side and the three-storied building of the *Morning Call* on the other. The ground floor of the *Call* building housed the printshop and the advertising department; its second floor was rented to a tenant; the newsroom occupied the third. Adjoining that was the United States Branch Mint, a beehive so overcrowded that its Superintendent, Robert B. Swain, had been forced to find quarters elsewhere for himself and his secretary. He was the tenant on the second floor of the *Call* building, and the secretary who shared his office was Francis Brett Harte, who supplemented his salary by writing poems and stories for the *Golden Era* under the pen name "Bret Harte."

In 1851, when he was prosperous, Joshua Norton was one of ninety-four prominent businessmen who had signed a petition to Congress, asking for a Mint to be built; now it was here, just a step from his door, and he was too poor for its treasures to be of any benefit to him.

The *Call* had borrowed its name from an unusual source. In 1856 five unemployed printers, meeting in the Blue Wing Saloon, discovered that they could raise enough capital between them to start a newspaper. Their only problem was what to call it. Leaving the barroom still undecided, they strolled along Montgomery Street, tossing names back and forth, until they came to the Metropolitan Theatre and there saw a playbill advertising the coming appearance of Mrs. Julia Dean Hayne in a comedy, *The Morning Call*.

Splendid name! Worth celebrating, that one. Back to the Blue Wing.

The first issue appeared that December under the capable editorship of Robert H. Newell. Newell stayed less than a year. George Barnes, one of the founding printers, took over as editor when Newell went on to New York and far greater fame as the political satirist Orpheus C. Kerr and later as husband of the notorious Adah Isaacs Menken, then shocking East Coast audiences with her pink tights.

Under Barnes the *Morning Call* prospered, partly because it was a lively paper, but chiefly because it cost half the price of any other. Of late, though, its circulation had been slipping, much of its liveliness having vanished when its resident humorist, Albert Evans, quit to take a job with the rival *Alta California*. Fred MacCrellish, the publisher of the *Alta,* concluding that the Mother of Newspapers was a shade too sedate for a city in love with a lunatic, had lured Evans from the *Call* by offering him something that was dear to the heart of every journalist—a by-line. Barnes had never permitted a reporter's name to appear on a story; MacCrellish, on the other hand, encouraged it. So Albert Evans became Fitz Smythe of the *Alta*. And now, without him, the *Call* seemed as flat as a pancake.

Barnes needed someone who could breathe life back into his paper. But who? Well, there was that fellow in Virginia City, the one on the *Enterprise* who sent him newsletters from the Comstock and contributed articles to the *Golden Era*. Now, some of those items were decidedly comical.

So George Barnes wrote to Samuel Langhorne Clemens.

* * *

"The *Call* has secured the services of 'Mark Twain' as its local reporter. His items already give evidence of a new hand at the bellows," the *Alta California* announced in June, 1864.

That gratuitous puff was the last favor Albert Evans would ever do for Sam Clemens. Within a month they would be at each other's throats, Twain sneering in the *Call* at Fitz Smythe's impoverished wit—"Dry as a squeezed orange must be the brain that moved the indicting of that paragraph"—and Evans retorting in the *Alta* that the "aborigine from the land of sagebrush and alkali" had been given his pen name by friends "for doing the drinking of two."

Twain shared a desk on the third floor with Franklin Soulé, who handled the telegraphic dispatches, a Forty-Niner with a reputation as a poet and local historian. The new reporter thought him "one of the sweetest and whitest & loveliest spirits that ever wandered into this world by mistake." They got along splendidly. Twain was delighted to learn, too, that another local literary lion occupied a den on the floor below; Barnes himself escorted him down the stairs to meet Bret Harte.

Mint Superintendent Robert Swain good-naturedly troubled his secretary as little as possible, giving him all the time he needed for his creative endeavors. Harte could easily spare an hour to talk; he was enthusiastic about a new venture. He and Charles Henry Webb, a columnist for the *Golden Era*, had recently forsaken that weekly to launch one of their own, *The Californian,* and Harte was seeking talent for the paper. He liked Twain's breezy, irreverent style and induced him to accept his offer of fifty dollars a month to write an article a week. Since Webb held the title of editor, Harte called himself the "editor-in-charge-of-Mark Twain." The two writers were friends then, but in time, after they had collaborated on a play that flopped, Twain would come to detest Bret Harte quite as much as he detested Albert Evans.

In a letter written six years later to Elisha Bliss of the American Publishing Company, which had just published *The Innocents Abroad* and was now considering the manuscript of a novel submitted by Evans, Twain dismissed Fitz Smythe as a "one-horse reporter who has been trying all his life to make a joke and never has, and never *will* succeed. . . . And don't he hate *me*? I should *think* so. I used to trot him out in the papers."

Why did he "trot him out"? There are reasonable grounds to suspect jealousy. George Barnes would not permit Clemens to use the by-line "Mark Twain" in the *Call,* or attach any other name to the items he scribbled (just as he had not allowed Evans when he worked for the paper), which must have been galling to a writer who had already established a local reputation with his droll sketches in the *Golden Era* and needed continual public recognition if he were not to wither on the vine. So there they were, two wags competing for the same laurel wreath, one with his pen name on everything he wrote, the other shrouded in anonymity. Indeed, one had to read other newspapers to discover that those comical local items in the *Morning Call* were written by Mark Twain.

As a matter of fact, Twain's first signed newspaper story, following his move from Nevada, actually appeared in the *Alta* a few days before he joined the *Call,* courtesy of Albert Evans, who had not yet learned to hate him. The steamship *Aquila,* bringing a monitor—a small, armed, ironclad craft—to San Francisco to protect the bay from Confederate raiders, had foundered in a storm the moment she docked, taking her precious cargo to the bottom of the harbor. A military officer trained in marine engineering, Major Edward C. Perry, had salvaged the monitor from the sunken vessel's hold, piece by piece, and Mayor Henry Coon had presented Perry with a cane, complete with engraved silver shield to acknowledge his accomplishment, on the stage of Maguire's Opera House, where the newly arrived Twain acted as master of ceremonies. He wrote an account of the presentation for Fitz Smythe, who put it on the local page with a preface that identified the author as "Mark Twain of Virginia City."

"The cane," wrote Twain, "weighs something less than twelve pounds and might have been copied from Emperor Norton's." How much less than twelve pounds he was careful not to say; the average reader would assume that it weighed just short of twelve pounds, never stopping to think that even one ounce is "something less than twelve pounds." Some readers must have thought that their city had not paid the major much of a compliment by giving him a cane too heavy to carry.

Now, Albert Evans would never have thought of that. And that brings us to another bone of contention between them: Which was the cleverer humorist?

Twain despised Fitz Smythe's flowery, overblown style. Why, the fellow even dragged in volcanoes just to describe a hat. And, what was unforgivable, he continually made jokes about Norton's lunacy. In fact, without the Emperor to poke fun at, Colonel Moustache really would be as dry as a squeezed orange. Twain's own often cynical writing disguised a compassionate heart. ("Those not familiar with this young man do not know the depth of tenderness in his nature," Frank Gross would comment in the *Bulletin*.) Twain felt genuinely sorry for Norton. This is evident in the letter he wrote to William Dean Howells years later: "I have seen him in *all* of his various moods & tenses, and there was always more room for pity than laughter."

However, it was not just pity that kept him from finding humor in Norton's eccentricity; from a journalist's point of view, there was a better reason. Albert Evans had cornered the market on Emperor Norton stories, and the public had come to regard "the Emp" as the exclusive property of the *Alta California*. No other reporter mentioned his name quite so frequently as Evans; no one else thought of inventing decrees even more hilarious than those composed by His Majesty for publication in the *Bulletin* (which indeed seemed rather dull by comparison). Twain could have written countless items about the Emperor, but that would have left him wide open to accusations of poaching on Fitz Smythe's preserve, and of copying him, if Twain had concocted proclamations for the *Call*, which of course was quite out of the question. Twain might drop Norton's name into a news item occasionally, but only because San Franciscans expected a humorist to mention His Majesty now and then, for to them "the Emp" was the funniest thing going. Twain, of course, had to be original, even though it meant raking the town for squibs that sometimes seemed hardly worth the writing.

At times, in despair, Twain sank to extraordinary depths, finding fun in the collapse of a drayhorse on a slippery street, a runaway buggy spilling its passengers, a man injured by a passing wagon, even an attempted suicide. Meanwhile, Evans continued to keep his readers laughing at the adventures of Norton the First. Fitz Smythe's wit might be pedestrian, but his subject was funnier by far. It would be a struggle to beat him with stories of runaway buggies.

But Norton was too much a part of the local scene for a reporter to ignore entirely, so Twain allowed him to creep into a sarcastic piece protesting military censorship. The Army, emboldened by the fact that Lee's retreat into Virginia after Gettysburg had caused public opinion in California to swing sharply in favor of the Union, had begun to harass Southern preachers who exercised their right of free speech in California. So, when a bishop was arrested at a camp meeting in Calaveras County and brought to San Francisco under guard, the press wanted to know the precise nature of his offense. They were told only that Bishop Hubbard H. Kavanaugh's church was the Methodist Episcopal Church *South,* which the Provost Marshal had deemed sufficient evidence of an unholy alliance with Dixie to justify incarceration in the Presidio. Twain thought that feeble excuse hilarious, although it disturbed him that the military could arrest a civilian and then refuse to talk about it. He revealed in the *Call* how all of his attempts to get the facts were frustrated:

> We started to the Provost Marshal's office, but met another reporter, who said: "I suppose I know where you're going, but it's no use—just come from there—military etiquette and all that, you know—those fellows are mum—won't tell anything about it—Damn!" We sought General McDowell, but he had gone to Oakland. In the course of the afternoon we visited all kinds of headquarters and places, and called on General Mason, Colonel Drum, General Van Bokkelen, Leland of the Occidental, Chief Burke, Keating, Emperor Norton, and everybody else that would be likely to know the Government's business. . . .

General Irving McDowell was Commander of the Department of the Pacific, General Mason was the Assistant Provost Marshal General, Colonel Drum was Chief of Staff at the Presidio, and General Van Bokkelen, the Provost Marshal of Nevada, was a guest at the Occidental Hotel, where Twain now lived. The others were unlikely sources of information. Police Chief Martin Burke was not at all involved in a strictly military matter; Jim Keating operated the Ivy Green Saloon; and Lewis Leland was the Occidental Hotel's owner-manager. Their names were merely tossed in for comic effect, but no doubt they appreciated the mention. As for the Emperor, well, he probably would not have minded in the least that the *Call* considered him an authority on governmental affairs. After all, he thought that himself.

The Army received such a ribbing that General McDowell begged Bishop Kavanaugh to return to Calaveras County and say no more about it. As a parting shot—a remarkably weak one for such a big gun—he did advise the bishop to drop the "South" from his church's name. And the bishop, in rich, round ecclesiastical tones, told him to go somewhere noted for its extreme warmth.

One might almost have thought that the Almighty, displeased with the rebellious cleric, had taken General McDowell's side in the matter, because at the very moment that Twain wrote that piece, at 10:40 P.M. on July 21, an earthquake rocked the city, the second within a month. Twain was in the newsroom at the time, scribbling that day's items, including the one about the general and the bishop:

> Up in the third story of this building the sensation we experienced was as if we had been sent for and were mighty anxious to go. The house seemed to waltz from side to side with a quick motion, suggestive of sifting corn meal through a sieve; afterward it rocked grandly to and fro like a prodigious cradle, and in the meantime several persons started downstairs to see if there were anybody so timid as to be frightened by a mere earthquake.

To which he added a complaint: "When we contracted to report for this newspaper, the important matter of two earthquakes a month was not considered in the salary. There shall be no mistake of that kind in the next contract, though."

The Emperor missed all the excitement. He had gone to Petaluma again. When he returned to his room in the Eureka he would probably find his collection of military caps all over the floor, shaken from their tenpenny nails, and Queen Victoria's tumbled portrait lying facedown on his bed.

There would be no "next contract" for Twain. After five months of scouring the town for what he called "lokulitems," he began to neglect his duties and was dismissed from the *Call*. But he was not quite finished with Colonel Moustache. Or with Emperor Norton.

Joshua Norton as a prosperous merchant and landowner about the time he joined the Vigilance Committee of 1851.

(The Society of California Pioneers)

The Emperor in full regalia, with his famous plumed hat.

Skin and bones. In his early days as Emperor, he was undernourished, as this picture shows. He wears a Confederate uniform here.

The Emperor in Union Army dress. Presumably he wore both uniforms to show his impartiality during the Civil War. He considered himself the Emperor of the whole nation and could hardly take sides.

(Top and bottom courtesy of California Historical Society)

Norton's signature (third from top) on a petition to Congress (partially reproduced here) signed by ninety-three prominent businessmen, asking for a Branch Mint to be established in San Francisco. The last to sign was Fred Marriott, publisher of the News-Letter.

City Hall with Portsmouth Square in the foreground. *The Emperor held court in the plaza daily and was briefly jailed on a charge of lunacy in the cells below City Hall. Mark Twain was jailed here, too, charged with drunkenness.*

Proclamation.

The following is decreed and ordered to be carried into execution as soon as convenient:

I. That a suspension bridge be built from Oakland Point to Goat Island, and thence to Telegraph Hill; provided such bridge can be built without injury to the navigable waters of the Bay of San Francisco.

II. That the Central Pacific Railroad Company be granted franchises to lay down tracks and run cars from Telegraph Hill and along the city front to Mission Bay.

III. That all deeds of lands by the Washington Government since the establishment of our Empire are hereby declared null and void unless our Imperial signature is first obtained thereto. NORTON I.

The proclamation ordering the bridge to the Farallones was a hoax by an Oakland newspaper. The Emperor's own decree in the Pacific Appeal, *shown here, was perfectly sane; it ordered the bridge to be built exactly where the Bay Bridge is today.*

The Emperor's first "love letter" to Minnie Wakeman. She turned down the chance to be Empress of the United States.

(Courtesy of The Bancroft Library)

Minnie Wakeman, at the tender age of seventeen, when the Emperor came courting.

(Courtesy of The Bancroft Library)

The famous "lunch counter" cartoon by Ed Jump that angered the Emperor and started the rumor that Bummer and Lazarus were his pets. In fact, he hated them.

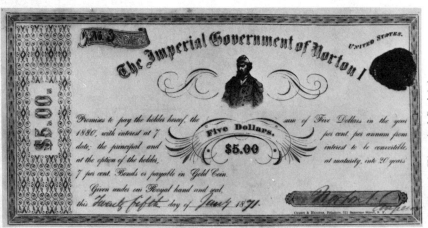

Five-dollar scrip sold by Emperor Norton in 1871. The smudge in the upper right-hand corner is the Emperor's "seal," made by smearing a coin with ink.

Left, *Mark Twain when he was with the* Morning Call. *Right, Albert Evans of the* Alta California, *Twain's bitter rival in the 1860s. Twain despised Evans for making fun of the Emperor in print.*

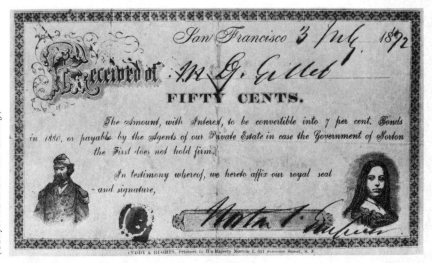

When this fifty-cent bond was issued it started an unlikely rumor that the Emperor would marry a notorious prostitute, Nellie Cole, star of the Bella Union Theater, whose picture appears in the lower right-hand corner.

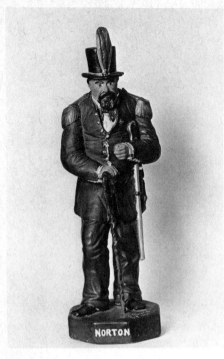

Colored figurines made of plaster, eighteen inches tall, like the one shown, were sold to tourists as souvenirs of Norton I.

(The Santa Rosa Press Democrat)

Sightseers board the Harbor Emperor, which has a figurehead of Norton the First on its bow, at Fisherman's Wharf for a trip to Alcatraz. The former penitentiary is a popular tourist attraction today.

Photo by Malcolm E. Barker

(The Society of California Pioneers)

No quotation marks question his right to a title on this monument over the Emperor's grave. Buried by millionaires in 1880, he was reburied in 1934 with civic and military honors.

Chapter 15

The Emperor's Secretary

The legitimate authorities of New York are hereby commanded to seize upon the person of one Stellifer, styling himself King or Prince of the House of David, and send him in chains to San Francisco.

—Norton I.

On February 2, 1865, another hoax appeared in the *Alta California*:

HIS MAJESTY'S BIRTHDAY

His Imperial Majesty, Norton I, Emperor of the United States and Protector of Mexico, commemorates his forty-eighth year on Saturday, February 4th, 1865. Owing to unsettled questions between His Majesty Maximilian I, El Duque de Gwino, The Tycoon, the King of the Mosquitoes, the King of the Cannibal Islands, et al, the usual display of bunting on the foreign shipping and public buildings will be omitted on this occasion.

Nobody knew the Emperor's age or the date of his birth. February 4 was significant for quite another reason. It was the fourth anniversary of the signing of a declaration of independence in 1861 by the first seven cotton states to secede: Mississippi, South Carolina, Alabama, Georgia, Louisiana, Florida, and Texas. Every year, on February 4, Southerners in San Francisco hung out rebel flags to celebrate the birthday of the Confederate States of America.

The Emperor's Secretary 111

The *Alta,* a staunch Union paper, was simply thumbing its nose at that display of Southern pride by pretending that the flags were flown to celebrate the birthday of a lunatic.

Such leg-pulling was commonly practiced by both sides. Southerners often tried to plant propaganda, thinly disguised, in Fred MacCrellish's paper. He once received a seemingly innocuous scrap of verse, seventeen lines in length, and might have published it exactly as it was written had he not noticed that the initial letter in every line, reading from top to bottom, spelled out "HURRAH FOR THE SOUTH." Before putting it in the *Alta* he made a couple of minor adjustments, changing only the first words in the thirteenth and fifteenth lines so that the acrostic now read: "HURRAH FOR THE NORTH."

Then he scribbled under it, "Sorry, Johnny Reb."

The Maximilian referred to in the Emperor's "birthday announcement" was the Austrian archduke recently installed as Emperor of Mexico by Napoleon III. "El Duque de Gwino" was a sneering reference to William McKendree Gwin, a former United States senator for California and the chief political foe of David Broderick. Gwin, a Mississippian, briefly imprisoned by the North for his loyalty to the South, was now in Mexico, where, it was falsely rumored, Maximilian had made him a duke.

That February 4, it so happened, was the Confederacy's last birthday. On April 9, at Appomattox, General Robert E. Lee surrendered his sword to General Ulysses S. Grant, and the war was over. And then, just one week later, in a theater in Washington, John Wilkes Booth fired his Derringer and Lincoln belonged to the ages.

Twain's contempt for Evans surfaced that week when Fitz Smythe, in a pitiful attempt to eulogize the fallen leader, went from bad to verse:

> Gone! Gone! Gone!
> Forever and Forever!
> Gone! Gone! Gone!
> The tidings ne'er shall sever!
> Gone! Gone! Gone!
> Wherever! Oh, Wherever!
> Gone! Gone! Gone!
> Gone to his endeavor!

112 Norton I

Twain, quoting the poem in a letter to the *Enterprise,* said it was lopsided: "There is too much 'Gone' in it and not enough 'Forever'." And when Evans dared to criticize an anthology of Californian poetry compiled by Bret Harte, Twain scoffed in another dispatch to Virginia City:

> . . . I attach no weight to Smythe's criticisms because he don't know anything about polite literature; he has had no experience in it further than to write up runaway horse items for the *Alta* [something Twain had done himself for the *Call*] and to act as Private Secretary to Emperor Norton. And even in the latter capacity he had never composed the Emperor's proclamations; his duties extended no further than to copy them for the Gold Hill *News,* and anybody could do that. As for poetry, he never wrote but two poems in his life. One was entitled, "The Dream of Norton I, Emperor," which was tolerably good. . . .

And the other? Well, the other had too much "Gone" in it.

But Twain was surely wrong in saying that Albert Evans had "never composed the Emperor's proclamations," only copied them for syndication, for the decrees that appeared in the *Alta* bore a much stronger resemblance to Fitz Smythe's style than to Emperor Norton's. The *Bulletin* was not the only paper to note that the Emperor's proclamations "were written in good style, grammatical and correct in orthography." Those in Fred MacCrellish's paper, on the other hand, were often inclined to be slangy. If Evans did not compose them, he certainly must have tampered with them, unless we are to believe that Norton himself deliberately added those farcical flourishes that made them even more ridiculous, and that he did this only for the *Alta* (since the manifestos published by the *Bulletin* were almost dull by comparison—so much so that George Fitch had stopped printing them, leaving the Emperor of the United States entirely to MacCrellish).

So the Mother of Newspapers, at this period of his life, was the only outlet for His Majesty's decrees, and his "private secretary" could do with them whatever he wished, even invent them. It's even quite possible that the Emperor, tired of Fitz Smythe's tinkering, did not write a single proclamation for MacCrellish's paper, but that Colonel Moustache composed *all* of them.

A case in point is the "royal ukase" published by the *Alta* when another mad monarch appeared on the scene, a rival to Emperor Norton.

As the rails of the Central Pacific crept slowly through the mountain passes of the Sierra Nevada to meet the tracks of the Union Pacific, crawling west, San Francisco began to develop an enthusiastic interest in tourism, a lucrative new industry that only the railroad could bring. The telegraph wires that stretched from ocean to ocean, no longer burdened with gloomy war news and free to deal with lighter matters, began to hum with stories from boosters, extolling the virtues of a golden city that soon would be within everyone's reach. It was probably inevitable that some of those dispatches to East Coast editors would mention the Emperor of the United States. And perhaps it was also a certainty that some Easterner, reading about him in a local paper, would be inspired to imitate him. In September the *Alta* announced:

ANOTHER EMPEROR IN THE FIELD
Since the advent of Maximilian we are having a heavy run of Kings, Emperors, and similar humbugs, and the disease threatens to become an epidemic in America. We would respectfully call the attention of our beloved Emperor, Norton I, to the case of a blackguard in New York who styles himself "Stellifer the King, Reigning Prince of the House of David and Guardian of American Destinies." This fellow, who appears to be a man of some education and luxurious tastes, has been boarding at all the leading hotels in Boston, New York and Saratoga, and other places, and when dunned for his bills agrees to settle when his stake of $3,500,000 was paid by the United States Treasury. His real name is D. Stellifer Moulton. . . .

D. Stellifer Moulton was the New York correspondent of the Boston *Traveller* before he became Stellifer the King. A religious fanatic, his association with that journal ended abruptly when the editor began receiving dispatches datelined Babylon and couched in the language of the Old Testament. Deprived of a newspaper's readership in Boston, he sought an audience in the synagogues of New York, which barred their doors when he interrupted the solemnity of a Rosh Hashanah service at the sounding of the ram's horn and was cast out of a temple on Nineteenth Street.

In a rambling letter to a New York paper, Moulton described the incident: "At the time of the horn-blowing, the power was great upon me, so I came down . . . and stood before the altar, and uncovered my head; and I commanded the horn-blowing to cease, and was about to speak before the teachers and congregation . . . when certain of the congregation seized me with violence and brought me out of the Synagogue, for I would not stoutly resist them."

There was more, much more, in the same aggrieved tone. And then Moulton had a favor to ask: he needed capital to start "a first-class daily newspaper for the advocacy of my ideas on religious and political matters." He had already written to Horace Greeley of the *Tribune* and James Gordon Bennett of the *Herald*, commanding each to contribute half a million dollars, but they were too shortsighted to perceive the advantage in financing a paper that would compete with their own, for he had not received a penny.

But he had developed a taste for expensive hotels; when a bill was tendered he simply signed it "Stellifer the King" and airily told the manager to charge it to the U.S. Treasury. And so he hopped from hotel to hotel, in city after city, leaving his worthless signature behind as evidence for any hotelier who wished to prove that "Stellifer the King slept here."

That fellow in the West who called himself Norton I, he told a reporter from the New York *Tribune*, was a fraud; he would soon cook *his* goose. The "imperial decree" that appeared next day in the *Alta* was so laced with slang—at least in its opening sentences—it is awfully hard to escape the conclusion that His Majesty's private secretary had more to do with its composition than the Emperor:

DOWN WITH USURPERS AND IMPOSTERS!

Off with his head! So much for cooking other people's geese. The legitimate authorities of New York are hereby commanded to seize upon the person of one Stellifer, styling himself King or Prince of the House of David, and send him in chains to San

Francisco, California, on trial before our Imperial Court on various charges of fraud, alleged against him in the public prints.

> NORTON I,
> Emperor of the United States
> and Protector of Mexico.

The phrase "Off with his head!" more properly belonged in *Alice's Adventures in Wonderland* (which, incidentally, had just been published that year) than the vocabulary of a man noted for his dignity.

King Stellifer *was* seized by the authorities of New York. The manager of the Fifth Avenue Hotel had him hauled before Judge Dodge at the Jefferson Market Police Court, who sent him to the lunatic asylum on Blackwell's Island.

And that was the end of Stellifer the First.

George Washington the Second was next.

Somebody was tearing down his posters, and he suspected Norton I. He went to City Hall to complain to Police Chief Martin Burke, but got no further than Chief Burke's clerk, Officer William Martin, who smilingly advised him that it was not a criminal offense to remove posters; if he wished redress he must bring a civil suit against His Majesty.

Lacking the funds to pay a lawyer, "Wash" called upon Fitz Smythe, hoping that a word in print might cause the Emperor to cease and desist.

Evans asked him why he suspected the Emperor.

"Because," said the Great Matrimonial Candidate, who had no good reason to suspect him at all, "he is jealous of my reputation with the fair sex."

At this point, Colonel Moustache's syndicated columns seem to have reached as far as the East Coast. A dispatch to the *Christian Enquirer* in Baltimore from a correspondent in San Francisco—surely Evans, since the identical piece appeared in the *Alta,* though the Eastern paper was credited as the original source and the author not identified—boasted that among the curiosities awaiting those who came on the train were two famous crackpots, one who imagined he was the Emperor of the United States and the other professing to be a reincarnation of the Father of the Country. The article specifically mentioned the Emperor's slovenliness—a most peculiar novelty to advertise as a tourist attraction—and "the light of insanity" flickering in Washington's eyes. When this was published in the *Alta* the pudgy phrenologist stomped into MacCrellish's office, banner in hand, boiling with rage, to let him know in no uncertain terms that he was *not* insane and furthermore resented being linked with that lunatic Norton. As he left, His Majesty entered on much the same errand.

Another decree immediately appeared in the *Alta,* directing the Chief of Police to "seize upon the person of Professor Coombs, falsely called Washington No. 2, as a seditious and turbulent fellow, and to have him sent forthwith, for his own and the public good, to the State Lunatic Asylum for at least thirty days."

Coombs, who must have read in the papers what happened to Stellifer the King when he dared to challenge the Emperor's authority, took off at once for his native New York, leaving the field to Norton I.

Meanwhile, Mark Twain was in hot water, having incurred the wrath of Police Chief Martin Burke by accusing him of protecting his men against complaints of police brutality. Twain suggested in the *Territorial Enterprise* that any officer who appeared before "Chief Burke's Star Chamber of Police Commissioners" for mistreating a private citizen could expect little more than a slap on the wrist no matter how strong the evidence against him: "If Pontius Pilate was on the police he could crucify the Savior again with perfect impunity."

Chief Burke got his revenge, making Twain spend a night in jail for being drunk and disorderly, much to the delight of Albert Evans, who was in court next morning when Twain appeared before Justice of the Peace Alfred Barlow. In his report Evans crudely compared the smell "which pervades the Police Court room when the Bohemian of the Sage-Brush is in the dock" to the stink of an abbatoir. Then his enmity went far beyond the bounds of good taste, when he learned that Twain had secured a contract from the Sacramento *Union* to write a series of articles about the Sandwich Islands (Hawaii). In a letter to the Gold Hill *News* he actually said that Twain, having lost forty dollars and a gold watch in a brothel but gained a venereal disease in exchange, was going to Honolulu "to get rid of one disease by catching another."

Naturally, he waited until Twain was safely at sea before that piece was printed.

In September the widowed Queen Emma of the Sandwich Islands, returning home from Europe after a summer spent visiting Napoleon III and Queen Victoria, arrived in San Francisco. General Henry W. Halleck was at the wharf to greet her when the distant guns of the Presidio, firing a royal salute, announced that her ship had entered the Golden Gate. A reporter, seeing the Emperor hovering on the fringe of the cheering throng when she came ashore with her entourage, and feigning surprise that he was not with the welcoming dignitaries, impertinently inquired whether it was not His Imperial Majesty's intention to receive the lovely young Queen.

"No," the Emperor replied. "General Halleck having ordered the salute without my direction, it would be improper for me to proceed further in the matter. But I shall call upon her privately, for she has been in Europe and will know how I am regarded in the courts of England and France."

His Majesty's conduct, the journalist commented, was "very correct." The Emperor was a stickler for protocol; Halleck should have awaited his order to fire the cannon.

Roos's windows were soon filled with portraits of Queen Emma, resplendent in court dress and diamonds. And so another framed lithograph went up on the wall of the Emperor's room beside that of his British cousin.

Bummer died in November, kicked to death by a ruffian, Henry Rippey, who was quickly jailed by the police before anyone could lynch him, although that did not save him from the wrath of a cellmate, David Popley, a popcorn seller, who "popped him in the smeller."

Some papers flatly refused to believe the news when Frank Gross reported it in the *Bulletin,* preferring to think the dog only injured.

"NOT DEAD!" roared the headline in the *Alta.*

"Bummer still lives, in spite of the endeavors of a certain vile mercenary sheet to kill him," sniffed the *American Flag*.

"Be easy, citizens—calm yourselves, calm yourselves, there is no truth in the item," piped up a cheeky little new daily, the *Dramatic Chronicle,* which ordinarily devoted its few pages to theatrical gossip but soon would broaden its interests and change its name to *The San Francisco Chronicle,* under which it still flourishes. The writer of the *Chronicle* squib was probably Mark Twain, who now reviewed plays for that paper and contributed snippets of gossip of a satirical nature, largely aimed at the *Morning Call,* which he nicknamed "the poor little Morning Squeak."

But the story about Bummer's death was true, and the Squeak confirmed it: "Notwithstanding a fellow feeling has made the reporters of a morning and an evening paper [Fitz Smythe and Mark Twain] cling to the hope that Bummer was one of 'the few immortal dogs that were not born to die,' yet he did and went the way of all dogs."

Twain, finally accepting the possibility that perhaps his successor on the *Call* was not such a dunce after all, gave in and admitted that Bummer breathed no more, even making it official by writing an obituary for the *Territorial Enterprise,* which Bret Harte reprinted in his weekly *Californian:*

> The old vagrant Bummer is really dead at last; and although he was always more respected than his obsequious vassal, the dog Lazarus, his exit did not make half as much stir in the newspaper world as signalized the departure of the latter. I think it was because he died . . . full of years, and honor, and disease, and fleas.

Several cartoonists produced lithographs of the dog on his bier for the print shops, caricatures of local street characters having become a thriving business since the advent of Ed Jump. But the new man on the *Call,* appointing himself art critic, voted Jump's the cream of the crop:

> JUMP UPON BUMMER—The best thing yet produced in respect to the memory of the late lamented Bummer is a lithograph by Jump, representing his unsouled tabernacle of clay lying in state. At each end of the four corners of the platform on which lies prone his mortal remains, stands a lighted candle, by the

funereal glare of which the observer may . . . see the spirit of Lazarus enjoying himself at a free lunch. Many might think it is the real Lazarus that is depicted; but it is not, gentle reader; 'tis only his spirit.

Jimmy Bowman, who had just quit the *American Flag* to join the fledgling *Chronicle,* pretended to take umbrage at the headline George Barnes had given that squib:

COWARDLY LITTLE "CALL"—Good kindly-hearted Bummer, the pet of the public, lies a corpse, and now, while the sorrow-stricken people bemoan his loss, the horrid, fiendish little *Call* publishes a paragraph which commences thus: "Jump upon Bummer." You'd like to jump upon him now he's dead, would you? You daren't do it while he was alive. "Jump upon Bummer!" Isn't this pretty advice to give to people who loved and respected him while alive, and now mourn his loss. We are not in favor of mob law, but—would it cause any surprise if an enraged populace demolished the office of the paper which dared to say "Jump upon Bummer"?

It is idle to speculate at this late date whether Bowman wrote the jibe at the cowardly *Call* out of loyalty to Twain, who was still smarting under the sting of being fired by Barnes, or because he hoped to impress the owners of the *Chronicle,* Charles and Michael De Young, that his own wit was every bit as entertaining as Twain's.

But, after all was said and done, the main thing was that Bummer was dead and would never pop up at a lunch counter to ruin the Emperor's appetite again. Still, Bummer's ghost would be back to haunt the Emperor, along with the shade of Lazarus, both wagging spectral tails, for Ed Jump had all-knowingly added another twist to the legend of Norton the First that would survive to this day. And even if it means getting ahead of our story a smidgen, at the risk of losing the thread, it's too good to wait for.

Chapter 16

Lazarus Redivivus

―――◆―――

Always with the Emperor were his two dogs, Bummer and Lazarus....

—Cora Older

When they were living they followed him everywhere....

—Fremont Older

In 1873, after the railroad reached the city, a young typesetter by the name of Fremont Older arrived on the train from Chicago, seeking a journalist's job. In time, when the *Morning Call* and the *Evening Bulletin* joined hands under the ownership of William Randolph Hearst, this same Fremont Older, now a seasoned veteran, assumed command of both papers and became the greatest of all of San Francisco's fighting editors. He fought fair, though, unlike the belligerent founder of the *Bulletin*, James King of William, and was much admired even by the politicians he caused to be jailed for graft. The word of such a man is not to be taken lightly, which may be why so many still accept as gospel the yarn he spun in the *Morning Call* in 1934 about Emperor Norton and Bummer and Lazarus. A snatch of it will suffice:

> When I came to the city in 1873 I met the Emperor on Montgomery street, walking slowly along, gravely returning salutes. His old pals, the two vagrant dogs, Bummer and Lazarus, were

dead when I arrived. When they were living they followed him everywhere, and the three were welcome in all of the saloons, where the "Emperor" fed himself and the dogs from the free lunch counter.

Pause a while now and admire that paragraph, for it is a veritable masterpiece of the art of telling tall tales; pause and digest, and then brace yourself for the rest:

> After Bummer and Lazarus died he traveled about alone. Lazarus was stuffed and placed in a glass case and hung on the wall of Van Bergen's saloon, on Sansome street, near Clay. It remained there until the fire [that came with the earthquake] destroyed it in 1906. I visited the place often, and on one occasion I met the "Emperor" there. He was eating solemnly at the lunch counter. Suddenly he turned his old wild eyes on the stuffed figure of Lazarus. The tears rolled down his cheeks and mingled with the crackers and cheese he was munching. "My old friend," he said, in a trembling voice.

The doughty old fighter *might* have seen the stuffed body of Lazarus encased in glass in Van Bergen's on Sansome near Clay, instead of in Martin & Horton's at Montgomery and Clay, where last we left it, for that corpse seems to have wandered the town over the years, like a spirit that can find no rest. But it's also possible that Older simply confused the two saloons, which would have been quite understandable, since he wrote that piece more than half a century later, when he was seventy-eight (though still keeping an eye on the *Call* and the *Bulletin* as editor in chief). But back in 1862, a full decade before Older came to town, His Majesty tried to shatter a shop window because a print-seller had dared to display a lithograph that implied he was a bummer, no better than the mongrels he mooched with. If he hated the dogs *that* much, one wonders how the story ever got around that he loved them, fed them, and called them his pets.

Fremont Older did not, and could not, pretend that he knew the Emperor well. He left the city shortly after arriving and spent the next eleven years with papers in other communities—Virginia City's *Territorial Enterprise* was one, Sacramento's *Union* another—returning to be a reporter for the *Alta California,* his first job as a journalist in San Francisco, two years after His Majesty was dead and gone. Just the same, the tale that he wrote about Emperor Norton and "his" dogs holds a firm place in the hearts of those who love legends and has often been repeated in print, even though a few killjoys on the *Chronicle* and the *Examiner* have been telling the town for years that, yes, it's a delightful story but not worth a tittle or a jot to anyone who has studied the facts on file in a newspaper morgue.

It's well-nigh impossible to shake a myth that was set down in black and white by a man who had seen the Emperor with his own eyes, and it is even harder when that man's wife backs him to the hilt by writing, in a book about the city, that most emphatically Norton I did indeed go everywhere accompanied by his dogs. Cora Older, who never met the Emperor, could only have heard that detail from her husband. And it's really quite easy to guess where *he* must have heard it, despite his claim that he got it from His Majesty himself, who sobbed like a child when he saw Lazarus on a taproom wall and said in a voice that trembled, "My old friend" (an utterance that, even in this phlegmatic day and age, deserves at least six exclamation points).

It all began with the coming of the railroad, bringing visitors from every corner of the continent to see the land of eternal summer they had only read about in books. Tourism had been impossible before, except for the idle rich who had the time and the money to travel by sea purely for pleasure. Few people of any means would have been prepared to endure a bone-shaking stagecoach ride of several weeks with all of its attendant ills—remember Greeley's boils, earlier?—to a city on the edge of the Pacific unless they planned to stay there for good. But the railroad changed all that, making it relatively simple even for folks of moderate resources to take a vacation trip to San Francisco and return home to tell the neighbors about it.

Now, imagine those vacationers getting off the train in Oakland and crossing the bay on the ferry to San Francisco, where they were certain to see Norton I in his ragged uniform and plumes, "walking slowly along, gravely returning salutes." Next, envision their astonishment when they saw the signs on the shops reading "By Appointment to His Imperial Majesty." And then picture them roaming the streets in search of mementos of their visit and discovering the Emperor's face in every print-seller's window. Well, now, prominent among those prints would have been the one that showed His Majesty lunching in a tavern with two dogs. When they asked the print-seller about those dogs, as they were sure to do, he would have had an explanation ready, knowing it is always easier to sell souvenirs if there is a good story attached.

"Oh," he would have said, "that's Bummer and Lazarus. They were *very* famous."

"Famous, were they? How famous?"

"Why, as famous as the Emperor. They were his own dogs, you see. Never went anywhere without them."

Well, a tourist couldn't argue with that, could he? Because there they were in the lithograph, three good friends sharing a platter, one for all and all for one.

And that's the tale that Fremont Older, just seventeen when he arrived from Chicago, would have heard and believed. The fib must have gained considerable currency by the time he reached town, three years after the first train brought the first sightseers, and there wasn't a merchant in all of San Francisco who would have told him anything different, since it fitted the legend that was important to the city's tourist trade, and surely no taverner would have squelched it while pouring a drink for a starry-eyed lad of seventeen who swears he is Older.

So, if that scenario is correct, the veteran journalist did not invent the tale he told in the *Call* sixty-one years later; he merely added a personal touch, putting himself in the picture, as raconteurs are apt to do when they are in the prime of their anecdotage and want to make a good story better. Nevertheless, our loyalty lies with the Emperor, God bless him, and we are obliged to give short shrift to the whoppers that tradesmen dreamed up to sell a souvenir, no matter how highly their testimony may be regarded by newcomers who thought it came straight from the horse's mouth when in fact it came straight from the ass's.

But we are getting ahead of our own story and must return to it. And we must go back in rather a hurry, because His Imperial Majesty has just been arrested.

Chapter 17

In Durance Vile

> "Detained for involuntary treatment of a mental disorder."
>
> —Police blotter, January 21, 1867

William Martin, the Police Chief's clerk, who had grown gray in the service of the city, heard the news as he sat at his desk in the anteroom of Room No. 11, the Chief's office on the ground floor of City Hall. He went at once to the gloomy jail in the basement.

"What's the charge?" he asked.

"Detained for involuntary treatment," said the desk sergeant, quoting the entry in the record.

"Who arrested him?"

"Armand Barbier, a local."

Officer Martin glanced at the clock on the wall. The *Evening Bulletin* already had the story; the news would be all over town in about three hours, when the paper hit the streets. He returned upstairs as fast as his tired old legs would travel to tell the new Chief, Patrick Crowley, that there was going to be trouble and that the cause of it was an overzealous young local.

The police department, limited by municipal ordinance to one hundred men, was twenty-eight short of that number, due to the providence of Crowley's predecessor, Martin J. Burke. Chief Burke had saved the city a great deal of money by supplementing a force of only seventy-two policemen with sixty-six uniformed auxiliaries, "special officers" paid by the property owners on the beats they patroled. An auxiliary wore the velvet-collared blue uniform and black top hat of a policeman, but unlike a regular patrolman, who could be assigned to any district, he was required to protect only the locality that paid him and for that reason was called a "local." The regulars, who suspected that a special earned much more from private sources than the $125 a month paid by the city, had no love for locals.

And so they were delighted when a local committed a blunder.

The facts came to light in due course. It seems that the Emperor, in search of a newspaper and comfortable chair, had wandered into the Palace Hotel (not the splendid and more famous Palace that will later play a part in this story, for that had not yet been built, but a smaller establishment of the same name). The proprietor, offended by his shabby presence, sharply ordered him off the premises, quite failing to realize that the public would deeply resent any insult to His Majesty if word of it ever reached the press. The Emperor demurred, declining to leave without an apology, so the hotelier summoned Armand Barbier, the local on duty in that neighborhood, to remove him. But the young patrolman, eager to prove he was worth every dollar the property owner paid him, did far more than that; he marched the unwanted intruder to the police station in City Hall, where he requested the desk sergeant to book him for vagrancy.

Now here was a marvelous chance for a regular to teach a local a lesson. Following proper procedure, the sergeant asked the bewildered prisoner to state his address and empty his pockets. Noting that the Emperor lived in a lodging house on Commercial Street and had a key to a room to show that he was a tenant, the sergeant counted the coins laid on his desk, found a total of $4.75, and told Officer Barbier—with a malicious smile, we may be sure—that a charge of vagrancy could not be preferred against a person who had a fixed abode and money to sustain him, the legal definition of a vagrant being a derelict who had neither a bed nor the means to rent one. The embarrassed special then cast about for another pretext to jail the Emperor and triumphantly found one. He had taken him into custody, he said, because he was of unsound mind and could be a danger to himself and to the community. That, at least, was enough to ensure that His Majesty would be held in a cell to await examination by the Commissioner of Lunacy.

So the desk sergeant wrote that charge in his blotter and sent a man upstairs to tell the Chief's clerk what was afoot, knowing full well there would be the devil to pay when Officer Martin relayed Barbier's cock-and-bull story to a publicity-conscious Pat Crowley.

Crowley had been elected on the strength of a pledge to reform the police department, which had earned a bad name during Martin Burke's eight years of office. Ed Jump's opinion of Burke's chance of reelection in the municipal battle for power showed in a print he produced before the voters went to the polls. His "Great Muni-Turn-Em-Out" depicted the incumbent city officials as knights in rusted armor mounted on chargers, lances poised to defend their posts against all challengers, while prominent in the foreground, sitting disconsolately on his dead nag, was an already vanquished Police Chief, toppled before the fight had even begun. Burke had gone off to be a real estate agent, and few regretted his going—certainly not Mark Twain, who had never forgotten his own night in the pokey. Now Chief Crowley, who was doing his best to give the police a better image with the press and the public, was about to learn that all of his efforts had just been sabotaged by the arrest of the people's pet on the preposterous charge of being himself.

There was little hope that the *Bulletin* would take care to point out that the fool responsible was a local, not a regular. To Frank Gross, who admired Twain and might be expected to share the writer's low opinion of the police department, a policeman was a policeman.

As Crowley had feared, the distinction between an officer paid by the city and an officer privately paid went unnoticed in a scathing editorial published by George Fitch:

> In what can only be described as the most dastardly of errors, Joshua A. Norton was arrested today in the Palace hotel. He is being held on the ludicrous charge of "Lunacy." Known and loved by all true San Franciscans as Emperor Norton, the kindly Monarch of Montgomery street is less a lunatic than those who engineered these trumped-up charges, as they will learn when His Majesty's loyal subjects are fully apprised of this outrage. Perhaps a return to the methods of the Vigilance Committees is in order. This newspaper urges all right-thinking citizens to be

in attendance tomorrow at the public hearing to be held before the Commissioner of Lunacy, Wingate Jones. This blot on the record of San Francisco must be removed.

But there would be no hearing before Commissioner Jones; the Emperor had already been released by an apologetic Police Chief. So relieved was the Emperor to be set free that he quite forgot to retrieve his wallet and room key from the property clerk and had to return for them next morning. Albert Evans was at the jail when His Majesty arrived, escorted from his park bench across the street by his "royal courtiers" (as the *Alta* reporter called the old Forty-Niners who gathered each day in the plaza):

> Yesterday he called at the Property Clerk's desk, received back the key to the palace and the Imperial funds, amounting to $4.75 lawful money, receipted for them in his bold hand, "Norton I, Emperor of the United States and Protector of Mexico," caused Ah How, his Grand Chamberlain, to witness his signature, and departed amid the acclamations of his devoted subjects.

Fitz Smythe applauded Pat Crowley's prompt action as just and proper, reminding his readers that "Norton was in his day a respectable merchant, and since he has worn the Imperial purple has shed no blood, robbed nobody, and despoiled the country of no-one, which is more than can be said for his fellows in that line."

It was Evans who belatedly explained to the public, presumably at Crowley's urging, that the patrolman who had jailed the Emperor was a local and not a regular. And to make sure the whole town knew that the regular police were faithful to the Crown, every man stationed on Montgomery Street took great care to salute His Majesty when he passed, so that nobody who chanced to be watching could possibly mistake them for locals (except that some of the locals started saluting too, hoping to be mistaken for regulars).

It's entirely possible, even probable, that the old-timers in Portsmouth Square would eventually hear from William Martin about the sharp reprimand young Armand Barbier received from Chief Crowley, because that same year, when Martin retired from the force, he moved from his room in Stone Alley to a cheaper chamber—fifty cents a night—on the third floor of Eureka Lodgings, just down the passage from the Emperor's, and became one of the Emperor's devoted band of courtiers, frittering away his days on a bench with the rest. Incidentally, the city directory that listed Martin's new address also gave His Majesty's proper occupation: "Norton, Joshua (Emperor), 624 Commercial."

His Majesty apparently forgave Officer Barbier, graciously granting him a royal pardon in view of his youth, for Barbier remained on the force for many a year thereafter, no doubt saluting the Emp like the dickens.

Mark Twain, happy in the knowledge of Martin Burke's defeat, had left for New York, sailing as far as Panama in the steamship *America,* under Captain Edgar Wakeman, who regaled Twain with old salt's tales during the voyage. For instance, there was that time in the Chincha Islands, off the coast of Peru, when some sea captains who had assembled to try a man for murder wasted so much time on such piffling nonsense as innocence or guilt that, while the court was still in session, weighing the evidence, Wakeman took the accused from his cell and hung him without further ado.

"He put the noose around the murderer's neck," Twain would later recall, "threw the bight of the line over the limb of a tree, and made his last moments a misery to him by reading him into nearly premature death with random and irrelevant chapters from the Bible."

Ned Wakeman did everything by the Good Book.

Ed Jump left soon after Twain, announcing his departure in a final lithograph that showed him soaring into the clouds in the basket of a balloon labeled "The Last Jump." He worked for a while on the staff of *Leslie's Illustrated* in New York, then went on to Chicago, a sensible city, where, finding little to tickle his fancy and make his pencil dance, he committed suicide.

The presence of a French army across the border, in Mexico, fighting to maintain the crown of Maximilian against a nation determined to have none of his alien rule, had been an additional worry for President Lincoln, who could do nothing about Napoleon III's invasion so long as his hands were tied by the conflict in his own country. Maximilian, however, was now in an untenable position, abandoned by Louis Napoleon, who had ordered his troops back to France when he saw that the war could not be won, leaving his Austrian puppet to the whim of fate.

In April, 1867, when Maximilian was besieged in Queretaro by the peasant army of Benito Juarez, the brilliant Indian leader in the struggle for independence, the *Alta California* could not resist publishing another fake decree, this time addressed to William H. Seward, Secretary of State, by an impatient Protector of Mexico:

To Mr. Seward:
   It is my desire that, in case Maximilian will surrender, he be sent here a prisoner of war, but that in the event of his continuing the war, or refusing to surrender, then he be shot.

Maximilian did not surrender. He was captured in June, taken to a hill outside Queretaro, and shot.

In San Francisco, on the wall of a cluttered cubicle lighted only by a candle that dimly flickered on the tin-framed faces of Queen Emma of the Sandwich Islands and Victoria of Great Britain, hung the portrait of Carlotta, widow of Maximilian, age twenty-seven. Unfortunately, she, poor thing, overcome with grief, had gone quite, quite mad.

Chapter 18

Railroad to Renown

His Majesty's full dress never-mention-'em's have lost their seat, and there is dangerous risk of the Empire being brought into contempt.

—*Evening Bulletin*

WHEREAS, *the* Evening Bulletin *newspaper has been goosey enough to join proscriptive traitors against our Empire;* **NOW, THEREFORE,** *we, Norton I, Gratia Dei Emperor, do hereby fine the said* Bulletin *$2,000; the amount to be appropriated to our Royal Wardrobe.*

—*Alta California*

If the Emperor seemed to be collecting royal widows, Robert B. Swain, the Superintendent of the U.S. Mint, adjoining the *Call* and the Eureka, appeared to be collecting unknown writers destined for fame. When a blond young man, discharged from the Army with a head wound and memories of a war that would sour his soul, came to Commercial Street in search of employment, the only job that Swain had to offer was that of night watchman. The macabre stories this newcomer wrote, when not patroling darkened corridors, would make the literary world sit up and take notice. His name was Ambrose Bierce. And he is the one who, after tasting the fruits of success in London with his *Cobwebs from an Empty Skull,* would one day write that the Emperor "lived in luxury." His forte, you see, was fiction.

His Majesty was painfully thin, wasted by malnutrition, his uniform deplorably threadbare. His ostrich plume, having waved in the wind too long and become worn to a frazzle, had given way to a hackle of peacock feathers mixed with rooster quills, and he no longer wore his baggy blue army trousers with the faded red stripes down the seams, as the *Bulletin* pointed out: "His Majesty's never-mention-'ems having lost their seat, the royal limbs are cased in a pair of civilian pants."

Frank Gross reported that the Emperor had petitioned the Board of Supervisors to supply him with clothes at the city's expense:

> . . . poor Norton humbly petitioned the Board as if he were asking for a new sidewalk before his palace, or gaslight at the street corner that his feet might not stumble upon returning late to lodgings after honoring his servants, the [theatre] players with his sacred person.

In the same petition His Majesty prayed that the Supervisors would compel one of the local newspapers to be his official journal and change its name to *The Imperial Gazette,* the only organ that would be empowered to publish his manifestos. The Emperor mistrusted MacCrellish's *Alta,* which too often exposed him to ridicule, and Fitch's *Bulletin* was still reluctant to print his proclamations so long as Evans was considered by the public to hold a copyright on the Emp.

To settle the matter, Deacon Fitch, taking a tilt at a rival in the afternoon field that seemed desperately anxious to increase its circulation, suggested in an editorial that the *San Francisco Examiner* might welcome a chance to brighten its pages, which he contended were awfully dull compared to his own paper's: "It would be a wholesome change especially to constant readers, as well as a relief to the editor, to devote the first column of the second page of the *Examiner* [the column reserved for editorial opinions] to advocating the Lost Cause of the Emperor Norton."

The Lost Cause was the Emperor's petition for a royal gazette and a suit. The Board ignored it, which afforded Fitz Smythe another opportunity to publish a fraudulent ukase, prohibiting the Mayor and Supervisors "from appearing in public with Coats on until the Emperor shall have been provided with suitable Imperial Raiment." Police Chief Crowley was commanded to arrest any city official found to be wearing a coat, presumably including himself.

For all of his monkeyshine manifestos, meant to mock His Majesty, Albert Evans was proud to announce that September:

> TESTIMONIAL—His Majesty, the Emperor Norton I, has received from a delegation of his faithful web-footed subjects an Oregon grape-vine cane, richly ornamented with a gold head and ferule, as a testimonial illustrative of the opinion held of him by the people of that moist country. His Majesty, with the wonderful condescension which has so endeared him to all his subjects, will cause the Minister of State [William Martin?] to make a suitable reply to the donors, and has been graciously pleased to accept the stick in the spirit in which it was given.

It was a handsome cane, its mahogany handle carved in the shape of a human hand grasping a writhing snake. The snake was fashioned from grapevine and was entwined around the cane's staff, which was hollow and contained buckshot, so that the reptile seemed to rattle when His Majesty walked.

His "scepter" the newspapers called that cane, though one writer named it his Serpent Scepter, and we will call it that to distinguish it from all of the Emperor's other insignia of sovereignty, for no other name will do half as well. Of all the dozen or more fancy sticks that he received from those who wished him well during the course of his reign, this was the one that he treasured most and kept for state occasions, such as when he went to Berkeley to inspect the cadets of the University Battalion. He often visited a school to address the pupils and counsel them to be good, advice deeply appreciated by the teachers, since the youngsters always listened to the Emperor with awe and respect.

Abraham Lincoln's successor, Andrew Johnson, thrust into the White House by the blast of an assassin's bullet (and thereby earning the derisive title "His Accidency the President"), was in deep trouble with his cabinet and with Congress. He had been in trouble since the day he took office, when it was charged that he had taken the oath at his inauguration in a state of intoxication, slurring his words and staggering. His supporters claimed that he was not inordinately fond of alcohol, as his detractors alleged, but had taken an extra tot or two of whisky before the inaugural ceremony because he was feeling unwell. Whatever the truth of that claim, the reputation of being a drunkard continued to haunt him.

This, though, was trivial compared to his present problem. The chief issue was the question of executive privilege, which had become a matter of grave concern to a legislative branch wrestling with the complexities of Reconstruction and divided in its opinions about what should be done with the South, whether to forgive and forget or to punish. President Johnson's adherence to Lincoln's policy of conciliation "with malice toward none, charity for all" aroused suspicions because he, Johnson, was a Tennessean (though loyal enough to remain in the Senate when his state seceded and to be nominated for the vice-presidency in 1864, when Lincoln ran for reelection against General George McClellan and won hands down). His conduct since the war had not allayed northern fears that the South might win back with words what it had lost with weapons, for he had not only declared himself willing to allow southern senators to resume their seats in Washington, but had told an indignant Congress that only he had the right to decide the future of the states that had rebelled. He had also made it abundantly clear, by vetoing the Civil Rights Act of 1866, which passed without his endorsement, that he was utterly opposed to granting suffrage to blacks.

For all of this Johnson was roundly denounced in a largely hostile press. The *Alta* had some fun with him, publishing another "proclamation" in the name of the Emperor that left no doubt—at least in a San Franciscan's mind—that the powers of executive privilege rested with His Majesty, not with His Accidency:

OFF WITH HIS HEAD!

> So much for Andy! The Supreme Court of the United States is hereby commanded to try Andrew Johnson for usurpation of our Imperial authority and prerogatives, and if found guilty, behead him or send him here to black the Emperor's boots.
>
> NORTON I

Not much doubt there that the Emperor's private secretary was up to his old tricks. Nor can there be much doubt that Fitz Smythe had grown extremely fond of the now popular phrase from Lewis Carroll's *Alice*.

The radicals in Congress found a way to get rid of Johnson. Since he had broken no law that would call for his impeachment, they passed a law that no president could obey if he were to insist upon maintaining executive privilege. A new Tenure of Office Act, passed over his veto, made it an impeachable offense for a Chief Executive to remove from office without the Senate's consent any person of cabinet rank appointed by himself, and the President at once fell victim to the Act when he dismissed Edwin M. Stanton, the Secretary of War. Victory for his political opponents seemed utterly assured when President Johnson was brought to trial in March 1868, as most of the senators who would try him were Republicans known to be wholly unsympathetic to him.

But they had not reckoned on the emergence of Sam Ward.

The defense team rightly argued that the case against the President was flawed, since Secretary Stanton had been appointed by Lincoln, not by his successor, who had every right to choose his own advisers. Sam Ward was hired to whip up support for the beleaguered Johnson, and a long and bitter battle ensued, lasting almost three months, during which it was openly charged in the House of Representatives that Ward had bribed some members of the Senate to alter their votes from "Guilty" to "Not Guilty," offering as much as thirty thousand dollars for any three votes changed in the President's favor.

However Ward did it, he did it, snatching Johnson from almost certain defeat by exactly one vote. After that, on Capitol Hill, little Sam Ward was known as "The King of the Lobby," a name bestowed in admiration by the Washington press.

The *Alta* had news of Professor Coombs from Mark Twain in New York, who had seen him on Broadway, still dressed as George Washington and "displaying his legs on street corners for the admiration of the ladies."

> Washington the Second had "cheek" enough before the Pacific Coast had yet to mourn his loss, but he has more of it now. When it was proposed to tear down the old William Penn mansion in Philadelphia to make room for some modern improvements, he

actually had the effrontery to carry a petition praying the authorities to . . . confer it on him, during life, on account of his resemblance to Washington, Franklin, and two or three others of America's great men.

As [he] failed to get the Penn mansion, it is said that he proposed to ask Congress to give him the Washington Monument. Congress might as well do it, for the ungainly old chimney that goes by that name is of no earthly use to anybody else.

Twain joined a cruise to the Holy Land that year in the steamship *Quaker City*, having first contracted with Fred MacCrellish to write a series of letters about the excursion for publication in the *Alta*. The tour's promoter, Captain Charles C. Duncan, a pillar of Dr. Henry Ward Beecher's Plymouth Church, had warned in a brochure that only the virtuous and righteous would be allowed to join the pilgrimage. Twain paid his deposit, submitted to "a pitiless Committee on Applications"—Captain Duncan himself—and was adjudged worthy on the strength of the references he had given.

"I referred," Twain told the readers of the *Alta*, "to all the people in the community who would be the least likely to know anything about me." He named his character references: President Andrew Johnson, General Ulysses S. Grant, and Emperor Norton. Two heavy drinkers and a crackpot.

Captain Duncan's pilgrims were a little *too* righteous for Twain. "The pleasure ship was a synagogue," he wrote, "and the pleasure trip a funeral excursion without a corpse." If he were to go on such a cruise again, and could choose his own traveling companions, he said, he would pick Captain Wakeman to lead it instead of the prudish Duncan and fill the ship with convivial Californians he had known. And he mentioned a number of San Franciscans he thought "could travel forever without a row and preserve each other's respect and esteem." Among them were Emperor Norton and "five delegates from San Quentin." Three hundred journalists, including himself and Bret Harte, would be consigned to steerage, Frank Soulé of the *Morning Call* apparently being the only one Twain considered fit to mingle with convicts and royalty in first class. That passage in the *Alta* was deleted when the letters were published by Elisha Bliss as *The Innocents Abroad*, as were all other paragraphs that could only amuse the West Coast, where the passengers he had named were well known.

The following year, 1869, with one best-seller behind him and *Roughing It* requiring only a polish, Twain wrote to Mary Mason Fairbanks of the Cleveland *Herald*, whose acquaintance he had made during the cruise of the *Quaker City*, to tell her that he was coming to Ohio to lecture on "Some Uncommon Characters I Have Chanced to Meet." The only uncommon character whose name he mentioned in his letter was "Emperor Norton, a pathetic San Francisco lunatic." Note that he had to explain the Emperor to Mrs. Fairbanks; the Californian chrysalid had not yet emerged as a North American Monarch.

Bethlehem, Pennsylvania, where Twain's lecture tour began, was the first Eastern city to hear about Norton I. But there nobody seemed to appreciate the Emperor; California still seemed as distant as the moon and might well be a monarchy for all that anyone in the Lehigh Valley knew or cared. When the topic also fizzled in Allentown, the newly married Twain wrote to his wife in despair: "Livy darling, this lecture will *never* do. I can't handle these chuckleheaded Dutch with it."

It would take more than a couple of lectures by Mark Twain to bring the Emperor of the United States to national attention. Indeed, it would take a great engineering feat, the completion of the transcontinental railroad.

But that was on its way.

After five years of tunneling through almost impassable mountain peaks, the tracks of the Central Pacific had crossed the mighty Sierras at last and were now marching at a much faster pace over the deserts of Nevada to meet the oncoming rails of the Union Pacific in Utah.

In a special edition published on the morning of May 8, 1869, the *Alta California* described the mounting tension as work crews graded the roadbed, laid the last ties, and bolted the rails into place. Squads of Chinese laborers set an astonishing record for speed, laying down as many as ten miles of track in a day, "as fast as the early ox-teams used to travel over the Plains" in Gold Rush times, said the *Alta*. Its reporter on the spot—not Albert Evans, since this was far from his beat—attempted a touch of Fitzsmythian humor:

> Passing along this line of Chinamen, I heard the [Irish boss] singing out, "Hurry up there, ye devils, shure we have no time

to lose," and the answer comes from the whole squad in a laughing manner, "Tach I Yah," which I inferred meant, "Ready and begorra, we do that same," for a closing up of the ranks, a brisker gait and a livelier movement of shovels and pick-axes immediately followed.

On May 10, when the rails from the East met those from the West at Promontory Point, north of the Great Salt Lake, a spike of Californian gold was brought from a safe in the railroad car that carried Leland Stanford, the president of the Central Pacific, from Sacramento. The golden spike would be driven into the last tie to lock the rails together. All over America reporters had gathered at the telegraph offices to await the tap of a key in Utah that would tell the world that the spike had been driven. In an office in Washington a correspondent of the New York *Tribune* waited beside the telegraphist whose duty it was to tell Congress and Horace Greeley (for this was the crowning achievement of Greeley's life, and he was on Capitol Hill with President Ulysses S. Grant, the victor at Appomattox, sworn into office just nine weeks before). Greeley's reporter told New York how the news, relayed by a telegraph operator in Chicago, came to Washington:

> After some little trouble in the Chicago office, and the closing of the circuit west of Buffalo the instrument here was adjusted, and at 2:27 P.M., Promontory Point, 2,400 miles west of Washington, said to the people congregated in the various telegraph offices:
>
> "Almost ready. Hats off; prayer is being offered."
>
> A silence for the prayer ensued. At 2:40 the bell tapped again, and the office at the Point said:
>
> "We have got done praying. The spike is about to be presented."
>
> Chicago replied: "We understand. All are ready in the East."
>
> Promontory Point: "All ready now, the spike will soon be driven. The signal will be three dots for the commencement of the blows."

Leland Stanford, in Utah, raised his hand and the assembled crowd of top-hatted railroad barons, Easterners and Westerners, as well as the blue-bloused Chinese who had tunneled so heroically through towering mountains and toiled so desperately through deserts, watched his hammer tremble in the air for a second and then swing down to make history.

There was a hush in the telegraph office in Washington, which was crammed with reporters, impatient to send their stories singing over the wires to their editors. Greeley's man was first in line, having been accorded that honor out of respect for the paper that had battled so long to make the railroad a reality. He said in his message to New York:

> For a moment the instrument was silent, and then the hammer of the magnet tapped the bell, one, two, three—the signal. Another pause of a few seconds, and the lightning came flashing eastward, vibrating over 2,400 miles between the junction of the two [railroads] and Washington, and the blows of the hammer upon the spike were delivered instantly, in telegraphic accents, on the bell here. At 2:47 P.M., Promontory Point gave the signal, "Done!" The continent was spanned with iron.

The word reached San Francisco in that very same moment.

Newspapers in other cities had frequently commented upon the condition of the Emperor's clothes—his linen "resembled the rarest, longest-unwashed old lace in color," the Cincinnati *Enquirer* had said—but when the *Evening Express* in Los Angeles, a piddling pueblo in Southern California that was getting a bit too big for its boots, sneeringly called His Majesty a "walking travesty upon San Francisco's shoddy spirit," it was more than any San Franciscan could reasonably be expected to bear. The local press, stung by the criticism, raised such an outcry that the Board of Supervisors, bowing to public pressure, finally voted to buy him new regimentals out of municipal funds. They bought the Emperor a new uniform and a beautiful new hat, a white beaver adorned with peacock plumes; but left him in broken boots.

Two photographers, who had just moved into new premises and were seeking a way to advertise that they were now located on Market Street in the only building in San Francisco that possessed an elevator, persuaded him to have his photograph taken. They seated him in a chair, snapped his picture, and made a print of unusually large dimensions, which they put in their window. Then they sent word of the photograph to Colonel Moustache, who gave them a puff:

> ROYALTY PHOTOGRAPHED—His Majesty, Norton I, our ever-beloved sovereign, has, at the request of many of his faithful subjects, consented to sit for his photograph, and Messrs. Bradley and Ruloffson have produced a mammoth picture of almost life size. His Majesty is *en grande tenue* [in full military dress], and the "divinity that doth hedge a King" stands out unmistakably in every feature of his noble face and every wrinkle in his coat.

Bradley & Ruloffson then arranged with a local printing firm to produce picture postcards from photographs they had taken of His Majesty. The tourists would soon be coming, and San Francisco meant to make the most of him.

Chapter 19

The Bridge to Nowhere

—⫸⫷—

Being anxious to have a reliable weekly imperial organ, we, Norton I . . . do hereby appoint the PACIFIC APPEAL our said organ, conditionally, that they are not traitors and stand true to our colors.

Norton I.

The Emperor was also awaiting the arrival of the Iron Horse with keen anticipation, for he had already foreseen a splendid new way to raise funds for the sadly depleted Imperial Treasury. The number of businessmen who had supported him for the past ten years, former colleagues in commerce who paid his tax out of pity, could never have been many, to judge by his emaciated appearance, and must have dwindled to even fewer during the course of the decade, as some retired to hometowns back East with their fortunes, or drifted off to seek silver in Washoe, or were killed in the war, or died in San Francisco. But now his troubles would soon be over.

Despite his delusion that he was royalty, His Majesty possessed a most inventive mind, as will become quite evident the further this story progresses. The possibility of increasing his meager income by taking advantage of tourism occurred to him shortly after Leland Stanford's gold spike was driven, either in June or early July at the latest, when he went to Cuddy & Hughes, the firm that was printing the picture postcards for Bradley & Rulofson, and ordered some "Imperial Treasury bond certificates," which he intended to sell to tourists.

The certificates, printed on white paper measuring about eight inches by four and decorated with all manner of ornamental scrolls and flourishes, carried this pledge:

THE IMPERIAL GOVERNMENT OF NORTON I
Promises to pay the holder hereof the sum of
FIFTY CENTS
in the year 1880 with interest at the rate of 7 per cent per annum from date, the principal and interest to be convertible at the option of the holder, at maturity, into 20 years 7 per cent Bonds, or payable in Gold Coin.
Given under our Royal hand and seal
this _____ day of _____ 18___
(Signed) _____

The certificates also bore a pen-and-ink etching of His Majesty's thin bearded face, obviously taken from an early newspaper engraving (he was portrayed wearing a Civil War kepi, which he had long ago discarded for his Kossuth). The printers probably designed the scrip themselves and furnished them without charge, being content to advertise their business in four-point type at the bottom of each certificate: "CUDDY & HUGHES, Printers to Norton I, 511 Sansome Street, S.F."

The real value of the scrip lay in the Emperor's autograph; he signed the bonds as he sold them (apparently carrying a bottle of ink and a pen in his pocket for that purpose), and the "seal" above his signature was made by smearing a coin with ink before applying it to the paper, which left rather more of a smudge than an identifiable imprint.

Fremont Older, who bought one of the Imperial bonds that day in Van Bergen's Saloon, when the Emperor supposedly wept with grief over a dead dog, remembered how His Majesty added the cachet: "He took my fifty cent piece, covered it with ink and smeared it on the bond as a seal. I should have kept that 'bond.' It would have become a valuable souvenir. But, being young and inexperienced, I tore it up and threw it away."

By then, presumably, the coin had already disappeared into an inky pocket.

Rivalry between San Francisco and Oakland grew more and more intense as the "city of oak trees"—once no more than a bedroom community for San Franciscans and a place to go for picnics—waited for the coming of the railroad that could mean instant prosperity. Battle was now joined in earnest, and the Emperor was caught in the middle, newspapers on both sides of the water freely making use of his name to poke fun at Oakland's dreams of dominating the bay or San Francisco's schemes to stop it. When one San Francisco paper suggested, with its tongue in its cheek, that the city should annex Oakland, "moving its commercial interests to the San Francisco side of the Bay," the Oakland *Daily News* replied with a "proclamation" ostensibly issued by His Majesty:

> WHEREAS, the Oaklanders are quite a well behaved people, and may remain so if not brought in contact with the vicious and profane, and
>
> WHEREAS, it is our purpose and desire that Oakland and San Francisco shall be neighborly, but view each other afar off;
>
> NOW, THEREFORE, we, Norton I, *Dei Gratia* Emperor of the United States and Protector of Mexico, do order and direct the city engineers of both cities shall cause the space between Goat Island and Oakland to be filled in with dirt taken from Mount Diablo [east of the bay], and that suitable wharves for ocean steamers be erected along the front of the same; whereof fail not under our royal displeasure.
>
> Given under our hand this 13th day of August, A.D. 1869, in the City of San Francisco.
>
> NORTON I.

The reference to Goat Island—officially called Yerba Buena Island, but known by an earlier name to those who still remembered it during the Gold Rush as a pasture for goats—was a jibe at San Francisco's proposal that the island be given to Leland Stanford as the most suitable site for his railroad terminal, which would then be closer to San Francisco than to Oakland.

The Oakland paper followed up this false decree with another, the most famous proclamation of all and one that lovers of legends still treasure as an example of the Emperor's lunacy. To fully appreciate that—and the hullabaloo it would later cause, in our own century—we will omit the opening paragraphs, which have nothing to do with the squabble with Oakland, and give only the part that matters:

> We, Norton I, Emperor of the United States and Protector of Mexico, do order and direct, first, that Oakland shall be the coast termination of the Central Pacific Railroad; secondly, that a suspension bridge be constructed from . . . Oakland Point to Yerba Buena, from thence to the mountain range of Saucilleto [now spelled Sausalito], and from thence to the Farallones, to be of sufficient strength and size for a railroad; and thirdly, the Central Pacific Railroad Company are charged with the carrying out of this work, for purposes that will hereafter appear. Whereof fail not under pain of death.
>
> Given under our hand this 18th day of August, A.D. 1869.
>
> NORTON I.

How they must have laughed in Oakland when that proclamation appeared in the *News*, for the bridge it proposed would have been an astonishing structure, meandering aimlessly all over the place from Oakland Point to Goat Island before wandering off to Sausalito in Marin County and then heading west for thirty miles beyond the Golden Gate to the Farallone Islands (a clump of rocks in the Pacific inhabited only by seals and seabirds, with one lonely lighthouse-keeper for company).

San Francisco's newspapers, hearing the titters that came floating across the bay, completely ignored the joke out of civic pride, refusing to reply to it and thereby acknowledge its existence. Today we might never have heard of it if a collector of Norton memorabilia, one Albert Dressler, had not found it in Oakland's archives and included it in a little book he published himself in 1927 under the truncated title *Emperor Norton of United States*. Dressler, who printed a facsimile of the original newspaper paragraph, was the first to suggest that the decree was genuine, saying: "San Francisco Bay was ordered bridged by Emperor Norton in 1869; the following Proclamation appearing in the Oakland Daily News, August 19, 1869." This claim caught the eye of an eminent historian, Robert Ernest Cowan, chief librarian and bibliographer of the Arthur Andrews Clark Library at the University of California in Los Angeles, who seemed to dismiss any quibble concerning the document's authenticity by saying, in a slim volume of limited edition published solely for collectors of Californian curiosa: "Whether or not it was drafted by the Emperor is insignificant, but its contents are extraordinary and of the greatest prophetic importance."

The entire tone of the paragraph in which Cowan made that comment, however, left the distinct impression that he did consider the manifesto to be authentic. In fact, he concluded with the surprising statement that, because Leland Stanford was "attempting to secure Yerba Buena, to make it a great terminal depot" for his Central Pacific, "the vision of the gentle old Emperor was not so fantastic after all," quite forgetting that any bridge that went traipsing off to a barren outcrop in the Pacific would have been truly fantastic and of no possible use to San Francisco or anywhere else.

Cowan's willingness to accept the proclamation as the Emperor's handiwork gave it instant credibility, for "Sir Robert"—as he was known among bibliophiles—was not only a respected archivist but could even claim a passing acquaintance with His Majesty. He was eight years old in 1870 when he and his parents met the royal ragamuffin on the station platform in Oakland, where they had just disembarked from a train that had carried them from Canada. The Emperor, he fondly recalled in a conversation with his publisher, Ward Ritchie, had patted his head and told him to be a good boy (after which, we may suppose, he turned to the lad's father, ink bottle in hand, to sell him a bond).

Then, in 1939, along came Allen Stanley Lane, who repeated the fable about the bridge to nowhere in a full-length biography, *Emperor Norton, Mad Monarch of America,* stating emphatically that the Emperor *was* the author of the Farallones proclamation, and furthermore had written the decree that ordered the bay filled in with dirt from Mount Diablo, extending Oakland's waterfront as far as Goat Island. In short, we were asked to believe that His Majesty took Oakland's side in the battle for the bay all along, a remarkably generous attitude considering Oakland's behavior at Camp Allen six years before, though most ungenerous to his own city, which had firmly supported him.

But that is not all. In 1964 Robert Cowan's monograph was

posthumously reprinted by Ward Ritchie as part of an anthology, *The Forgotten Characters of Old San Francisco*, and so a later generation came to hear about the delightfully dotty idea attributed to the Emperor by an Oakland journalist who had intended it only as a spoof and could never have imagined that anyone would actually believe it.

Now that we've let the cat out of the bag, it's time to examine what the Emperor *really* said about the bridge, for it is certainly true that he ordered one built, although his decree was a great deal saner than the one invented by Oakland. Here it is, precisely as it appeared in the San Francisco *Pacific Appeal*, not in 1869 but on March 23, 1872:

PROCLAMATION

The following is decreed and ordered to be carried into execution as soon as convenient:

I. That a suspension bridge be built from Oakland Point to Goat Island, and thence to Telegraph Hill; provided such bridge can be built without injury to the navigable waters of the Bay of San Francisco.

II. That the Central Pacific Railroad Company be granted franchises to lay down tracks and run cars from Telegraph Hill and along the city front to Mission Bay.

III. That all deeds of land by the Washington Government since the establishment of our Empire are hereby decreed null and void unless our Imperial signature is first obtained thereto.

NORTON I.

Another fraud? Not at all. It is entirely in keeping with his sense of dignity—"written in good style," as the *Bulletin* once said, "correct in orthography"—and does not contain a foolish threat like Fitz Smythe's "Off with his head!" or Oakland's "Fail not under pain of death." But the best assurance of all lies in the fact that it appeared in the *Pacific Appeal*, a weekly paper that the Emperor himself had appointed his royal gazette on the strict understanding that its editor, Peter Anderson, would never tamper with his public pronouncements.

In 1936, when the San Francisco–Oakland Bay Bridge was completed, it followed exactly the route the Emperor had suggested.

One of its approaches begins at the end of Broadway on the slope of Telegraph Hill and the bridge then crosses almost a mile of water to Yerba Buena Island and from there travels more than two miles farther to Oakland Point (or in the Emperor's decree, which merely reverses the direction, "from Oakland Point to Goat Island, and thence to Telegraph Hill").

But wait, for here is another surprise for those who thought the Emperor was too crackbrained to order the bridging of the bay.

Today a tunnel runs under the waters of the bay, carrying commuters by the thousands into San Francisco every day from Oakland and more than a score of other cities east of the bay in swift electric trains.

The tunnel was the Emperor's idea, too. The proof may be found in a proclamation that appeared in the *Pacific Appeal* on September 21, 1872:

> WHEREAS, we issued our decree ordering the citizens of San Francisco and Oakland to appropriate funds for the survey of a suspension bridge from Oakland Point *via* Goat Island; also for a tunnel; and to ascertain which is the best project; and whereas the said citizens have hitherto neglected to notice our said decree; and whereas we are determined our authority shall be fully respected; now, therefore, we do hereby command the arrest by the army of both the Boards of City Fathers if they persist in neglecting our decrees.
>
> Given under our royal hand and seal at San Francisco, this 17th day of September, 1872.
>
> NORTON I.

The earlier decree referred to in this manifesto has not been found. If he sent it to the *Appeal*—one of the few papers to survive the 1906 disaster that destroyed so much of the city's written history—it was never published, which could explain his impatience, ostensibly with the Boards of City Fathers but more likely with an editor he thought could be trusted. His stern admonition, "we are determined that our authority shall be fully respected," could have been a warning to Peter Anderson that the Royal Warrant which granted his weekly journal the privilege of publishing

His Majesty's bulletins would be rescinded if he neglected his duties again. Anderson must have heeded the warning, too, because in the years that followed he printed an astounding number of proclamations, as many as five in a single issue and rarely fewer than two, never letting a week go by without some word from the Emperor.

His Majesty's long struggle with the *Alta* for serious recognition of his imperial authority was over—and he had won.

Albert Evans retired from the city beat and went off to seek a "lost Spanish galleon" reported to have been sighted in the Salton Sea, a landlocked body of water in the Colorado Desert, only to discover when he got there that the mysterious ship was nothing more than a broken barge. He now disappears from these pages, twirling his moustaches and flicking the dust of a desert from his British tweeds, though he goes in the bitter knowledge that the editor who had lured the Emperor away with a promise of fair play was an intimate friend of his enemy, Mark Twain. Once, he had reported in the *Alta*, as if it were the most astonishing thing in the world, that Anderson and Twain had been seen together on Montgomery Street, strolling along arm in arm. That was it, the entire item, and it must have puzzled the reader who did not know that Peter Anderson was a black man whose newspaper advocated civil rights for blacks. In Fitz Smythe's opinion, by linking arms in a spirit of brotherhood, the Bohemian from the Land of Sage and the editor of the *Pacific Appeal* were carrying racial equality much too far, which tells us rather a lot about Colonel Moustache's bigotry.

But again the pen is racing ahead of the tale, for you have not yet been told the rest of what happened in 1869, the year that the railroad came and madness gave way to genius in more ways than you've heard so far.

Chapter 20

Possible Dreams, Reachable Stars

———◆———

> *There has been no great genius without a touch of insanity.*
>
> —Seneca

Alfred Babcock sold Eureka Lodgings that year to David and Eva Hutchinson, a pleasant pair, newly married, he twenty-five, she but sixteen. Eva was a happy addition to the household, the only woman. Her feminine eye permits us a glimpse into the Emperor's domestic life (though she kept her tongue still for a decade, saying nothing until the night that he died, when she found herself besieged by newspapermen eager to know more about him and obligingly tattled). According to the *Morning Call* of January 9, 1880, she talked mostly about His Majesty's underwear:

> The landlady says that he never allowed anything to be moved, and a few months ago, when she took the liberty of carrying off some very dilapidated garments, he expressed deep displeasure. He was in the habit, every morning after he awoke, of visiting the room of an old friend near his own, who always buttoned his shirt-collar for him. Whenever he wanted a woollen undershirt, he issued a proclamation to the manager of one of the woollen mills, directing him to furnish the garment required. For some time he had trouble with the Chinaman who did his washing—the Mongolian not recognizing the imperial authority but demanding the same pay for washing the linen of the Emperor as he received from his other customers. In order to placate him and

humor his weakness, the proprietor of the lodging-house at length had his washing charged to his own bill.

That reporter could have used a lesson in racial harmony from Mark Twain and Peter Anderson. The *Call,* which was blatantly biased against the Chinese, frequently used the derisive term "Mongolian" to describe them. Twain claimed that he was actually fired by George Barnes for writing items that protested ill treatment of Chinese by hoodlums, whose favorite sport was to catch two Chinese and tie their queues together before sending them off with blows and kicks.

The old friend who fastened the Emperor's collar stud for him was William Martin, the retired policeman, who had found a new job since the Hutchinsons took over the Eureka; they employed him as their clerk, presumably letting him keep their account books in exchange for his room. It would not have been an arduous task, since the hotel was so small, and he could still be found on a bench in the plaza every morning with His Majesty.

But the Emperor's world was not confined to a park bench and a lunch counter. His afternoons were usually spent at the Mechanics' Institute on Post Street, reading books, playing chess, or writing proclamations on the Institute's handsomely engraved stationery. "He was seen daily in the chess-room of the Mechanics' Library," remembered the *Call,* "and there were few who could beat him at the royal game."

The great library housed the finest collection of technical books to be found on the Pacific Coast, a veritable treasure house of precious volumes dealing with science and the arts. Under its huge-domed roof, in high-vaulted chambers and marble-floored corridors lined with glass-cased displays of scientific apparatus, the Emperor would meet some of California's most gifted inventors, among them Andrew Hallidie, the Scottish wire-rope manufacturer who soon would conquer the city's hills with his unique cable cars; Eardweard Muybridge, the society photographer who was about to give the world its first motion picture (a few flickering shots of Leland Stanford's favorite racehorse trotting down a track); and Frederick Marriott, the ingenious publisher of the weekly San Francisco *News-Letter* (whose airship would be the first powered craft ever to fly). Men of that caliber would hardly have tolerated the company of such a scarecrow if all he had on his mind was the notion that he was an emperor.

The bylaws of the Mechanics' Institute stated: "Any person may become a member, *being acceptable to the Board of Trustees* [emphasis added] and paying an initiation fee of one dollar and one dollar and fifty cents quarterly in advance." Six dollars a year would not have been too steep even for a pauper's purse, if he were thirsty for knowledge, but apparently the Emperor was acceptable whether he paid the dues or not. The fact that Joseph Eastland was on the Board of Trustees may have had something to do with it. Eastland could have testified from personal acquaintance that His Majesty's mind was sound enough to merit membership, and the quarterly dues could have been waived through Eastland's kind intercession, just as the theater managers and the riverboat owners excused the Emperor from payment as a privilege of rank.

Even if the Emperor's scientific knowledge was "sometimes mixed," as Benjamin Lloyd said in his book *Lights and Shades in San Francisco,* his reasoning was not as disordered as others have since claimed without the benefit of firsthand experience; it was they who misunderstood him. Take, for example, the decree he wrote ordering the winding course of Petaluma Creek to be "straightened." Now that, like the bridge to the Farallones, has been gleefully produced by modern writers to show the extent of his lunacy, for whoever heard of anyone unwinding a river that twisted and turned? But it could be done and it was.

Norton was particularly fond of Petaluma because of the way he was treated there after he straightened the creek and thereby substantially improved the town's economic growth. Charles Chaffee Champlin, a rancher prominent in local politics (one of only nine Republicans in that hotbed of Democrats and proud of the fact that he was the first to cast a vote for Abraham Lincoln), vividly recalled when the stream was as crooked as a Democrat's tongue until the Emperor worked his magic. He and his wife, Sarah, used to look forward to His Majesty's visits to their ranch in the Sonoma Valley. We have this from their grandson, the Reverend Charles C. Champlin, a minister of the Congregational Church in

Possible Dreams, Reachable Stars 151

Sonoma before he retired to Oakland. He told a Sunday supplement writer of the Oakland *Tribune* in 1955, shortly before his own long life came to a close:

> Every few months he would board the steamer *Gold* at the Jackson Street wharf [in San Francisco] and steam up Petaluma Creek. He would disembark at Lakeville, a few miles this side of Petaluma, and walk up the Stage Gulch Road to the old Hinkston ranchhouse, then wander into the Sonoma Valley another few miles to the Champlin ranch. Always welcomed by the Charles Champlins, the affairs of Europe and the Norton empire would be discussed far into the night. Then Emperor Norton would be escorted to the best bedroom in the house. No money was ever accepted for transportation, food, entertainment or clothes from so eminent a personage as Emperor Norton.

Petaluma Creek, in those days, could only be used by hayscows and similar craft of shallow draft, due to the continually shifting silt that gathered at every bend, making it impassable for paddle wheelers that might have carried Petaluma's poultry and dairy products to San Francisco and other markets beyond the bay. Charles Minturn's little steamer, *Gold*, could travel upstream only as far as Lakeville, where her passengers transferred to stagecoaches for the rest of their journey to Petaluma, seven miles up the Stage Gulch Road. The stage line thrived, but Petaluma's farmers might have fared better if the serpentine creek had been straighter, the little Concord coaches being much too small and too light to carry commercial cargoes as well as passengers.

A small railroad had operated briefly between the town and the steamship landing, until one dreadful August day in 1866 when the boiler of its only locomotive exploded in the depot at Petaluma, beheading the engineer and badly injuring several passengers. After that, four mules pulled the cars to and from Lakeville, walking two abreast between the rails. Restless commuters fumed at the languid pace, impatiently waiting for Minturn, who owned the railroad, to make good his promise that the improvised muletrain was merely a temporary inconvenience until a new engine, "already contracted for, can be placed on the tracks." That pledge was never kept, because the train became unnecessary when the silt-choked creek was straightened out, making dredging relatively easy.

Today, if you glance at a map of Sonoma County, you can see at once how it was done. The narrow river still twists and turns, like one letter "S" following another, but now a channel runs through each S-bend as a slash runs through a dollar sign. This was probably not Norton's idea, but the papers of that time often gave him the credit for ideas he merely agreed with.

When the channel was excavated the steamship *Gold* passed by Lakeville with no more than a toot on its whistle. The little town began to dwindle to the couple of houses that stand there now, wistfully dreaming of long-gone neighbors, while the Emperor had no further need to sleep overnight at the Champlin ranch on the almost deserted Stage Gulch Road to Petaluma, because any hotelier in that flourishing city would have given him a supper and a bed free of charge. Charles Minturn dared not demand that the Emperor pay his passage, either, or he would have read in the local *Argus* what an ingrate he was after all the valuable time and money that His Majesty's genius had saved him.

The Emperor was also convinced that, one day soon, men would fly in the sky. Americans had cherished that hope for years. In 1849, before James Merritt Ives became his partner, Nathaniel Currier had issued a lithograph for sale in New York, captioned "The Way They Go to California." The print depicted a futuristic airship over the Hudson River, bound for the newly discovered goldfields. That same year, when thousands were plodding across the plains in covered wagons or boarding ships for the long voyage around Cape Horn, a New York publisher, Rufus Porter of the *Scientific American,* designed a cigar-shaped dirigible, eight hundred feet long, which he advertised in New York's papers as "Porter's Aerial Locomotive." The gondola beneath its gasbag, he claimed, would be large enough to support a steam engine and its boilers as well as "from 50 to 100 passengers" who would travel to California in comfort at speeds ranging from fifty to one hundred miles an hour. Porter formed a stock company to build his airship but found too few investors.

There were other attempts to fly, some by San Franciscans. On November 17, 1856, the local *Herald* announced that a Professor Wilson had ascended in a balloon from the roof of a hotel and landed about a mile away "without injury to himself or his machine." But a balloon flight of one mile, with just one man in the basket, was a far cry from a gondola large enough to transport a hundred passengers over a continent three and half thousand miles wide.

Fred Marriott, the publisher of the *Weekly News-Letter,* thought it possible. What is more, he had limpid blue eyes, cherubic cheeks, and a halo of golden hair turning white, the look of an angel who could fly to heaven on just one wing if he chose, so his appearance of honesty and innocence helped him in financing his project. He confided in Andrew Hallidie and got his backing. Together, Englishman and Scot, they formed the Aerial Steam Navigation Company to build the curious combination of dirigible and stub-winged monoplane that Marriott called the "Avitor."

On July 2, 1869, at Shellmound Park, a racetrack near Oakland, the machine was given its first test, watched only by journalists. One spectator, a correspondent of Rufus Porter's *Scientific American,* reported back to New York:

> The morning was beautiful and still—scarcely a breath of air stirring. The conditions were favorable to success. The gasometer was fully inflated and the model floated out of the building. In six minutes steam was got up—the rudder set to give a slight curve to the course of the vessel—and the valves were opened. With the first turn of the propellers she rose slowly into the air. . . .

No pilot sat in her gondola. Marriott hoped that by achieving two flights—the first unmanned, the second with passengers—he would be able to raise enough funds to build a machine four times larger than this forty-foot prototype. The test flight was a success; Avitor circled the racetrack twice, steered by the fixed rudder, as two men holding ropes fastened to bow and stern followed her around at a jog trot.

Despite all the praise in the papers, Montgomery Street's speculators made no concerted rush to invest in the Aerial Steamship Navigation Company, prompting a decree from the Emperor:

PROCLAMATION.

Whereas, we, Norton I, "Dei Gratia" Emperor of the United States and Protector of Mexico, being anxious for the future fame and honor of the residents of San Francisco, do hereby command all our good and loyal subjects to furnish the means and exert their best skill and advance money to make Mr. Marriott's aerial machine a success.

NORTON I.

Given at San Francisco, Cal., this 25th day of July, A.D. 1869, in the seventeenth year of our reign.

Two weeks later, Marriott announced that the second flight would be made on Saturday, August 14, with passengers in the gondola. Sam Tetlow, seeking publicity for his Bella Union as always, told the *Herald,* that "if it does not make a successful voyage, each and every person [aboard] will be presented with a ticket for the evening performance" of *Red Hot, Hottest,* a bawdy musical comedy starring Nellie Cole. He stood to lose nothing whether the flight was a success or a failure. If the Avitor flew he kept his tickets; if it crashed there would not be a soul alive or fit enough to watch Mrs. Cole's naughty performance.

The Avitor didn't fly. Someone with a match got too close to it on the night before the test flight and its gas-filled envelope collapsed in a burst of flame. Anyone with a calendar could have prophesied that disaster; it chanced to be Friday the thirteenth.

But let's take a closer look at that last proclamation, for it seems to confirm something about Norton's earlier years that so far we have only been able to guess at. If he had really been in "the seventeenth year of our reign" in 1869, as he said in that decree, he must have donned his invisible crown in 1852, though still keeping it a secret from his friends in Pike Street and giving them only the merest glimpse of his innermost thoughts when he said: "What this country needs is an emperor. Now, if I were Emperor of the United States . . ." Why, even as he talked with Hall McAllister and Joseph Eastland over brandy and cigars after dining on Sam Ward's delicacies, in the darkest corners of his mind he already *was* an emperor. The Emperor spoke the truth in that proclamation; he had been an emperor for seventeen years. And here, all along, we've been thinking it was ten.

We have not yet finished with the saner side of the Emperor's mind, however, for there is still another story to tell, which may explain why Joseph Eastland considered him worthy of membership in the Mechanics' Institute.

For months, ever since Fred Marriott hired him to write a column for his *News-Letter,* Ambrose Bierce had been titillating the town with his savage wit. For example: "A man in Vermont was recently hanged by the neck until he was dead, dead, dead, and for the trifling offense of stealing another's shirt. He had previously removed the head that the garment might not be soiled with hair oil." No woman, he said, could keep a secret: "There is positively no betting on the discreet reticence of any woman whose silence you have not secured with a meat ax." He affected to dislike small boys: "The fact that boys are allowed to exist at all is evidence of a remarkable Christian forbearance among men . . . we should devour our young, as Nature intended."

Yet Bierce confessed to be at an utter loss to understand a notice that had been pasted on a wall of the railroad depot in Oakland following the collision of two local trains. Quoting it in full, he asked the stationmaster across the bay for a translation:

> Hereafter, when two trains moving in opposite directions are approaching each other on separate tracks, conductors and engineers will be required to bring their respective trains to a dead halt before the point of meeting, and will be very careful not to proceed until each train has passed the other.

Only an Oaklander, Bierce, felt could explain how two trains could pass each other at a standstill.

A railroad employee's faulty timepiece was apparently to blame for the crash. A switchman, who was supposed to haul his lever so that an idling locomotive could move into a siding to make way for an oncoming freight train, thought his turnip watch was keeping good time when in fact it was running slow. Believing he had several minutes to remove the obstruction from the track, he dawdled over his coffee, leaving the switch untouched, only to hear a few moments later the frantic shriek of a whistle, the screaming of brakes, and the awful sound of tearing metal.

There had to be a better way to run a railroad; the safety of passengers could not depend upon a switchman's faith in his watch. The Emperor found the solution, a switch that worked by itself, and the news was announced in a journal that every member of the Mechanics' Institute read and respected, *The Mining and Scientific Press:*

> Emperor Norton has invented a Railroad Switch, a model of which is now being made. It consists of a novel application of a spiral or elliptical spring, operated by the weight of the passing train, by which the Switch is turned off or on as desired. Patent applied for.

That notice, reprinted in the *Pacific Appeal,* was followed by a brief proclamation in the same issue of Anderson's paper:

> The Emperor desires that there should be a thoroughly practical and mechanical Switch, and his ideas improved upon so that Europe will be glad to pay America for the patent.
>
> NORTON I.

There was just one snag. When the Emperor asked Andrew Hallidie to make him a model in his machine shop, to demonstrate that his switch could be operated by the mere presence of a train on the track, without the aid of human intelligence and muscle, the careful Scot advised him that it would cost a hundred dollars. When the Emperor wrote a draft for that amount and presented it to the First National Bank, it was refused (so much for Mrs. Neville's belief in the beneficence of bankers). Another decree quickly appeared in the royal gazette:

> WHEREAS, the First National Bank refused to honor a small check of $100, to pay the value of a model for a Railway Switch invented by us, thereby endangering our private personal interest to a large estate:
>
> AND, WHEREAS, it is publicly notorious that one or two of the Directors have large amounts in trust belonging to our personal estate;
>
> NOW, THEREFORE, we, Norton I, Emperor of the United States and Protector of Mexico, do hereby decree the confiscation to the State of all the interest of said Bank as security for any losses we may sustain by reason of their acts.
>
> NORTON I.

It is not known for certain whether a model ever was built, or a patent applied for (if so, it wasn't granted), but the parsimony of a fellow inventor and the closed purse of a banker may have deprived mankind of a safety device when it was most sorely needed.

On October 29, 1869, the last rails of the Central Pacific were laid in Oakland, and on November 8, when the first overland passenger train pulled into the terminal, the Emperor was there, with his sword and his scepter, his bonds and his ink bottle, to greet the travelers who poured from its cars.

Chapter 21

Birth of a Legend

My dear Senator Sherman,
   I have to apologize for not replying to your letter sent me some time back. In fact, my love & esteem for ruling over this nation is fast oozing away. All I do for you only ends in ingratitude. No pay, no clothing, no palace....

   —Letter to Senator John Sherman,
   brother of General William T. Sherman,
   from the Emperor of the United States

"There is almost nothing to see in San Francisco that is worth seeing," Anthony Trollope reported to the Liverpool *Mercury* in 1875. "There is a new park in which you may drive for six or seven miles on a well-made road . . . an inferior menagerie of wild beasts, and a place called the Cliff House, to which strangers are taken to hear seals bark."

If that tireless English traveler found so little to write home about in 1875, he would have discovered even less had he arrived with the herd of reporters who came riding the rails five years earlier, whisked in a matter of days over mountains and prairies that had once taken half a year to cross in an ox-drawn wagon. The seals were there in 1870, barking at the Cliff House from the ragged rocks below, and Woodward's Gardens on Mission Street had its zoo, but the Golden Gate Park with its well-made roads did not exist, just a desert of sand and a rough path of planks from the city to the sea.

The junketing journalists were unimpressed. Not wanting to admit in print that they had traveled so far merely to look at lions and sea lions, they begged to be shown something truly unique, some wonder of the Golden West that could not be found in the East.

"Anything beside seals?"

"Why, of course," said the townsfolk, on the defensive. "There's the Emperor. You could write about him."

And there he was, strolling the streets in his hat with the rooster feathers, armed with his rusty sword. They had madmen back home, kept in cages like the beasts at the zoo, but none like the Emperor of the United States, who could roam wherever he wished, acknowledged by all as their liege lord (or so it was said), even saluted by the police.

So they wrote about Norton the First.

Others who came after them would tell his tale too, spreading his name and fame all over the land, until in time he came to symbolize San Francisco in much the same way that the quaint little cable cars and the bridge that turns to gold in the setting sun symbolize that city today.

Among the first to arrive by train were "General" Tom Thumb and his wife, Lavinia Warren, both less than three feet tall, engaged to appear at Maguire's Opera House. The *Alta California* called General Thumb "second in command of His Majesty's troops." The paper did not trouble to explain to the newcomers who His Majesty was, simply assuming that by now everyone must know. Those who did not would soon be enlightened when they asked why so many shops in San Francisco seemed to bear signs saying: "By Appointment to Norton I."

Bradley & Ruloffson did rather well with their postcards.

"The velocipede mania is upon us," cried the *Chronicle* as daring young men on wood-rimmed wheels began to be seen on the streets, even skimming at breakneck speeds down the steepest hills, from the crest of California Street to Kearny at the bottom, and down the slope of Powell as far as Market.

At the Mechanics' Institute, under the great dome of its pavilion, a "Grand Velocipede Tournament" was held. "The occasional falls were very pleasant," in the opinion of one reporter, who did not have to suffer them but thought it pleasant to watch others tumble. "Some riders have legs too long, some legs too short. There was no betting and very little real test of speed. To our amazement the best velocipedist present was a Doctor of Divinity, Reverend Horatio Stebbins, who rode at a mad pace when it suited him. Never have we witnessed such speed in a pulpiteer."

Twain had liked Dr. Stebbins; it was possible to pull his leg without offending him. Once, while reporting the events of an earthquake that had rocked the city on a Sunday, Twain had written to the *Enterprise* that the popular pastor of the First Unitarian Church "did precisely what I thought of doing myself but had no opportunity—he came out of his pulpit and embraced a woman. Some say it was his wife." Later, in a letter to the *Alta* after his "funeral excursion" in the *Quaker City* with Captain Duncan and his sanctimonious pilgrims, he had included the Reverend Stebbins on the list of congenial Californians he said he would prefer to join on a cruise to the Holy Land with Ned Wakeman and Emperor Norton.

The Emperor was an ardent admirer of Dr. Stebbins, preferring the freewheeling pulpiteer to any other. Charles A. Murdock, a staunch Unitarian who taught Sunday School in the minister's church on Geary Street, recalled in his memoirs:

"He often attended the service of the Unitarian church, and expressed his feeling that there were too many churches and that when the empire was established he should request all to accept the Unitarian church."

The reason the Emperor favored the teachings of Dr. Stebbins should have been apparent to anyone who knew His Majesty's somewhat radical views on religion. The Unitarian doctrine of reason and tolerance must have seemed to him about as close as mankind ever would come to realizing his own dream of ecumenical brotherhood, though the Reverend Stebbins stopped far short of advocating the establishment of a state church in which Protestants and Catholics would worship with Jews and none would be able to claim to be closer to God than another. Dr. Stebbins urged the unification of all Christian churches, without giving a thought to synagogues.

The Emperor's rather more liberal vision of unification was made obvious when he decided to abolish a city ordinance that forbade shops to open on Sundays while permitting them to trade on Saturdays, the Hebrew Sabbath. There had been complaints from Jewish merchants that the law was prejudicial to their interests, presumably since it gave non-Jews six days in which to conduct their business and Jews only five:

> WHEREAS, it is our intention to endeavor to obtain some alteration in the doctrine of the Church, by which the Hebrew and Christian faiths will become united; as also by which the foreign churches will become Americanized; now,
> THEREFORE, we, Norton I, Emperor [etc], do hereby prohibit the enforcement of the Sunday Law until our object is obtained and one Sunday established.

Here the Emperor's sympathies clearly lay with the Jewish shopkeepers. When he had succeeded in founding his state religion, he would decide which day should be given to God, the Sabbath observed by Christians or the Sabbath he had been taught to revere as a child. In the meantime, the shops could stay open on a Sunday.

His Majesty also espoused a movement to have the Bible "purified" of certain passages that some thought conflicted with the tenets of their own particular creed, maintaining that the questionable passages should be either amended or expunged. Dr. Stebbins would certainly have approved of that. One has only to read Charles Murdock's biography of his pastor, *Horatio Stebbins, His Ministry and His Personality,* to understand that the minister did not regard the Bible as the cornerstone of truth.

"The Bible," Stebbins said, "is not an infallible book. Some, thinking so, have taken the book instead of God. It is history, literature, law, and religion. There is much in it from which we gain little . . . there is much in it that is not true."

The Emperor expressed himself rather more eloquently in the *Pacific Appeal:*

> WHEREAS, there are great commotions in different quarters of the terrestrial globe, arising from discussing the question, "The Purification of the Bible—its True and False Lights," and fears are entertained that a war may break out at some remote point

and spread all over the world, carrying in its winding course death, pestilence, famine, devastation and ruin;

WHEREAS such a state of affairs is to be deplored by all liberal-minded Christians, who oppose bigotry, charlatanism and humbuggery, and who follow the golden maxim of the lamented Lincoln, "With malice toward none—with charity for all";

AND WHEREAS, Religion is like a beautiful garden, wherein the False Lights may be compared to the poppies, which fall to the ground, decay and are no more, the True Lights . . . bloom in everlasting etherealism, blessing forever the Creator and the Christian world by their Love and Truth;

NOW, THEREFORE, we, Norton I [etc], do hereby command that all communities select delegates to a Bible Convention, to be held in the City of San Francisco, State of California, U.S.A., on the second day of January, 1873, for the purpose of eliminating all doubtful passages contained in the present printed edition of the Bible, and that measures be [adopted] towards the obliteration of all religious sects and the establishment of an Universal Religion.

Take note of those last two words; it is not merely a state religion that the Emperor now has in mind, but a religion preached and practiced in every corner of the world.

His Majesty attended the tournament at the Mechanics' Pavilion and was photographed on a velocipede. It was one of the saddest pictures ever taken by Bradley & Rulofson, showing him at his thinnest, a skeleton on a bicycle, rather like a gaunt Don Quixote astride his bony Rosinante.

But he was about to blossom.

The bonds made all the difference. He no longer had to rely on the generosity of bankers and merchants, for he could now make as much money in a minute from a tourist as he had from a banker in a month.

Though his income was now secure, his needs remained quite modest; he spent not a cent on clothing, but sold just enough scrip every day to pay his rent and perhaps add a cheap supper to his free lunch (which would explain his spreading girth in all of the photographs taken after 1870). Only the better class of restaurant would have turned him away; there must have been many an inexpensive cafe whose proprietor would have admitted him, now that he was becoming so famous, putting a card in his window: "Caterer to His Majesty." A four-course dinner in such an establishment would rarely cost more than twenty-five cents, even with a pint of red wine. The Emperor could easily have afforded that; just four bonds, at fifty cents each, would have fed him for a week, with a quarter left over for a tip. The wise restaurateur, eager to please his working-class customers, who thought the world of the Emperor, might willingly have accepted a bond in payment from His Majesty to induce him to return.

Those who thought the Emperor's scrip worthless must have been astonished to read in the press that one fifty-cent certificate, offered at auction in 1870 to raise funds for charity, actually sold for one hundred and fifty dollars. The auction took place at the French Fair, held at the Mechanics' Pavilion, and was reported by most of the newspapers in the dry and dull prose usually reserved for such functions. Only the *Chronicle* thought it funny that a pauper should do something for charity:

> Emperor Norton I, San Francisco's privileged bummer, wishing to contribute his mite to the good cause, liberally donated his check on his private banker for $1,000,000. His High Mightiness confidently believed it would sell for at least fifty million dollars; but . . . the check had to submit to a slight shave, bringing the moderate sum of $50.

The item was so inaccurate that any reporter who could confuse a half-dollar bond with a personal check for a million dollars could never have attended the auction but must have found his facts in the bottom of a tankard at a tavern. The Emperor quickly set him right in the *Appeal:*

> WHEREAS, the *Chronicle* of last Sunday, in the course of noticing the events which took place on Saturday afternoon and evening at the French Fair, then being held at the Pavilion, [referred] to us personally as "San Francisco's privileged bummer," making false representations as to the value of our national scrip, thereby hoping to injure our person and prevent the sale of the scrip;
> NOW, THEREFORE, we issue this decree to correct the erroneous impression which the *Chronicle* sought to create. Our

scrip sold at $150 premium, which the purchaser generously donated to the Fair. As to the *Chronicle* calling us names, we would deem this attack too contemptible and beneath our notice, if it were not for the proscriptive policy of the press, with few honorable exceptions, which is undermining our government.

But here is something that the *Chronicle* apparently failed to realize: the Emperor had signed that bond "Norton I"—which means he wrote just seven letters—and the bidder who had bought it for $150 had actually paid more than twenty-one dollars a letter! Surely, there was never an author alive who could command that kind of pay for his pen (nor any today for that matter). The reporter who wrote that slur would have had to scribble all day long from morning till night for almost three weeks to earn even "the moderate sum of $50." Fremont Older, who came along shortly afterward, looking for a job on a paper, had good reason to remember what journalists were paid then: "Most of the men received $18 or $20 a week." The Emperor did better than that; he could have earned twenty dollars in a single day simply by selling forty certificates.

On August 1, 1870, the Emperor's title was finally recognized by the United States Government. That was the day the federal census taker came to 624 Commercial Street. Under its roof Assistant Census Marshal J. Ellis Hill found thirteen lodgers, all of them male and all of them white, according to David Hutchinson, whose duty it was as "head of the household" to answer the questions put to him. Of these thirteen only five were known to be American citizens; seven were registered aliens. The thirteenth was Joshua Norton, whose citizenship was not clear to anyone; nevertheless, the enumerator put him down on the rolls as a "Male citizen whose right to vote is denied or abridged." In the column for occupation, the census marshal wrote "Emperor." And in another, explaining why the right to vote was denied and headed *Whether deaf and dumb, blind, insane or idiotic,* he wrote: "Insane."

What an irony! A federal officer acknowledges freely, in writing, on a U.S. government document, that Norton was an emperor—and yet brands him as insane for believing it himself.

Chapter 22

Old Queen Cole

> *Who has not heard of the Bella Union? Go to the furthest edge of our sage brush in the mountain country, and you will meet some antique miner of the primeval days who will tell, with glistening eye, of the many queer sights he enjoyed at the Bella Union.*
>
> *—Morning Call*

Old Mammy Hopkins had sinned too often to know which of her many lovers had fathered her offspring, Sterling and Nellie. When her faded charms forced her to retire from active service as a whore, the children inherited her business, Sterling bringing in the clients to be entertained by Nellie. That was their occupation in 1856 when Willis Cole, a grocer catapulted into temporary prominence as the quartermaster of the Vigilance Committee, was sent to check on the health of Sterling Hopkins, who lay abed, his neck swathed in bandages, stabbed by Judge Terry.

The visitor, smitten by Nellie's beauty, returned again and again, professing great concern for the welfare of her wounded brother, though he spent less time in the sickroom than he did behind closed doors with the sufferer's sister. One day, when it seemed that Sterling was likely to recover and thus deprive the vigilantes of an excuse to hang his assailant (and their quartermaster of a pretext to continue his amorous visits), Cole proposed marriage to Miss Hopkins, quite failing to notice that her waistline seemed to be swelling. Three months after the wedding, when she gave birth to a child, he divorced her on the grounds that she had deceived him in regard to her innocence, which must have astonished every rake in town who knew the nature of her calling. To his dismay she kept his name when she became the star of the Bella Union. The champagne flowed freely behind the drawn drapes of the private booths in the auditorium whenever the playbills outside announced that Nellie Cole was the featured attraction.

Because of the plumes she liked to wear on her gown or in her hair, Mrs. Cole was known as "Lady Peacock." Sam Tetlow probably suggested the plumage and gave her the nickname to boost his business, for he would do anything to advertise his melodeon and its prima donna, never hesitating to lie when it suited him. He even concocted a rumor that romantically linked the daughter of Old Mammy Hopkins with the Emperor of the United States.

Love came to the Emperor late in life; he was fifty-two when the word got around that he was actively seeking a soulmate. He talked about it to Charles Murdock, whom he came to know rather well when he joined the flock of Dr. Horatio Stebbins. Murdock remembered the occasion in his autobiography, *A Backward Glance at Eighty:*

"He once asked me if I could select from among the ladies of our church a suitable empress. I told him I thought I might, but that he must be ready to provide for her handsomely; that no man thought of keeping a bird until he had a cage, and that a queen must have a palace."

His Majesty must have taken Murdock's advice to heart, because he began to seek better living quarters, demanding in the *Pacific Appeal* that a suite of rooms in the newly opened Grand Hotel on Market Street, facing the foot of Montgomery, be converted to his use as a palace:

> WHEREAS, our friends and adherents are dissatisfied that we are not better lodged, and hold that we ought to have had a suitable palace years ago;
>
> WHEREAS, the treasonable proscriptive acts of some of the hotel keepers of this city have kept us out of decent rooms for

our accommodations, so that we have been unable to make our family arrangements in order.

NOW, THEREFORE, we do hereby command the proprietors of the Grand Hotel to forthwith furnish us with rooms, under penalty of being banished.

September 21st, 1870.

NORTON I.

The words "family arrangements" alerted the press that the Emperor was contemplating matrimony. Editorials appeared in several papers, each trying to guess the identity of his intended consort, the most popular theory being that he was pledged to wed Victoria, the Widow of Windsor, to cement an alliance between the United States and the United Kingdom. The *Chronicle* warned that an America ruled by two English sovereigns was likely to find itself reduced once more to the status of a British colony. The *Call* conjectured that a more suitable candidate might be Carlotta, the banished Empress of Mexico, she having much in common with His Majesty, both being as mad as March hares and therefore compatible. Nobody thought of Nellie Cole until Sam Tetlow suggested it.

Surprisingly enough, the Emperor himself seemed to confirm that unlikely choice by ordering a new set of Imperial Treasury bonds from his printers, certificates that bore not only his own portrait but also a companion picture of Mrs. Cole, or somebody suspiciously like her. It may have been merely the likeness of some unknown young woman whose long black tresses resembled Mrs. Cole's, printed from an engraving that Cuddy & Hughes happened to have on hand. But it also could have been an actual sketch of Lady Peacock, supplied by the wily Tetlow as part of his scheme to have the actress promoted to empress. Tetlow did have some posters printed, which he displayed at the entrance to the Bella Union, announcing the opening of a new revue starring Her Majesty "Old Queen Cole" (a parody on the popular nursery rhyme that Lady Peacock would have had a right to resent, since she had yet to see her thirtieth birthday).

His Majesty was furious. He withdrew the offensive bonds from circulation, discharged Cuddy & Hughes from his service, and appointed a more conservative printer in their place, a respectable churchgoer who would never do anything to besmirch his good name—none other than Charles Murdock.

Charles Albert Murdock, a former reporter of the *Morning Call* (only one of several who had occupied that position since Mark Twain's ignominious dismissal), owned a print shop in Clay Street. His doorway served as a sort of unofficial employment bureau, where pressmen in search of a job with a newspaper would gather every morning. They hoped that some editor who needed a hired hand would come along and find a man on Murdock's front step who might fill the bill. Fremont Older said that he found a job there setting type for the *Call* when he arrived in 1873 (before he learned that a paper in Redwood City, down the peninsula, was looking for a reporter).

Murdock redesigned the imperial scrip several times during the years he served the Emperor, improving their appearance considerably, even printing a seal to replace the ink smear, and making it unnecessary for His Majesty to soil his fingers. On one batch of certificates he imprinted the Great Seal of California. On another batch he used Napoleon Bonaparte's royal insignia, the letter "N" enclosed within a wreath of laurel (the initial now standing for Norton's name). Never once did Murdock attempt to advertise his business by adding a line at the bottom to say that he was His Majesty's printer, as Cuddy & Hughes had done. We know this only because Murdock said so in his memoirs:

"I was his favored printer, and he assured me that when he came into his estate he would make me chancellor of the exchequer."

The new bonds were issued in three denominations—fifty cents, five dollars, and ten dollars—although it must have seemed unlikely that a purchaser would have been willing to pay five or ten dollars for His Majesty's autograph when he could have had it for fifty cents. Even so, among the few examples of the Emperor's scrip still in existence, guarded by California's archivists as carefully as the crown jewels in the Tower of London, are at least two of the higher-priced certificates, each bearing the imperial signature and the date on which it was sold.

His Majesty's bonds are collector's items today, treasured by all Emperor Norton buffs, whose numbers are legion in California and Nevada. But the rarest of all is the Nellie Cole scrip, worth fifty cents before Sam Tetlow made it the subject of scandal and God knows what price when it was suppressed to stop the gossip. Now it would be worth a king's ransom.

One of the most popular acts at the Bella Union was the comedy team of Magilder and Murray. Philip Magilder was the star turn, Larry Murray the butt of his jokes. Tetlow's audiences would roar with glee when Magilder, his face blackened with burnt cork and wearing a robe of many hues, appeared onstage as Alamagoozalum Whangdoodlum, an Eastern potentate of unfathomable origin who spoke a jargon all his own, meant to be pidgin English (or perhaps pidgin Hindu). One day, just for a lark, he and Murray concocted a royal proclamation, signed it with the Emperor's name, and sent it to the *Pacific Appeal,* where it must have escaped the eye of Peter Anderson, because it appeared on the front page:

PROCLAMATION

WHEREAS, one Philipmagilder Alamagoozalum Whangdoodlum Larryum Murrayum is engaged in plotting with conspirators to usurp our prerogatives and is a traitor to our person and scepter; and

WHEREAS, all movements of such nature tend to weaken the stability of our government at home, and cause it to fall into contempt and ridicule with foreign Nations;

NOW, THEREFORE, we, Norton I, Dei Gratia Emperor of the United States and Protector of Mexico, hereby decree that said Philipmagilder Alamagoozalum Whangdoodlum Larryum Murrayum be appointed Chief of Police to ex-Emperor Louis Napoleon Bonaparte, and that he forthwith leave our realm to fill such an appointment.

NORTON I.

September 13, 1870.

The proclamation's presence in the *Appeal,* despite Anderson's promise to keep such claptrap out of its pages, can easily be explained: Anderson never saw his paper until it was published, but simply assembled the editorial matter and sent it out to be printed, trusting others to set the type and run the press. So that it was always possible for something to slip in that had never passed his desk.

Louis Napoleon, by the way, had no need of a police chief; he was now a prisoner of war, captured by the Prussians at Sedan less than two weeks earlier, on September 1. The empire of Napoleon III had collapsed. He would be sent to England, where he would die in exile like Louis Philippe. And another portrait would hang on the wall of a tiny room on Commercial Street, that of the banished Empress Eugenie of France.

Every Friday morning, when the Board of Supervisors met in council, the musicians of the Bella Union would assemble on the sidewalk in front of City Hall to play catchy tunes on their instruments, another idea conceived by Tetlow to draw attention to his theater, which stood close by. The music certainly captured the attention of His Majesty, holding court in the park across the street; he could hardly hear himself speak above the noise. Since the Supervisors seemed unable to stop it, there being no law that forbade music being played in the streets, the Emperor issued a sharp order to Tetlow in the *Pacific Appeal:*

"The music in front of the City Hall, being a nuisance to the Board of Supervisors during the hours of session, is hereby prohibited, under penalty of closing the Bella Union Theatre, for whose benefit it is performed."

Of course the music continued, possibly even louder than before, until at last the Emperor, unable to bear it any longer, was compelled to seek refuge elsewhere.

"The Emperor's rendezvous on Friday mornings for the present will be at the City Gardens," announced the imperial gazette.

It is hardly likely that the Emperor's courtiers would have welcomed his decision to move, their ancient legs being rather too wobbly to carry them so far. The City Gardens stood on Folsom Street, south of Market, almost a mile from Portsmouth Square. His presence on Friday mornings must have been sorely missed by the old Forty-Niners until the Board of Supervisors, frustrated by the din under their windows, passed a Noise Abatement Act that banished the band from Kearny Street and brought peace to the plaza once more. His Majesty returned to the bench in the park with a carnation in his buttonhole from Marcelin Aurignace's flowercart.

There remains only one thing more to say here. In 1880, shortly after the Emperor went to his heavenly reward, Sam Tetlow shuffled off this mortal coil himself, doomed to dance for the Devil on the coals kept stoked for the damned.

Herbert Asbury described Tetlow's last days in a book, *The Barbary Coast:*

> [He] shot and killed his partner, Billy Skeantlebury. Tetlow was acquitted on a plea of self-defense. A few months later he sold the Bella Union and retired to private life, but his wife died, and he became enamored of a chorus girl, who soon reduced him to poverty. He died a pauper.

This is the first we have heard of Billy Skeantlebury, who must have been a silent partner in the business since he appears in none of the stories that the newspapers told about the Bella Union, silent until the day that Tetlow closed his mouth forever with a bullet. In the gaudy history of San Francisco he lives only in death.

What happened to Lady Peacock was never recorded, though it's safe to assume that she was not the scatterbrained chorus girl whose carelessness with a dollar reduced Sam Tetlow to rags. By 1880 she would have been close to forty, which was no age for Old Queen Cole to be kicking up her legs in a chorus.

Chapter 23

Don't Call It 'Frisco

Honored and Respected Sire:

We, your unhappy subjects, do hereby ask your gracious Majesty to give us a sign that we are in favor by writing to us; that we may feast our eyes on your handwriting, and know that it was you who had grasped the pen that wrote it.

—Six citizens of San Mateo

Not being personally acquainted with the writers, and not having received any tribute from them (to the best of our recollection), we shall willingly accord the request asked upon receipt of fifty cents each, by mailing our scrip of that denomination.

—Norton I.

Leland Stanford had used his considerable influence as Governor of California to acquire, at absolutely no cost, almost twenty-four million acres of public land for his Central Pacific Railroad, contending that the C.P.R. would need so much property to operate its trains. But no sooner was the railroad completed and the trains began to run than the company started to sell off most of the land to the thousands of immigrant farmers who came in search of their own place in the sun. And in 1872, when Stanford increased the tariff on freight, forcing the farmers to pay more to send their produce to market, which in turn raised the cost of living, Californians were fit to be tied. Angry editorials appeared in the press, denouncing the "robber baron" who had boondoggled the state out of land worth sixty million dollars and now waxed fat on the profits. Ambrose Bierce called him £eland $tanford and Stealin' Landford and many other harsh names besides.

His Majesty was incensed, claiming that Stanford had robbed him, too:

> Whereas, one third interest in the Central Pacific Railroad, being held in trust for us in the name of President Leland Stanford, and whereas it is necessary in order to give credit and prestige to our Empire that we should have absolute possession of the said interest; now, therefore, we . . . do hereby command Mr. Stanford to forthwith grant us possession and save the trouble of legal proceedings.

The Central Pacific could not have picked a worse time to cross swords with the Emperor of the United States.

One day, in 1872, a C.P.R. conductor in Oakland, unimpressed by His Majesty's claim that his rank entitled him to travel without charge, sharply ordered him to purchase a ticket or get off the train. Tourists, who had been told that the Emperor could travel anywhere he pleased as the railroad president's guest, must have been sorely disillusioned to read this in His Majesty's gazette:

> WHEREAS, the directors of the Central Pacific Railroad are guilty of insurrection and rebellion against our personal prerogative and dignity by allowing their employees to tax us on making use of their road; and Mr. Stanford is guilty of fraud in illegally taking possession of our interests and refusing to account to us;
>
> NOW, THEREFORE, we, Norton I, do hereby command our personal friend, Hon. Mr. Luttrell of Siskiyou, to forthwith bring articles of impeachment to compel him to give us our rights.

174   Norton I

The Emperor's choice of a champion was rather shrewd. Siskiyou County, on the Oregon border, derived no direct benefit from a railroad so far to the south, which considerably reduced any chance that its representative in Sacramento was in the former governor's pocket.

£eland $tanford was in trouble enough without giving the press another excuse to needle him. The Emperor was quickly given a free pass.

Theodor Kirchhoff, in a book published in Germany in 1886, *Californische Kulturbilder,* related an incident that occurred aboard a train to Sacramento when he was the Emperor's table companion in the dining car (English translation by Rudolph Jordan):

> I was in the act of appropriating an excellent Hamburg steak with fried potatoes, and . . . indulging in the panorama of the lovely California landscape flitting by the window, with Mount Diablo in the background, when the well-known figure of the Emperor of the United States and Protector of Mexico came in with great dignity from the car ahead, and seated himself at my table opposite me.
>
> Norton the First commanded a waiter to bring him immediately some lamb chops, with vegetables, oyster patties and a bottle of Rhine wine. The waiter, however, took no notice of him, and even had the audacity, after a loud and huffy repetition of the demand, to ask him if he had sufficient money in his pocket to pay for the meal!
>
> The indignation of His Majesty was boundless. Beating his knotted bludgeon on the table, he snarled furiously at the frightened waiter and in his rage commanded that he be served in a hurry, threatening to disfranchise the Pacific Railroad within the boundaries of his empire. Thereupon several California traveling companions interceded in his behalf and started a collection with the splendid result that a truly royal service was obtained, enhanced by two bottles of Champagne to pacify the perturbed soul of the Emperor. Norton the First deigned to fill the glasses of all present, including [myself], with the sparkling wine.

"He was not fully satisfied, however," said Kirchhoff, "until the repentant waiter had apologized, and the conductor, who had entered in the meantime, had promised him most submissively that a similar disrespect as just now shown him would never be offered again on any train of the Pacific Railroad."

San Francisco's gift shops were filled with souvenirs of His Majesty: Ed Jump's lithographs, Bradley & Ruloffson's postcards, Emperor Norton statuettes, Emperor Norton dolls, Emperor Norton mugs and jugs, Emperor Norton Imperial Cigars. The newspapers wrote about him constantly, to keep the visitors amused, which was easily done in a day when primitive jokes and pedestrian puns flourished as wit. The *Jolly Giant,* a new magazine, published a caricature of His Majesty on its cover with a cartoon of his royal coat-of-arms, a shield emblazoned with a knife and fork crossed over a plate of beef and cheese, and the motto "Free Lunch." The story inside began:

> One of the most prominent men of San Francisco is Emperor Norton. He possesses the following titles: Emperor of Merry Hingland by birth, King of Hingland by right, Emp of Hamerica by title, and Protector of Mexico by appointment. The Emp said his Empire was in a flourishing condition as a general thing, but he had some trouble with the Irish and Hinglish subjects, as they all wanted to be rulers.

False decrees and spurious reports of the Emperor's activities frequently appeared in the press. A favorite hoax was to publish a "telegram" supposedly from abroad, usually in the name of some harassed European monarch faced with a crisis and desperately in need of His Majesty's advice. "Victoria Regina" bombarded him ceaselessly with questions concerning international affairs, seemingly unable to make even the smallest decision without first asking him what she should do. He often complained about such forgeries in his letters to the *Pacific Appeal:*

> WHEREAS, there is every now and then a street report that the Emperor has received a telegram, or that he has done so and so, and on investigation found to be without foundation or fact;
> WHEREAS, we are anxious that there should be no deception, and also that no imposter should make use of our authority;
> KNOW, THEREFORE, all whom it may concern that no act is legal unless it has our imperial signature.

Visitors made fun of him, too. Once, aboard the ferry to Oakland, just as the side-wheeler was docking to discharge some tourists returning home on the evening train, the Emperor was approached by a man from Chicago with an offer to buy one of his bonds. His Majesty, who had not anticipated such a request, being bound for Sacramento that day to attend the opening of the State Legislature, replied that he had none to sell. The Chicagoan said he was sorry to hear that because he had hoped to show the Emperor's autograph to his friends in the Middle West. Could he perhaps give him a written receipt for his fifty cents? That would serve his purpose just as well as a bond. The gangplank had already been lowered and the passengers were streaming ashore, but the Emperor, courteous as ever, accepted the proferred pencil and paper and began to write, pausing only to ask the man his name, to which he replied: "I. M. Short." His Majesty finished writing the receipt and handed it to the buyer, expecting him to produce the promised coin. Instead, the fellow hurried away, explaining as he vanished among the crowd on the wharf: "I told you, I am Short—short of funds, don't you see? Toodle-oo."

The Emperor, failing to find the rascal in the railroad carriages he searched, sent a telegram to Peter Anderson, who received it just in time to publish it in his paper the following day:

> On the seven o'clock ferry with the passengers for the overland train, a tallish, knavish-looking fellow, representing himself as Mr. Short (short of honesty), a grain merchant of Chicago, fraudulently got possession of the following document written in pencil:
>
> San Francisco, May 6, 1872,
>
> Received of Mr. Short, fifty cents, the amount with interest to be converted into 7 per cent bonds in 1880, or payable by the agent of our private estate, in case the Government of Norton I does not hold firm.
>
> In testimony whereof, we affix our Royal Seal and Signature.
>
> Any person who will catch the fellow and make him pay something to the poor, and return our receipt, will do a service to the honor of
>
> Norton I, Emperor.

There was one thing about the tourists that the Emperor simply could not abide; they called the town " 'Frisco," which no true

San Franciscan ever did, thinking it smacked of blasphemy to nickname a city that had been christened in honor of a saint (although they did not mind in the least if a visitor from St. Joseph, Missouri, called his own hometown "St. Joe"). His Majesty proclaimed:

> Whoever after due and proper warning shall be heard to utter the abominable word "Frisco," which has no linguistic or other warrant, shall be deemed guilty of a High Misdemeanor, and shall pay into the Imperial Treasury as penalty the sum of twenty-five dollars.

The railroad was really to blame. "FRISCO" was the code name chalked or stenciled on goods that crossed the continent in freight cars, much as the baggage of airline passengers bound for San Francisco is today labeled "SFO." Visitors still say 'Frisco, much to the townsfolk's profound disgust, but perhaps they find it easier to pronounce than "SFO."

In May 1872, Andrew Hallidie commissioned Charles Murdock to print a prospectus that announced "the formation of a company to construct a new type of street-car, to be propelled by wire cable running in a conduit [beneath] the street and reached by a grip through a slot."

Hallidie laid the slot on Clay Street, between Jones and Kearny where the grade was steepest, and built a small powerhouse to run the endless belt of cable in the conduit just below the street. The cable car actually consisted of two cars, one towing the other. The leading car, called the "dummy," carried the driver and a heavy wheel that operated a large screw, which raised or lowered the grip under the dummy, clutching the racing cable to make the cars move or releasing it to allow them to stop. Both vehicles had seats for passengers; the dummy had benches for eight, even ten at a squeeze, whereas the car in the rear could accommodate twelve or fourteen.

At daybreak on August 1, 1873, before the town was astir, Hallidie demonstrated his invention in the presence of a single reporter, who described the occasion in *The Mining and Scientific Press:*

> It was a gray morning, and the fogs were hanging around the hills, the ground slippery from the moisture. The engine [in the

> powerhouse] was started, and the rope, which was 7,000 feet long, moved through its long tube under the surface of the street quietly and satisfactorily. The dummy was brought to the brow of the hill looking over the bay, and the grip lowered into the tube containing the moving rope. A consultation was held, and it was determined that the trial had to be made, and the man detailed to take the dummy down the hill turned pale, and succumbed to the prospect of possible disaster. Seeing the man's fear, Mr. Hallidie took charge of the dummy, and, fastening the grip upon the rope in the tube, went over the brow of the hill. . . .

Not a thing went wrong, the little car stopping smoothly when Hallidie turned his wheel to disengage the grip, continuing each time he rotated the screw to snag the wire rope. When he reached the end of the line, at Clay and Kearny, the dummy was reversed on a turntable and attached to its companion car for the trip back up the hill, the inventor again taking the wheel while six of his workmen clambered aboard, their spines considerably stiffened by the knowledge that the contraption had worked without a hitch.

"By this time," the paper reported, "some of the residents had been aroused from their sleep, and one man, appearing at the window, enthusiastically cheered, and threw to the company on the dummy a bunch of flowers."

Clay Street was jammed with spectators that afternoon, at three o'clock, when a second demonstration was made with the rear car attached to the dummy.

> It was the intention to take the car up empty, and to permit three or four of the public to stand on the dummy; but the desire of the people to ride was so great that the doors were forced open, and the car was crowded to far beyond its capacity. In like manner, people clung to the dummy, so that about 60 persons managed to get a free ride at their own risk; and when she started, and moved about 20 feet, cheer after cheer rang through the air, and the surging crowd ran up Clay Street, keeping pace as well as it could with the progress of the car.

The Emperor was not impressed; he inspected the conveyance and pronounced it unsafe:

> Whereas we are informed that the screw which works the Clay Street Railroad is not strong enough for that purpose, and that it

is, consequently, dangerous to the lives of the passengers; also that the dummy is a useless appendage. Now, therefore, the Directors of the company are hereby ordered to see that precautions are taken to make travel on said railroad perfectly safe by using a screw with at least twenty-four inches diameter.

The dummy *was* a useless appendage, although Hallidie was slow to see that. It was not until many years later, toward the close of the century, that the two cars finally merged into one. The screw, however, disappeared fairly quickly, to be replaced by a lever and a much more efficient method of gripping the cable. So perhaps His Majesty had been quite correct about both the dummy and the screw.

The celebrated Chapman sisters, Ella and Blanche, arrived in 1873 to appear at the Metropolitan Theatre on Montgomery Street, choosing "a new and original burlesque" titled *The Gold Demon* for their opening performance on March 18. A star was born that evening when an unknown youth named David Belasco, nineteen years old, his beardless face heavily disguised with greasepaint and whiskers of horsehair, made his stage debut in a comic uniform and waving plumes. "D. Belasco took the house by storm with his make-up for Emperor Norton, which was quite a feature of the piece," said *Figaro*.

So began the dazzling career of New York's future "Bishop of Broadway."

Chapter 24

Captain Stormfield's Daughter

> *He fancied many of San Francisco's belles deeply in love with him, and on all occasions exhausted his skill and invention in making himself agreeable. He was the recipient of numerous tender missives on pink paper....*
>
> —Morning Call, January 10, 1880.

> *The good will of the ladies was at all times of importance to him, and he always courteously tipped his hat to those of his acquaintance, in passing.*
>
> —Addie L. Ballou

Addie Lucia Ballou led an active life. She was a writer, a poet, a painter, a lecturer, a suffragette, a civil rights worker, and a Methodist preacher, all this in a day when it was commonly supposed that it was the duty of a wife to cook and clean, bear children, and meekly submit to the will of her husband. Mrs. Ballou did bear three sons and a daughter, although nothing is known about a spouse today other than that she was married in Wisconsin at the age of fifteen. It is almost certain that she lost her husband in the Civil War, when she served as a nurse with the 32nd Wisconsin Volunteers.

We know far more about her battles to abolish capital punishment. She marched all over the country, trying to save those condemned to hang on the gallows. Her powers of persuasion were astonishing. In the case of one young murderer, Jesse Pomeroy, doomed to die in Boston, she actually had the gall to plead that, since his mother had "frequently assisted her husband in butchering cattle while the unborn boy was beneath her bosom," it was not his fault that he came into the world with a perfectly natural aptitude for slaughter. The Governor of Massachusetts, touched by her eloquence, conceded the point and commuted the youth's sentence to life imprisonment.

We also know something about Mrs. Ballou's paintings, some three hundred of which were purchased for the Stanford Gallery in Melbourne, Australia, by Leland Stanford's younger brother. And we know for a fact that she painted the portrait of the Emperor of the United States, the first of several artists who committed his face to canvas.

"He was a faithful artist's model," she wrote in the *Morning Call* many years later, "and when the portrait was completed he drew up a check for $250 dollars on the Nevada bank, which was more honored in the preservation of as a relic than in the cashing. . . ."

Alone together in the artist's studio on Market Street, while he posed and she painted, the Emperor spoke to Mrs. Ballou about his fruitless quest for an empress. In the *Call* she touched on this very topic, passing on what she had heard from His Majesty's own lips:

> [He] confessed to a personal diffidence with the fair sex, inasmuch as they all seemed very modestly "shy" of him, but acquiesced to the suggestion that they were naturally embarrassed and awed at any personal attentions from royalty . . . and the matter of a conjunction with anything regal must at once appeal to their sense of delicacy.

But surely, she chided gently, it was not the shyness of the fair sex alone that was the stumbling block; if he "failed to pursue his suit" due to his own diffidence, how could he ever hope to convince a woman that he meant business? Faint heart ne'er won fair lady, so to speak, and so on and so forth.

"He thereupon concluded," Mrs. Ballou continued, "that it would be more in keeping with his exalted position to appoint a chamber of deputies, whose duties would require their immediate conference and action in the matter."

Mrs. Ballou was the only woman known to have visited the Emperor in his lodgings (apart from his solicitous landlady, going about her daily duties).

"His room," she wrote, "small and obscure, even to dinginess, was quite too limited to serve as the abode of an empress. His couch lacked much of the regal and consisted of an antique and very much worn frame, ricketty springs and badly soiled and shabby upholstering." No doubt she avoided it, preferring to trust her bustle to the one hard chair rather than sink into a sofa with creaking coils and unappealing fabric. "His limited wardrobe depended from tenpenny nails driven into the walls, and was varied and sacred through tradition and long usage."

A female visitor, especially one with an artist's sharp eye, who discussed with him in private the subject of his search for a consort, would hardly have failed to notice the lithographs on those walls—Queen Victoria's, Queen Emma's, Carlotta's, and Eugenie's. They slipped her mind, though, when she described his room in 1908, by which time her memory must have been failing. The newspapermen who followed her to Eureka Lodgings would supply those missing details.

Addie Ballou's portrait of Norton I still exists (in the Society of California Pioneers' collection of Nortoniana). In it he wears his new hat of white beaver, presented to him by the city, and holds in his hand the famous Serpent Scepter. It is a haunting picture, depicting His Majesty in an abstract mood, staring vacantly into space, as if wondering whether he would ever have the courage to ask a lady for her hand in marriage.

He was fifty-seven before he found the nerve, and the object of his affections was a sixteen-year-old schoolgirl, Ned Wakeman's none too flattered daughter.

Captain Wakeman was dead, the victim of a stroke that had crippled his huge body. Unable to earn a living, he had come so close to poverty that Mark Twain, hearing of his plight, had written to the *Alta California,* urging its readers to contribute to a relief fund for the once fiery mariner "now lying paralyzed and helpless at his home in your city" (actually in Oakland, but what San Franciscan would rush to the rescue of a man who was fool

"Gentlemen, that is my wife. If, when she opens her eyes, she be not swivel-eyed and with all her head-nails rotted out, I shall marry that girl, if I have to kill eleven men before breakfast to get up an appetite."

Sam Clemens was right; Wakeman *did* have a way with words.

Mary Lincoln, the daughter of a San Francisco businessman, was on her way to a finishing school in Boston, traveling without an escort. Taking her aside, he proposed to her on the spot and gave her three days to make up her mind whether she would marry him or not. On the third day, when he asked for her answer, she lowered her eyes and shyly replied: "The last words my mother spoke me were not to engage myself to anyone."

But her answer was: "Yes." And he did not even have to kill eleven men to get it.

Mary Lincoln married the captain on Christmas Eve, 1854 (or, as he put it, "she tied a knot with her tongue that she could not untie with her teeth"). A year or so later, sailing the Pacific with him in the clipper ship *Adelaide,* she gave birth to a daughter, who lived no more than six months, saddled with the names Adelaide Seaborn, and was buried at sea. Mary Wakeman spent five years wandering the globe with her husband, but after the storm-tossed birth of a second daughter, whom they christened Minnie, she quitted the sea the moment she found she was pregnant again. In the little village of Fruitvale on the edge of Oakland, amid meadows and orchards, Ned built her the cottage that Twain thought looked more like a ship—with "all a ship's appointments, binnacle, scuppers, and everything else"—and there she gave birth twice more, producing a daughter named Keith and then a son called Eddie, after his father.

Keith, who was fourteen in 1875, when her father died, would grow up to be an actress and tour the East with Edwin Booth and Lawrence Barrett; Eddie, then twelve, would turn to journalism and become the first biographer of Allan Pinkerton, the founder of Pinkerton's National Detective Agency. But it is Minnie, age sixteen, going on seventeen, whom we are most concerned with here, for she is the one who caught the Emperor's eye and made his aging heart dance such a jig that he finally summoned up the courage to overcome his shyness and speak the words that he had never before dared utter.

Isobel Osbourne, the future stepdaughter of Robert Louis Stevenson, knew Minnie Wakeman; they were neighbors and attended school together. She was "a tall, beautiful creature," Belle wrote sixty years later, "who had lovely dark blue eyes with fringed lashes and long curls that were the admiration of the whole school."

Those eyes and curls so bewitched Oakland High that the class of 1874 had not the slightest trouble choosing a beauty queen. One young beau wrote to Belle: "Will you except [sic] me for your nite at the May Day picnic? Minnie Wakeman will be Queen."

Belle was greatly impressed with the May Queen's intellect. Minnie, she said, was "the leader of the highbrows at school." But she also revealed that even a queen with brains can dream those delicious dreams that tickle and torment every red-blooded girl who has passed the age of puberty.

"She wrote poetry and sometimes condescended to walk with me and tell of her sad, sad lot," recalled Isobel Field, the former Belle Osbourne, in her autobiography, *This Life I've Loved*. "There was a gallant horseman who galloped past her window every night. Looking out, she saw his shadowy form. But she would never meet him or know who this mysterious lover was. Ah, me! It was all very tragic and romantic. After swearing me to secrecy, she usually ended by reading me a poem on the subject."

Ah, me, indeed.

The Emperor may have seen the captain's lovely daughter when he attended the Graduation Day ceremonies at Oakland High School, where she graduated with honors. Some two months after her father died, the Emperor wrote her a note, sealed it in an envelope, addressed it quite simply to "Miss Captain Wakeman, Oakland," and mailed it to the cottage in Fruitvale. It read:

> My dear Miss Wakeman:
>
> In arranging for my Empress, I shall be delighted if you will permit me to make use of your name. Should you be willing, please let me Know but Keep Your Own Secret. It is a safer way I think.
>
> Your Devoted loving friend,
> The Emperor.

There was little doubt that Miss Minnie would keep his proposal a secret; her mother would see to that. Mary Wakeman, still in mourning black for the husband she had lost in January, was in no mood to see the family's name held up to ridicule by insensitive reporters. She knew the newspapers would not allow a widow's grief to stand in the way of a good story. Minnie, then busy editing her father's memoirs for publication, found the time to write a short letter, thanking His Majesty for graciously thinking her worthy of his attentions but advising him that she was already betrothed. This happened to be true; there was a handsome young man named William Bostwick Curtis whom she was engaged to wed.

If the Emperor had been in San Francisco when her letter arrived, the matter might have ended there. But he had gone to Sacramento, and it was almost two weeks before he returned by train to Oakland, quite unaware that he had been rejected. Instead of transferring from the train to the San Francisco ferry, as he normally did, he boarded a streetcar for Fruitvale.

Mrs. Wakeman must have been horrified when Norton I came trudging up her garden path. His timid knock would have been answered by the widow herself rather than her embarrassed daughter. And it may be assumed that her younger children, Keith and Eddie, were watching from behind the window curtains with Minnie, nudging each other and giggling, when the forlorn old man, thwarted on the doorstep by that unyielding sentinel in black bombazine, retreated disconsolately down the lane to catch the omnibus back to Oakland and the ferry.

The Hutchinsons may have retired for the night by the time the Emperor reached his lodgings, because it was not until the following day that they gave him the mail that had accumulated during his absence. Miss Wakeman's letter must have depressed him considerably. His state of mind is revealed in the note that he composed in reply. Instead of his usual literate, well-rounded sentences, he wrote in the terse, tight style more commonly used in a telegram:

> My dear Miss Minnie:
>
> I did not receive your note until this morning, having been absent nearly a fortnight attending the Legislature. Otherwise would not have been so rude as to have called on you yesterday. Regret extremely your previous engagement. Hope is if anything

should occur to break it off, you will think of one who loves you to distraction.

The State expects me to get my Lady and travel to Washington and I must look to the Ladies to answer.

Yours faithfully,
Norton I.

The Emperor's unhappiness was surprisingly brief. The very next day another message was dispatched across the bay to inform the greatly relieved schoolgirl that his heart now belonged to another:

My dear Miss Minnie Wakeman,

The Ladies of S. F. have declared Miss B. Marig Empress Norton I. Hoping to have your consent.

I am, your affectionate friend,
Norton I, Emperor.

Miss Marig, whoever she was, must have been the victim of a joke, played by someone who hoped that His Majesty would publicly announce their engagement. If so, the prank was a failure. Not a word appeared in the press. Perhaps the Emperor had written to request her permission to "make use of your name," as he had done with Miss Captain Wakeman, in which event he would certainly have met with a flat refusal. And so the lady, passing up a chance to go down in history, remains an enigma.

Ned Wakeman's daughter also kept her secret well. In fact, it would never have come to light at all if His Majesty's love letters had not found their way into the Bancroft Library's archives at the University of California at Berkeley when Minnie Wakeman Curtis died in 1933. Norton the First might not have impressed her as a suitor, but apparently she treasured his letters.

Chapter 25

Emperor of the World

His dementia was of a mild and harmless type, his ruling idea being that he was Emperor of the world.

—*The New York Times,*
January 10, 1880

    The poets and painters of the Bohemian Club should have understood the Emperor better than anyone else; he was a dreamer and so were they. In their library, as proud testimony of their regard for him, hung a portrait of His Imperial Majesty by California's leading artist, Virgil Williams.

    The character of the Bohemian Club has changed beyond all recognition since its founding in 1872 by a group of artists and writers who met in rented rooms above a market on Pine Street. Today the club occupies a stately building at Post and Taylor and is the preserve of men of power and wealth, patrons of the arts rather than artists. Actually, even in the earliest days of its long history, probably none of its members would have fitted the description of a Bohemian as *Webster's Dictionary* then defined the term: "A person, especially an artist or literary man, who leads a free, vagabond, often dissipated life, having little regard for what society he frequents and despising conventionalities generally." One of their guests, Oscar Wilde, would tell the San Francisco *Examiner* in 1882: "I have never seen so many well-dressed, well-fed Bohemians in the course of my whole life." So far as anyone could tell, from reading the Bohemian Club's annals, there was not a single dissipated vagabond in the lot (though several were newspapermen, a species that comes dangerously close).

It has been said that the Emperor was a member, but that seems rather doubtful since he lacked the qualifications necessary for membership, being neither an artist nor a writer (or, rather, he was not recognized as a writer despite the hundreds of proclamations that he composed for publication in the press). There is, however, a strong possibility that he was permitted to use the club's library.

We already know that the Emperor frequented the Mechanics' Library on Post Street and the Mercantile Library on Bush—he had "free access to all the libraries and reading-rooms," Benjamin Lloyd said in his book—and it simply would not have occurred to His Majesty that he might not be welcome to use the Bohemian Club's, too; after all, he was the Emperor, and emperors may go wherever they please. Besides, one member of the club, Timothy Reardon, an attorney who had been a journalist on the staff of the *Overland Monthly* when Bret Harte was its editor, was in charge of the Mercantile Library. If Tim Reardon was willing to admit the Emperor to his own reading rooms, he surely would not have objected to his browsing in the one that displayed his portrait.

And if anyone else had protested His Majesty's presence, a word from the artist who had painted the portrait should have been enough to soothe the complainant and smooth the Emperor's ruffled feathers. Virgil Williams, a founder and former president of the Bohemian Club, wielded considerable influence in all of its affairs.

There was something rather curious about that portrait, by the way. Williams had refused to emphasize his sitter's eccentricity by painting him in his feathers and uniform, as other artists did, but posed him in a slouch hat and a civilian suit. This was remarkable, for without his plumes and epaulets there was nothing to distinguish His Majesty from the common herd. Here, in fact, was a perfectly ordinary man in his fifties, thoughtfully smoking a pipe and looking very much like the merchant that Joseph Eastland and Hall McAllister had known in Gold Rush days. The odd thing is that Emperor Norton was never known to smoke a pipe or to wear anything but a Kossuth, a kepi, or a white beaver hat. It may be that the artist painted him that way to tell the world that Joshua Norton was not the clown that everyone supposed.

Had he wished to use the club's library, it's fairly certain that Virgil Williams would have arranged it, just as he arranged it for another nonmember, Robert Louis Stevenson, who was not nearly so well-known as Emperor Norton when he arrived in San Francisco to marry Fanny Osbourne, whom he had met in France.

The Emperor was still in search of a gilded cage for the bird he hoped to keep. He had dismissed the notion that the Grand Hotel on Market Street might provide suitable accommodation for an empress, the management having answered his decree with complete and utter silence. For that, he had punished the owners, William C. Ralston, the president of the Bank of California, and the Comstock millionaire, Senator William Sharon:

> Whereas, the Grand Hotel, hitherto our headquarters, is in rebellion; now, therefore, we, Norton I, do hereby command the Water Companies to close down on them, and the Gas Company to give them no light, so as to bring them to terms.

The last part of that decree was intended for the eyes of an old friend. Joseph G. Eastland was now a powerful man, able to plunge both sides of the bay into darkness at night, for he was not only the secretary of the San Francisco Gas Lighting Company but also president of the company that illuminated Oakland's buildings and streets. In time, when gas pipes were laid in other cities and the two utility companies acquired the rights to use Thomas Edison's incandescent electric bulb, invented in 1879, the two companies would merge to become the gigantic Pacific Gas & Electric Company that today supplies every therm and watt of heat and light used on the Pacific coast.

But the Emperor's eyes were now on much more splendid lodgings. Next door to the Grand, Ralston and Sharon were building a palace that soon would dwarf every hotel in America; even New York's magnificent new Grand Union had only 450 rooms. San Francisco's glittering white-and-gold Palace Hotel, built at a cost of nearly five million dollars, would have eight hundred. *Harper's Weekly* told its readers: "An exchange informs us that the head waiter of the new Palace Hotel, San Francisco, will wear a purple velvet suit, powdered wig, silk hose and pumps. He will receive guests at the dining-room door to the sound of opera music and gently assign them seats by a slight inclination of the head and a graceful wave of his hand. On Sundays he will walk on rosewood stilts. . . ."

At the opening banquet, said Fred Marriott's *News-Letter*, "all the entrees [will be] sprinkled with gold dust" and the hotel's manager and head chef would enter "on solid bonanza silver velocipedes."

His Majesty, suitably impressed, issued a proclamation:

> Whereas, it is our intention to take an Empress, and in consideration of the visits by the Royalty abroad, we, Norton I, Dei Gratia Emperor of the United States and Protector of Mexico, do hereby command the builders of the Palace Hotel to fit up a portion of their building for our Imperial Residence, as becoming the dignity of a great and hopeful nation.

And then the Emperor made a grave mistake. Another proclamation managed to slip past the editor of the *Appeal* and onto the front page undetected. Anderson was horrified when he read it next morning:

> WHEREAS, a person styling himself Charles R. Peters was at the time of the drawing at the Mercantile Library lottery accused of appropriating the capital prize, which was won by Norton I, and intended by the Emperor for charitable distribution;
> AND WHEREAS, the said Peters is now attempting by misrepresentation and false assertions to induce emigrants to purchase worthless land at a "town" which he calls Newark (but which has neither local habitation nor name outside of the imagination of said Peters);
> NOW, THEREFORE, this is to caution all persons against being misled or deceived by the said Peters, and the Grand Jury is hereby instructed to inquire into said matters, and to bring said Peters to trial.

There was no signature attached, and really no proof at all that His Majesty had written it, but Anderson believed him to be the author. When the land developer sued for libel and demanded a retraction, the editor placed the blame squarely on both the Emperor and the printer:

> An article appeared in the *Appeal* some two or three weeks ago, written by "Emperor Norton," or "Norton I," reflecting on the excursion made to Newark under the proprietorship of Mr. Charles R. Peters, the eminent and enterprising Real Estate Broker, the article being put in the paper by a compositor in the establishment where we get our paper printed. The said journeyman printer also took the "Emperor's" *nom de plume* from the bottom of the article, thus leaving the article without signature. As we have been imposed upon by the journeyman compositor, as also an offense has been given to Mr. Peters against our wishes or will, we take this occasion to retract the said article by Emperor Norton, and forbid him hereafter bringing anything to our office for publication. . . .

That was the end of His Majesty's happy association with Peter Anderson. Not that it mattered much; half a dozen papers, undeterred by the prospects of a libel suit, immediately began to compete for the honor of being the royal gazette.

The Emperor, incidentally, was entirely wrong about Newark. Far from having "neither local habitation nor name outside the imagination of said Peters," Newark stands today on the east side of the bay, south of Oakland, a thriving salt-processing center with a population of about ten thousand.

"I am quartered at the Palace Hotel, one of the greatest hostelries in the United States," a correspondent wrote to the *Hoboken Democrat* in Hoboken, New Jersey. "The way I happen to be here is because Senator Sharon and my father used to be licked by the same schoolmaster in their native New England village and consequently were bosom friends. The Senator had known me from boyhood, in fact considered me a genius, and when I met him on Sansome Street, shortly after my arrival here, he shook me by the hand, took me to his hotel, and instructed the clerk to give me the best room in the house, No. 24,999."

The year was 1876, the gates of the Palace were open, and the nation's humorists at the top of their form:

Captain Stormfield's Daughter   183

enough to live over there?). At Twain's home in Connecticut, hidden from the censorious eyes of his God-fearing wife, Livy, was the first draft of *Captain Stormfield's Visit to Heaven,* an impious satire on nineteenth-century notions of eternal bliss, based upon a dream the sailor had once told him about. Both men would be dead long before Twain's autobiography disclosed that Captain Stormfield was really Ned Wakeman. But the stricken giant was hardly the sort who would be content to appear in print under a fictitious name. When, in time, he recovered sufficient use of his left hand, he set himself the laborious task of scratching out his memoirs.

It was an immodestly heroic opus, full of blood and thunder, although Wakeman showed remarkable restraint in dealing with the gruesome events of 1851, dismissing his own part in that sorry episode in less than one brief paragraph:

> I will not attempt to describe the exciting times that prevailed in San Francisco in particular, and in California, in general, at this period. Suffice it is to say that I took a lively part in all that I thought would conduce to the welfare of the State. Of course, I joined the Vigilance Committee and acted as sheriff at the hanging of Jenkins and Stewart.

That last sentence, the only one that mentions hanging, contains just eighteen words. Wakeman used more than that to express his remorse at needlessly shooting a monkey for sport in Nicaragua, as though the monkey at least had deserved a trial, and a better one than English Jim Stuart got (at the insistence of a madman who believed in justice).

Every line in Wakeman's *Log of an Ancient Mariner* reads like a dime novel, even his account of meeting the girl who became his wife. This meeting occurred when he was in command of the paddle wheeler *New Orleans* during a passage to Panama. One morning, while making a tour of inspection, he saw a pretty passenger lying asleep in a deck chair.

"Who is that?" he asked the purser.

"That," he was informed, "is a passenger whom you have not seen before, as she has been confined to her berth with seasickness."

Captain Wakeman "took a good look at the pretty thing, with her hair stuck up, and then, being impelled by a sort of mysterious presentiment," he said:

In the large dining hall, two acres square, 2,000 waiters dash about recklessly on skates. They are of all nationalities, and are required to be accomplished skaters. There is a circular railway on every floor to enable ladies and people in delicate health to visit each other while stopping at the hotel. A band of 250 pieces performs on the roof every evening, and at sunset a park of 100 cannon is fired off. The effect is grand. It is astonishing that in such a vast caravansary so few people get hurt. Only about a dozen a day are killed.

But the eyes of the world were on Philadelphia and its great Centennial Exposition. That city was crammed to bursting, every hotel booked to capacity, its coffers filled with tourist dollars. In San Francisco the boosters worked hard, turning out thousands of words in the hope of capturing some of the overflow of visitors from overseas who poured into the City of Brotherly Love to celebrate the nation's one hundredth birthday. They talked about the Palace Hotel, the splendid new park, the zoo, the seals, and the Cliff House, and of course Norton the First. Philadelphia's stories were hard to beat, but they tried. God, how they tried! One of the tales they told has never been forgotten and deserves to be remembered here because it is now firmly embedded in folklore and no book about Norton the First would be complete without it.

It is said that when Dom Pedro II, the Emperor of Brazil, had seen all that there was to be seen in Philadelphia, he decided that he must visit the wondrous City by the Golden Gate before he went home. And that, when he arrived, he asked to meet the Emperor of the United States, about whom he had heard so much. The two emperors met, the newspapers reported, in the royal suite at the Palace and talked for more than an hour.

The legend was now in full flower.

Chapter 26

The Palace of Truth

Of all our visitors, I believe I preferred Emperor Norton.

—Robert Louis Stevenson

On December 26, 1879, Robert Louis Stevenson wrote to a friend in London: "For four days I have spoken to no one but my landlady or landlord, or to restaurant waiters. This is not a gay way to spend Christmas, is it?"

Stevenson was in a sorry plight. Almost penniless, living in cheap lodgings, he had rationed himself to one meal a day in a cafe that charged no more than twenty-five or fifty cents. He spent his mornings in bed, working on a manuscript, or on a bench in Portsmouth Square, watching the passing parade (and dreaming up the stories, it is said, that would one day make him famous). Meanwhile, he needed a job. He had already offered himself as a reporter to most of the papers, but the best he could hope for was an occasional fee from George Fitch, who had suggested that he might submit a few pieces about San Francisco, as seen through a visitor's eyes, for possible publication in the *Bulletin*. Perhaps he should write about Norton the First. He had seen this fairy-tale monarch in the plaza, holding court every morning, as solemn as any European sovereign and quite unaware of the comical spectacle he presented.

One day, when all the world knew the name Robert Louis Stevenson, he *would* write about the Emperor, not in a newspaper

The Palace of Truth 195

article but in a book, with Fanny Osbourne's son as his collaborator.

"Merry Christmas, Emperor," everyone said. And then, a few days later, "A Happy New Year to Your Majesty."

But it wasn't a happy New Year. January 1 was the day of reckoning. For ten years the Emperor had been selling his bonds, payable at seven percent interest in 1880, and now he had to redeem them.

The street urchins had begun to tease him: "Hey, Emp, it's time to pay up. Let's see the color of yer money. You ain't goin' to bilk us, are yer?"

He tried to ignore their mocking cries, but couldn't. What if everybody who had bought his scrip demanded payment? He had sold hundreds of Imperial Treasury certificates in the past decade, perhaps even thousands, and all of them had now matured. The interest alone would be ruinous.

There was only one thing to do: try to pay off the old bonds with new ones. He went to see Charles Murdock and had some more certificates printed, payable at only four percent interest in 1890.

It was a wretched January night. William Proll, showcase manufacturer, locked the door of his shop on California Street, bending his head against the driving rain as he began the arduous climb up the slanting sidewalk to the Academy of Natural Sciences at California and Dupont, two blocks up the hill. There was to be a debate of the Hastings Society that evening, scheduled to begin at eight o'clock sharp, and he did not want to miss it. Ahead of him, toiling slowly up the slope, he saw a familiar figure, a plumed head shielded from the storm by a Chinese umbrella of red-and-green varnished paper, the Emperor's usual protection against inclement weather; he owned no overcoat. The showcase maker guessed, correctly, that he was on his way to the Academy. His Majesty always attended the Hastings Society's lively monthly discussions; Proll, a member of the Academy, saw him seated in the audience whenever a debate was held.

The Emperor never reached the hall, but paused a few steps from its door, seeming to stagger for a moment, the parasol falling from his hand to roll into the gutter as he faltered and then suddenly slumped in a heap on the sidewalk. Proll stooped to grab the umbrella as it wheeled toward him in a gust of wind, pressing the catch on its bamboo haft to close it while he hurried to the Emperor's side.

He was unconscious, his eyes closed, breathing painfully through lips already coated with froth. Proll propped him up on the sidewalk, rested his head against a wall, where he looked like an old rag doll.

A cable car stopped at the corner to disgorge its passengers, and a crowd began to gather, unmindful of the downpour.

"Fetch a hack," said Proll. "He needs to go to the hospital."

But it was too late for that. The clock of Old St. Mary's, across the street, marked the moment of his passing. It was a quarter after eight. The bonds in his pocket would never be redeemed in 1890. Death had released him from his debts on the eighth day of 1880.

The stagedoor-keeper of the Baldwin Theatre, just two blocks from the city morgue, heard the news from a rain-soaked pedestrian within minutes of the dead-wagon's arrival. He passed it on to a stagehand, who told the stage manager, who relayed it to the leading lady, who took an unseemly number of curtain calls before she announced it to the audience. Somewhere along the line, between the street and the footlights, the news must have reached the ears of the assistant stage manager, David Belasco, who might have heard it from the prompt box under the proscenium (since his chief function at the Baldwin was to whisper lines from the script whenever an actor forgot them).

The playgoers filed out quietly, the night's frothy comedy forgotten. The play was *The Palace of Truth*; tomorrow the press would reveal the truth about Norton's palace. Eureka Lodgings was already filled with reporters, who came straight from the morgue to Commercial Street to see for themselves how he had lived. They described his room in detail, from the frayed uniforms and hats hanging on the walls to the lithographs of his "royal equals, including Queen Emma of the Sandwich Islands and the Empress Eugenie."

> Suspended from a nail was his sabre with his silk sash and rich tassel pendants . . . in one corner was a group of walking-sticks,

the handles carved in fantastic shapes, and adorned with silver plates on which were engraved his name and titles.

"In a drawer of the small table at the head of the bed," the man from the *Call* noted, "were a number of letters, telegrams and newspaper clippings, some bearing date in Oakland, others in Sacramento, Petaluma and surrounding towns."

The Hutchinsons and their lodgers were interviewed: "A general feeling of sadness was noticeable among the habitues of the Eureka House when they heard of the Emperor's death. His old friend, Mr. Martin, was particularly down-hearted."

William Martin was, in fact, stunned. "It only goes to show," he said, "that there is nothing certain in this world. I walked along Montgomery Street with the Emperor at five o'clock this afternoon and he seemed perfectly well and in good spirits."

Only Eva Hutchinson had noticed something that suggested the Emperor's health might have been failing: "He usually retired at ten or eleven o'clock, unless he attended the theatres, and always got up before eight, but in the past two or three months he did not rise before nine or nine-thirty."

They would know more after the autopsy the next day.

Dr. William A. Douglass, Professor of Clinical Surgery at the Medical College of the Pacific, performed the postmortem in the presence of several students he had brought from the college to watch. The city's derelicts, more useful in death than in life, were the professor's guinea pigs, and the Emperor of the United States was a specimen he had long coveted.

The brain was removed and placed in the pan of a medical scale; it weighed fifty-one ounces, an ounce and a half more than average but not enough to occasion surprise in view of the amount of blood found in its cells as a result of the stroke the Emperor had suffered.

Dr. Douglass sutured the wounds, leaving the mortician to bandage the head while he washed his hands and put on his Prince Albert frock coat and his tall silk hat before making his way to the front office, where reporters were waiting to hear his verdict.

"The cause of death was sanguineous apoplexy," Douglass announced.

But they wanted to know more than that.

"Did you examine the brain, sir?"
"I did."
"Find anything unusual?"
"Nothing abnormal."
"No sign of lunacy, then?"
"No pathological evidence of insanity was discovered."

Some people, reading that in the papers, would infer that it meant the Emperor was perfectly sane, as they had always suspected.

The news flashed across the continent that Friday would be in *The New York Times* the next day:

> For 25 or 30 years this eccentric man has wandered the streets of San Francisco, given a "square meal" whenever he asked it, endowed with a certain income from easy-going citizens and tolerated because he was a public character it pleased the popular whim to encourage. Among the old Californians there were not a few who humored the old vagrant's fancy and gave him a quarter of a dollar when his pressing needs compelled him to remind his subjects that the "Imperial Treasury" was in need of funds.

Mark Twain relived his memories in a letter to a good friend, William Dean Howells, the editor of *The Atlantic Monthly*. "O, dear," he told Howells, "it was always a painful thing for me to see the Emperor begging. . . ."

Twain used that last word loosely. The Emperor was hardly a beggar, certainly not in the ordinary sense. He had never solicited coins on street corners, humbly, cap in hand, but levied his "tax" like imperial Caesar exacting tribute. If he was a beggar, he was surely the only one ever accorded the distinction of an obituary in *The New York Times*.

Here is the Emperor in Robert Louis Stevenson's novel *The Wrecker*, collecting his revenue from a delinquent merchant:

> His Majesty entered the office—a portly, rather flabby man, with the face of a gentleman, rendered unspeakably pathetic and absurd by the great sabre at his side and the peacock's feather in his hat.
>
> "I have called to remind you, Mr. Pinkerton, that you are somewhat in arrears of taxes," he said, with old-fashioned, stately courtesy.

"Well, Your Majesty, what is the amount?" asked Jim, and when the figure was named (it was generally two or three dollars), paid upon the nail and offered a bonus in the shape of Thirteen Star [brandy].

The Emperor had taxed only those who could well afford it, the bankers and the merchants who had profited most from his mad career (and who, for that reason, probably *should* have paid his tax); fifty cents a month was a mere pittance to businessmen who reaped the benefits of tourism.

In point of fact, for the past ten years of his life, the Emperor had supported himself by selling his bonds. Stevenson, who arrived by train from New York, might have seen him hawking his scrip at the depot in Oakland, as he had been doing for a decade, yet he said nothing about that in *The Wrecker,* preferring to stay with the legend told by Bowman and Biggelow—and wondrously burnished by Bierce—about a city so friendly and sentimental that it kept a poor lunatic in "luxury and idleness without physical or mental toil," which scarcely did justice to the madman who had lived by his own ingenuity and helped fill that city's coffers with gold.

San Francisco had lived off Emperor Norton, not Norton off San Francisco.

That thought may have occurred to the president of the Pacific Club, Joseph Eastland, as he sat reminiscing about the good old days with the treasurer, Rolla Brewster, who said it was a pity that a man once worth a quarter of a million should now be worth only a pauper's coffin and a pauper's grave.

"Perhaps we should do something," said Eastland.

The time had come to pay a debt long overdue.

And so a final flourish was added to the legend.

"The man of imaginary majesty, prospective consort of the Queen of Great Britain and Empress of India, narrowly escaped burial in a plain redwood box," Jimmy Bowman reported next day in the *Chronicle.* The Emperor would be interred in a casket of rosewood ornamented with silver.

"Mr. Eastland took upon himself the task of securing for his old friend a funeral in some degree suited to his former circumstances," wrote Bowman. "He and Mr. Brewster at once drew up a subscription paper to procure a fund, headed it handsomely themselves, and taking it down to the Pacific Club, soon had all the money they deemed necessary.''

Joseph Eastland, a charter member of Occidental Lodge No. 22, Free and Accepted Masons, owned a burial plot in the Masonic Cemetery; the Emperor, a former lodge brother, would be buried there.

The news that millionaires had rescued a beggar from common clay came as no surprise to a city accustomed to fairy tales.

The undertakers prepared His Majesty for a grave far from Potter's Field. They trimmed his unkempt beard, clipped the thicket of gray curls that grew wild about his ears, scrubbed away the dust of two decades, and dressed him in the cerements of Victorian respectability—a black robe, a starched white shirt, and a black bow tie. His uniform lay in a locker under coroner's seal with his battered boots, his foolish hat, and his sword, relics of a golden age to be preserved in a museum forever (or at least until a great fire and earthquake destroyed the city and all of its wonders).

The Cincinnati *Enquirer* predicted what would become of the Emperor's Serpent Scepter, found in his room by the reporters who went there: ''There will be a lively struggle between the Society of California Pioneers and the Bohemian Club for this relic. The former will claim it as connected with the antiquity of California; the latter because Emperor Norton was a Bohemian of the Bohemians.''

There was really no struggle; the Bohemian Club was quite content to have the painting by Virgil Williams in its library and another by Benoni Irwin in its chess room. The Pioneers got the scepter, the sword, the hat, and the regimentals, which were put on display in a glass case beside another cherished keepsake that the Society had recently acquired—the moth-eaten carcass of Lazarus. And so you might say that, in a way, the Emperor of the United States was united at last with an old enemy. All that remained, that is, of both.

Jimmy Bowman had seen many strange things in his time but nothing quite like the scene at the morgue on O'Farrell Street that Saturday, the day of the funeral, not since James King of William was shot and half the town turned out to watch his assassin die.

''The number who called to view the remains during the day,''

Bowman wrote, "was estimated at fully 10,000." This in spite of a cloudburst that drenched the city all day. "The removal of the body was delayed for half an hour after the appointed time, and finally the door was closed on a constantly increasing throng, which not only filled the doorway but covered nearly every foot of the sidewalk and filled the windows and doorsteps of houses on both sides of the street."

And then it was time to send him to glory.

"The funeral cortege that followed his body to the grave was two miles long," the *Daily Intelligencer* told Seattle, Washington.

Some traveled in carriages, some walked in the rain.

Nobody realized, until the coffin was covered with earth, that they had forgotten to order a tombstone to show where the Emperor lay. That omission was quickly remedied by the minister who read the burial service over his remains. The Reverend Githens passed a collection plate among his flock at Sunday services next day and raised enough money for a simple marker, a Christian cross to remember a Jew who had strayed far from his faith.

That Sunday, it so happened, was reserved by the heavens for a special gesture of farewell. For, believe it or not, at 2:39 P.M., even while Joseph Eastland, a vestryman at the Church of the Advent, was handing the silver salver around and the dollars and dimes clinked and tinked as it passed from pew to pew, the world grew dark and the sun passed into total eclipse.

Chapter 27

The Controversy

No more through the crowded streets he goes,
With his shambling gait and shabby clothes,
And his furtive glance and whiskered nose—
  Immersed in cares of state.
The serpent twisted upon his staff
Is not less careless of idle chaff,
The mocking speech or the scornful laugh,
  Than he who bore it late.

  —From a poem by Dr. George Chismore, recited at the Bohemian Club's annual Low Jinks, January 31, 1880

Salmi Morse, the editor of the *Wasp*, an illustrated weekly magazine that published a portrait of the Emperor on its front cover the Saturday following his burial, was the only man in America who pointed out in print that Joshua Abraham Norton, born a Jew and still a Jew (never having converted for all of his praying in churches on Sundays) was "buried in a cemetery not dedicated for the burial of Jews," contrary to Jewish rites.

Morse castigated the Jewish community of San Francisco for permitting it to happen: "We have traveled far and wide, and never yet met with an incident to compare with the present. We have seen members of various religious denominations die strangers in foreign lands, with none to mourn except those of their own belief, and have never yet heard of the instance when co-believers did not step to the front and claim the remains as their own!"

Salmi Morse was a renegade, a Jew turned atheist. Six days after his editorial appeared, Abe Seeligsohn, who edited *The Jewish Progress,* took him to task for it. Morse, he wrote, "belches forth a torrent of abuse which holds in its vulgar embrace all the Israelites of this city and crushes them with a volume of nauseous poetry" (a reference to the doggerel that Morse was prone to inflict upon his readers).

In 1934, when San Francisco demolished its burial grounds to make room for the living, the Masonic Cemetery was ploughed under but the Emperor's bones were saved. His casket was taken to Colma, a necropolis in San Mateo County but close to town, where he was reinterred with civic and military honors in Woodlawn Memorial Park. The San Francisco Municipal Bond played suitable dirges, the Third Battalion of the 159th Infantry fired three volleys in salute, and a bugler sounded taps. Then he was laid to rest again, this time under a monument properly inscribed:

NORTON I
EMPEROR OF THE UNITED STATES
AND PROTECTOR OF MEXICO

JOSHUA A. NORTON
1819–1880

No quotation marks surround those titles to throw doubt upon their authenticity. The Emperor Norton Memorial Association that commissioned the epitaph respected his idiosyncrasy even though he was no longer there to demand it.

In 1974, another Jew broached the matter of the Emperor's burial by Christians, which had managed to avoid a public airing in all of the many newspaper articles written about Norton the First during the ninety-four years since Seeligsohn's quarrel with Morse. Professor William M. Kramer of California State University wrote a monograph on the subject, *Emperor Norton of San Francisco,* the only book ever published that did not treat the Emperor as a clown. He wrote:

When the old Masonic Cemetery where the royal remains had been interred was abandoned, the body of Emperor Norton was removed after fifty-four years and found intact, parchment tag and all, and placed in a temporary holding vault in San Mateo County. Once more, no Jew stepped forward to claim the traditional divine imperative (a "mitzvah") of burying a Jew in the way of his people.

Professor Kramer continued: "One can only speculate that the Jews of San Francisco were embarrassed by the eccentric Norton. They knew themselves to be a community which merited being taken seriously. Perhaps they could not see themselves as being associated with the monarch of madness." But he suggested another possibility, that "far from ignoring Emperor Norton, the Jews of San Francisco may have withheld their services in order to honor his wishes." And to support that theory Kramer quoted Rabbi Isaac Mayer Wise's newspaper in Cincinnati, *The American Israelite,* which had said of His Majesty in 1869:

He entirely ignores his Hebrew origins, arguing with due regard to logic, "How can I be a Jew, seeing I am so nearly related to the Bourbons, who it is very well known were not Jews?"

Even so, Professor Kramer lamented the fact that no royal Star of David adorned the monument over the Emperor's body in Colma, concluding his book with a bow to both hypotheses: "Either [San Francisco's Jewry] didn't do their Jewish duty or they respected his fantasy to the end."

The professor, a rabbi, did what was necessary. With his head covered and a fringed tallith over his shoulders, he stood before that Christian grave and solemnly intoned the Kaddish, knowing that the God of Abraham and of Joshua would hear it and take a lost sheep back into the fold:

Yisgaddal,
Veyiskaddash,
Shemay rabbah. . . .

Epilogue

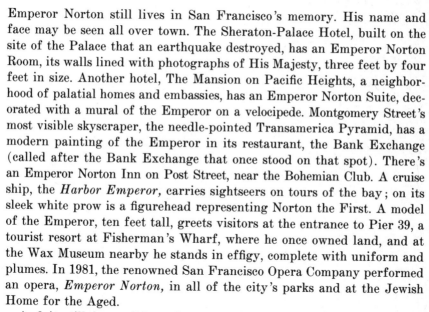

Emperor Norton still lives in San Francisco's memory. His name and face may be seen all over town. The Sheraton-Palace Hotel, built on the site of the Palace that an earthquake destroyed, has an Emperor Norton Room, its walls lined with photographs of His Majesty, three feet by four feet in size. Another hotel, The Mansion on Pacific Heights, a neighborhood of palatial homes and embassies, has an Emperor Norton Suite, decorated with a mural of the Emperor on a velocipede. Montgomery Street's most visible skyscraper, the needle-pointed Transamerica Pyramid, has a modern painting of the Emperor in its restaurant, the Bank Exchange (called after the Bank Exchange that once stood on that spot). There's an Emperor Norton Inn on Post Street, near the Bohemian Club. A cruise ship, the *Harbor Emperor,* carries sightseers on tours of the bay; on its sleek white prow is a figurehead representing Norton the First. A model of the Emperor, ten feet tall, greets visitors at the entrance to Pier 39, a tourist resort at Fisherman's Wharf, where he once owned land, and at the Wax Museum nearby he stands in effigy, complete with uniform and plumes. In 1981, the renowned San Francisco Opera Company performed an opera, *Emperor Norton,* in all of the city's parks and at the Jewish Home for the Aged.

And it still is possible to buy Emperor Norton Brand Cigars, even Emperor Norton Coffee, in the city that treasures a legend born of a moonstruck dream.

Appendix A

The Clampers

―――――◆―――――

> *The Order ... laid claim to the greatest names in history: Daniel Webster, Ned Buntline, Henry Ward Beecher ... Norton I, Emperor of the United States. ...*
>
> —George Ezra Dane,
> *Ghost Town*

There exists in California and Nevada a remarkable society of history buffs called The Ancient and Honorable Order of E Clampus Vitus. It is a fairly large organization; each of its thirty-six chapters has at least a thousand members (none of whom, though, can tell you with any degree of confidence what E Clampus Vitus means, since those who coined the name never troubled to explain it, and they've been dust in their graves for more than a century).

The Order was born in a gold camp on a wintry night in 1851 when some miners, imprisoned in their mountain diggings by snow, decided to form a fraternity dedicated to drinking and devilment but pledged to help widows and orphans. When spring came and the snow melted, opening the trails to the valleys, word of this bibulous brotherhood spread, carried by mule from camp to camp and by stagecoach from town to town, later crossing the Sierras to Washoe with the silver miners, until by the end of the decade there was hardly a community on either side of the mountains that did not have a chapter of E Clampus Vitus.

A long tin trumpet, called the Hewgag, was used to rally the lodge brothers whenever they were needed, whether it was to put out a fire, capture a thief, pass the hat for a widow, or merely to indulge in horseplay. Most often the trumpet's bray meant that a stranger, newly arrived, had expressed a wish to join the Ancient and Honorable Order. The candidate was usually a drummer—a traveling salesman—who had found it impossible to sell his wares in any Clamper stronghold unless he could prove membership in one lodge or another. The wise drummer quickly enlisted when he found that virtually every storekeeper on his route was a Clamper and would do business only with Clampers.

One fledgling drummer, William Turner Ellis, left a vivid account of his own induction. In a buckboard loaded with goods, he had left Marysville and followed the north fork of the Yuba River as far as Downieville in the folds of the Sierra Nevada, which ought to have welcomed any peddler bringing supplies at that time of the year, since it was snowbound and difficult to reach. But a Clamper town, young Ellis discovered, would rather do without food than fun. He was given the usual ultimatum—join or go without orders—and a triumphant blast on the Hewgag told Downieville his decision.

In a large hall filled with Clampers, he was led before the Noble Grand Humbug, who asked "some very embarrassing questions" and then, apparently satisfied with his answers, inquired of the assembly: "What is the will of the lodge?" And a hundred voices roared back: "Initiate the sonofabitch." So it was done. First he was blindfolded and then:

> . . . for about two hours I was put through various hazings, from being dropped from a coffin suspended in the air . . . into a tank of cold water, to crawling through what was called a "noiseless cavern," which consisted of a long pipe, just wide enough to crawl through, and when I got to about the middle of the pipe, several husky fellows commenced to roll it back and forth the hall's length, all the time belaboring [it] with clubs, which made it anything but "noiseless." The finishing touch was trying to ride the back of a large stuffed bear in my birthday suit, the bear being so adjusted that it would buck me off quite frequently.

Still naked but bathed in sweat, he was then led outside and thrown into a bank of snow to cool him off, after which he was rubbed down with a towel, the blindfold was removed, and he was allowed to put on his clothes. Every lodge brother, he wrote, then "welcomed me and shook my hand, each apparently trying to outdo the other in the violence of the handshake, which left my hand sore for a week."

Ellis later became the Mayor of Marysville and lived to a venerable age, a Clamper to the end.

E Clampus Vitus still torments initiates and flourishes in spite of that, although the public knows it best as a fraternity that strives to preserve the memory of olden, golden days by parading in red shirts, like those worn by the miners of 1849, and erecting bronze plaques on places deemed to have some historical significance.

It is a democratic institution, no member ranking higher than another no matter what his standing in the community at large. Some are journalists, some lawyers, some policemen, some plumbers, some doctors, some dentists, some bankers, and some bakers of bread. All are of equal indignity in the eyes of Clamperdom. And any Clamper will tell you, with his hand upon his heart, that the Emperor of the United States was a Clamper, too. That claim, on the face of it, seems highly improbable; the Emperor's profound sense of dignity would scarcely have permitted him to submit to the clownish antics that a drummer had to suffer for the sake of a sale. But the Order's motto is *Credo quia Absurdum* ("I believe because it is absurd"), and that alone would be enough to settle the matter to any Clamper's satisfaction; the very thought of His Majesty having ridden a bear in his birthday suit would seem much too ludicrous to be untrue.

There is a possibility that the Emperor became a Clamper, though entirely without his knowledge.

E Clampus Vitus occasionally does induct a "Poor Blind Candidate" without bandaging his eyes and making him suffer, provided he is a man of some importance whose membership would be valued, a senator, say, who is willing to join but declines to play the fool. The usual procedure in such a case would be to have him kneel on a cushion and then dub him a Clamper by touching his shoulder with the Sword of Mercy, a wooden sword seven feet long, usually sheathed in velvet and decorated with the mystical symbols of the brotherhood.

But when might the Emperor have been inducted, and by which chapter? That's not hard to guess. Remember those men from Marysville who escorted him from Sacramento in a stagecoach to attend the opening of the railroad to Oroville? They, like the guard of honor that marched beside his carriage in the grand parade next day, were almost certainly Clampers. So, it could have been on the night of February 14, 1864, at the Western House where he spent the night as a guest, that his epauletted shoulder felt the touch of the Sword of Mercy.

But how to perform even that harmless ceremony without His Majesty knowing that he was joining an order famous for its practical jokes? Simple. Those who had him kneel before a solemn-faced Noble Grand Humbug could have told him that they were the town's leading citizens (as well they might have been, like William Turner Ellis, who remained a Clamper when he was Mayor of Marysville), come to confer upon him the Freedom of the City. The Emperor would have understood that. There was no reason why he should *not* have believed them. Unlike today's Clampers, they wore no scarlet shirts and lodge pins to betray their membership in the Order, just everyday clothes, which if they were men of position in the community would have been top hats and frock coats. The only sign that they were pranksters would have been their colored sashes, embroidered with the name of their lodge, which they would have removed anyway. How was the Emperor to know that Marysville did not grant civic honors with a wooden sword seven feet long? He believed something much stranger than that; he believed he was the nation's ruler.

So the Emperor could have become a Clamper and never known that he was one, because nobody ever told him, just the sort of tomfool thing any Clamper would do. In any case, the Ancient and Honorable Order insists he was a Clamper, and that's the end of the discussion so far as E Clampus Vitus is concerned. Being a Clamper myself and bound by the Order's rules, I have no choice but to accept it. I merely explain here how it could have happened to satisfy those skeptics who are not Clampers and do not subscribe to the age-old creed, "I believe because it is absurd."

Depend on it, the Emperor was a Clamper, whether he knew it or not.

That is why, every year on or about January 8, the anniversary of his death, the call of the Hewgag summons the red-shirted brethren from far and near to pay homage at his grave. It is also why they erected a plaque to his memory, though they hung it in quite the wrong place. And with it hangs a story that should make every loyal San Franciscan weep for very shame.

Mounted on a pedestal close to the toll plaza of the Golden Gate Bridge is a bronze statue of Joseph B. Strauss, the man who built the bridge, and cemented to a concrete wall beside "the eternal rainbow that he conceived" is a plaque. The plaque was placed there by the Native Sons of the Golden West when the bridge was opened in 1937 "as tribute to the engineering genius which gave the State of California the Golden Gate Bridge, the longest bridge span in the world."

The bridge spans the bay at its narrowest point and is less than a mile from shore to shore. East of it, where the bay is wider by far, stands another bridge, more than three miles long, completed and opened eight months before "the longest bridge span in the world." No plaque adorns that bridge to commemorate the fact that the genius who ordered it built was the Emperor of the United States, so one should not expect to find a statue of His Majesty there.

The San Francisco–Oakland Bay Bridge is a monarch, a splendid double-decker carrying more than six times the traffic that the single-decked Golden Gate Bridge can bear on its busiest day. But the latter gets all the glory simply because it bears a more romantic name and is painted red so that it gleams like gold when the sun sinks into the Pacific. The

Bay Bridge, painted gray, the color of the fog that creeps through the Golden Gate after sunset, never gets into the travel brochures or appears on television like the bridge it dwarfs. Look what happened in the 1960s, when the popular TV series, "Bonanza," decided to devote an entire episode to Emperor Norton and his bridge. In that story, still shown nationwide in reruns, the Emperor—played by Nehemiah Persoff in a beautifully plumed top hat and a uniform much too neat—arrives at the Ponderosa Ranch near Virginia City with a model of the span he wants to build, hoping that the Cartwrights will invest a few thousand dollars in his dream. And what does he show them? Why, a miniature Golden Gate Bridge.

So now we come to the fine old brouhaha that an Oakland newspaper's prank caused ninety years after it was printed, when an attempt was finally made to give His Majesty proper credit for his role in bridging the bay.

In 1959 the Ancient and Honorable Order of E Clampus Vitus tried to place a plaque on the bridge to honor Norton the First, a fine bronze plate bearing a portrait of the Emperor—with Bummer and Lazarus, of course—and these words inscribed below:

>
> PAUSE, TRAVELER,
> AND BE GRATEFUL TO
> NORTON I
> EMPEROR OF THE UNITED STATES
> AND
> PROTECTOR OF MEXICO, 1859–80
> WHOSE PROPHETIC WISDOM
> CONCEIVED AND DECREED
> THE BRIDGING OF SAN FRANCISCO BAY
> AUGUST 18, 1869
> DEDICATED BY E CLAMPUS VITUS, FEB. 25, 1959
>

A fitting memorial, the editorialists said, let it be put on the bridge. But the Bridge Authority denied permission, arguing that the Emperor had nothing to do with the bridge. There was an awful fuss; everybody wanted the plaque on the bridge and only the bridge directors opposed it. But the Bridge Authority had all the power and the fake decree to uphold their claim that His Majesty had merely commanded that a span be built from Goat Island to Sausalito and the godforsaken Farallones. Even E Clampus Vitus could not argue with that evidence, because they had put on the plaque that he ordered the bay to be bridged on August

18, 1869, the date on the only proclamation then known to exist and nobody knew it was a fraud.

So the history buffs gave up and installed the plaque in the lobby of the Cliff House at Seal Rocks, a restaurant that boasts of a tenuous connection with Mark Twain (Twain had eaten breakfast in an earlier Cliff House on the same spot and given the place a puff in the *Morning Call*). That's where the plaque is today, on the wall of a resort that never saw His Majesty's face, because the Cliff House that knew Mark Twain was much too far from Montgomery Street. It was six or seven miles from town, along a plank road laid over sand dunes, and the streetcars that might have taken him there, without charging a cent, never went anywhere near the place. He would have had to hire a horse and carriage.

But the Emperor *did* order that bridge to be built, and also commanded that a study be made to determine whether a tunnel might be feasible, as we have already seen. The plaque should be taken down from the wall at the Cliff House and placed where it rightly belongs, either at the Telegraph Hill approach to the bridge or at the entrance to the tunnel at Montgomery Street and Market, opposite the Palace Hotel, where it can plainly be seen by the thousands of commuters who travel under the bay every day.

More than that, the bridge ought to be renamed.

The San Francisco–Oakland Bay Bridge is a clumsy name, anyway. Nobody calls it that, because it's much too long to pronounce; you can't get your tongue around it without swallowing twice. People on both sides of the water simply call it the Bay Bridge, a name equally without charm, as gray as the paint on its girders. Its name, like its color, makes it no match for the gilded and more poetically named, though smaller, span that crosses the strait called the Golden Gate. The Emperor Norton Bridge has a better ring to it, and that should be its name.

Then, perhaps, that bridge too will get into travel brochures and onto the television screens, and the Emperor's name will once again be known all over the land.

Strangely enough, in spite of all that the Emperor meant to the city in days gone by, and all that he did for its tourist trade, there is not a single plaque to remember him by in any of the streets that he walked— only the monolith over his grave in Colma, across the county line, and that sadly misplaced memorial out where the seals bark at passing ships.

There should at least be a plaque on a wall of the office building next to the old U.S. Mint on Commercial Street (now a part of the Bank of Canton), to show where he lived for seventeen years. And a tablet set in the sidewalk on the southeast corner of California Street and Grant Avenue (formerly Dupont Street), the gateway to Chinatown, to show where he died. The tourists could pay for them with a fine of twenty-five dollars whenever they utter the abominable word " 'Frisco," as His Imperial Majesty decreed long ago.

Appendix B
The King and Huck Finn

Greatening Truth thou teachest, Emperor,
That the Real is ghost and shade;
While the shadow, made ideal,
Likewise is immortal made.

—William McDevitt, 1880

On Thursday, January 8, 1880, the day that His Majesty died, Samuel Langhorne Clemens wrote to William Dean Howells from his home in Hartford, Connecticut: "Am waiting for Patrick [his coachman] to come with the carriage. Mrs. Clemens and I are starting (without the children) to stay indefinitely in Elmira."

The Clemenses were in Elmira, New York, next day when the Associated Press learned of the Emperor's death in a telegraphed message from San Francisco and relayed it to newspapers all over the East, many of which published it on Saturday. Clemens himself might have read it in *The New York Times,* which would have been shipped to Elmira by an early train that Saturday morning and could have been delivered to the home of his wife's parents, whom they were visiting, in plenty of time to give the humorist a lively topic with which to entertain the Langdons at dinner, telling them all about the royal ragamuffin he had often seen with his own eyes.

I mention this only because, within a week or two of his arrival in Elmira, Mark Twain started work on *The Prince and the Pauper,* which leads me to wonder whether he might not have been inspired to begin that novel because his memory of a princely pauper had been jogged by Joshua Norton's obituary in the *Times.*

Back in Hartford at the end of January Twain wrote to tell Howells about the story he was working on: "It begins at 9 a.m., January 27, 1547, seventeen & a half years before Henry VIII's death, by the swapping of clothes *and places* between the prince of Wales & a pauper boy of the same age and countenance. . . ." Actually, Twain had conceived the idea two years before, briefly summarizing the plot in a notebook on November 23, 1877: "Edward VI and a little pauper exchange places by accident. . . ."

Now, it may be of no great significance that he jotted down that note when Norton was at the height of his fame, and it may be only a coincidence that he began the book just a few days after the papers announced the Emperor's death. But there is perhaps rather more significance and less coincidence if we consider Justin Kaplan's observation that Twain wrote *The Prince and the Pauper* because he "had found the confusion of dream and reality to be a subject for comedy." It was precisely the Emperor's own inability to distinguish dream from reality that had made him the subject of comedy in the press, as Twain had seen when he worked for the *Call* on Commercial Street and His Majesty lived next door.

There can be no doubt that Twain was utterly fascinated by the Emperor of the United States; proof of that may be found in his notebooks and in his letters to Howells. Indeed, if we follow his progress since his departure from California we shall see that His Majesty was seldom far from Twain's thoughts.

This book began, you may recall, with a quote from a letter to Howells in which Twain said he found it odd that "no professionally literary person in San Francisco has ever 'written up' the Emperor Norton." Twain named four who had known the Emperor well enough to do it: Franklin Soulé, Bret Harte, Charles Warren Stoddard, and himself. Of those four Frank Soulé would have been the logical choice for royal biographer; Twain and Harte had not seen the Emperor for many a year and could only have written tidbits dredged from a distant past, while Charley Stoddard's forte was writing about the South Seas. But Frank Soulé was still in San Francisco, much closer to the subject; as a journalist, and as chief compiler of *The Annals of San Francisco,* a treasure trove of early Californiana culled from the city's old newspaper files, he would have had easy access to everything that had ever been published about the Emperor and might even have known Joshua Norton when he was wealthy and thought to be sane. What was more important, Soulé, "one of the sweetest and whitest & loveliest spirits that ever wandered into this world by mistake," would have treated a fellow wanderer with proper compassion.

In 1880, unfortunately, Frank Soulé was squandering his life away on poetry that nobody wanted. Howells rejected the verses he submitted to *The Atlantic Monthly.* Soulé might have been better employed writing about Norton. And that is just what Twain seems to be driving at in his letter. "O, dear," he begins, "it was always a painful thing for me to see the Emperor (Norton I, of San Francisco) begging; for although nobody else believed he was an Emperor, *he* believed it. And Frank Soulé believes himself a poet (& many others believe it, too) & it is sad enough to see him on the street begging for the charity of mere notice." From there Twain goes on at length about Norton, expressing his wonder that no professional writer had ever "written him up." All in all, the letter has every appearance of being an attempt by Twain to bring a respected periodical, a qualified author, and a remarkable subject together.

Twain may have been hinting at himself as the author if Soulé did not suit Howells. See how he emphasizes his own qualifications in his letter: "I have seen the Emperor when his dignity was wounded and when he was both hurt and indignant at the dishonoring of an imperial draft; & when he was full of trouble and bodings on account of the presence of the Russian fleet, he connecting it with his refusal to ally himself with the Romanoffs by marriage & believing these ships were come to take advantage of his entanglements with Peru & Bolivia; I have seen him in *all* his various moods & tenses, & there was always more room for pity than laughter." (The italics are his.)

But there is more than that to suggest that Twain was probably thinking of the Emperor as a subject for his own pen.

In 1882, when Frank Soulé's sweet spirit wandered out of this world forever, leaving His Majesty's tale untold, Twain wrote Norton's name in one of the several notebooks that he kept filled with ideas for stories. That entry—just "Emperor Norton"—immediately followed another: "Bummer and Lazarus" (the two mongrel dogs that were supposed to be the Emperor's pets). Although he never wrote an article about Norton for *The Atlantic Monthly* (or if he did Howells never published it), it is my belief that he did put the Emperor into his fiction.

Perpend:

In 1874, Twain had written a very odd letter to his wife. He was in Boston, nursing blisters after a hiking trip. It was November 16, his thirty-ninth birthday, but he dated the letter November 16, 1939, the centennial of his birth, and pretended that he had seen great changes during his hundred years on earth. The United States was no longer a republic; it was now an Irish monarchy. New York City had been renamed Dublin, Boston was now called Limerick, Twain was the Earl of Hartford, and William Dean Howells was the Duke of Cambridge, Massachusetts. The Emperor of the United States was O'Mulligan the First.

That rambling letter makes little sense unless it is recognized as the skeleton of a story Twain was thinking of writing. Twain often tried out a story idea on Olivia Clemens or Howells, whose opinions he trusted. In this instance he not only sent the letter to Livy but mailed a copy to Howells, evidently fishing for the blessings of both.

Why an *Irish* monarchy? I can only guess. The papers at that time were filled with reports of the upcoming graft trial of William Marcy Tweed, whose powerful Irish faction in Tammany Hall dominated New York's politics. Twain, I believe, was satirizing the extent of "Boss" Tweed's influence, implying that if the Tweed Ring had its way the entire country would be ruled by the New York Irish. If that hunch is correct, then Twain was already thinking of writing a comic fantasy with social overtones somewhat along the lines he would later pursue in *The Prince and the Pauper* and *A Connecticut Yankee in King Arthur's Court*.

The story was never written, possibly because Boss Tweed was sent to prison and the Tweed Ring lost its power, which took all the sting out of the tale. Still, Twain liked the basic idea and five years later used it as the theme of a humorous sketch, "The Great Revolution in Pitcairn," which Howells published in the *Monthly*. In this version, an American named Butterworth Stavely, marooned among the descendants of the *Bounty* mutineers on remote Pitcairn, seizes control of the Pacific island's happy-go-lazy government and proclaims himself Emperor. Norton I, however, with a free pass to travel California's railroads, was a lot better off than Butterworth I, whose subjects trundle him around his tiny empire in a "gilded imperial wheelbarrow."

But Twain wasn't finished with Norton. Surely that's the Emperor's tattered ghost that appears as the hobo "King" in *The Adventures of Huckleberry Finn:* "Yes, gentlemen, you see before you, in blue jeans and misery, the wanderin', exiled, trampled-on, and sufferin' rightful King of France . . . the pore disappeared Dauphin, Looy the Seventeen, son of Looy the Sixteen and Marry Antonette."

True, that doesn't sound like Norton. According to all who knew him, his diction was refined and his vocabulary large. By contrast, the King in *Huckleberry Finn* is an ignorant lout, without even the thinnest veneer of culture. However, it must be remembered that the narrator of the story, Huck Finn, is an illiterate country boy whose final comment is: "If I'd 'a' knowed what trouble it was to make a book I wouldn't 'a' tackled it, and ain't a-going to no more." The language he puts into the mouth of "Looy the Seventeen" could hardly be more sophisticated than his own.

Twain told the Portland *Oregonian* that he borrowed his fictional characters from life. "I don't believe an author ever lived who created a character," he said. "It was always drawn from his recollection of some one he had known." And as Professor Walter Blair says in his *Mark Twain and Huck Finn*, "Characters usually had much more than their names changed." Nature never produced a masterpiece that Twain could accept as a finished work until he had made a few major alterations. To my mind, there can be little doubt that the Emperor of the United States was the prototype of the "pore disappeared Dauphin."

The disappearance of the eight-year-old Dauphin, in or about 1794, started a vogue for missing princes that lasted well into Norton's time and became a favorite theme of Victorian novelists and dramatists. The nineteenth century spawned a host of cheap books and melodramas in which a handsome but humble hero, despised by all for his poverty, was revealed in the final chapter or the last act to be the long-lost heir to a great estate and a title by the fortuitous discovery of a "strawberry mark" on some hitherto hidden portion of his anatomy, where only a misplaced aristocrat could be expected to have a skin blemish.

Though Norton claimed to be a Crown Prince of France, he did not mean he was the Dauphin, Louis XVII, but another French prince whose identity he would not divulge. Perhaps he was sane enough to know that he could not pretend to be a prince who had vanished long before he was born.

I really cannot accept Professor Blair's theory that "Looy the Seventeen" was modeled on Captain Duncan of the *Quaker City*. Blair offers too little evidence to support it. Comparing the Captain's piety with the Mississippi scalawag's "soul-butter and hogwash" sermonizing simply isn't enough, and cannot be supported by so weak a prop as Twain's 1877 letter to the New York *World,* in which he said of Duncan, "I knew him to be a canting hypocrite, full to the chin of sham godliness." That remark was written in revenge; Twain had just learned that Duncan, then on the lecture circuit, was calling him a drunken liar, telling audiences that Twain had applied for the trip to the Holy Land as "a Baptist minister cruising after health" and had polluted the Captain's office with the fumes of bad whiskey (which did not discourage Duncan from issuing him a ticket).

Huck's King is not a full-time gospeler, forever spouting soul-butter. "Preachin's my line, *too,*" he says (my italics). He will do anything to bilk the gullible, whether it be kneeling tearfully before a congregation of Holy Rollers to confess that he is a repentant pirate (which nets him kisses and a hat full of money), playing a bearded Juliet to the scruffy Romeo of his vagabond companion, the "Duke of Bridgewater," or capering about on a stage, naked and painted with stripes, as a cameleopard or Royal Nonesuch.

Captain Duncan at least gave his passengers full value for their $1,250 fare. Twain admits that in *The Innocents Abroad.* "I have no fault to find with the manner in which the excursion was carried out," he says in the concluding chapter, adding that "if the *Quaker City* were weighing her anchor to sail away on the very same cruise again, nothing could gratify me more than to be a passenger. With the same captain and even the same pilgrims, the same sinners." Yet in the original version, the one published in the *Alta California* before the book was pruned, Twain had picked a very different skipper—the colorful, hard-swearing Captain Ned Wakeman of San Francisco.

Professor Blair's only other evidence that Duncan and Looy were one and the same lies in his comparison of their physical appearances. He quotes Huck as saying that Looy is "seventy, or upwards," has "a bald head and very gray whiskers," and wears "an old longtailed blue coat with slick brass buttons." Then Blair adds that an ink portrait of Captain Duncan in the first edition of *The Innocents Abroad* "shows a thoroughly bald, gray-whiskered oldster in a coat which (if it resembled those of other ship's officers pictured) is long-tailed, probably navy-blue and brass-buttoned."

Well, we don't know for sure that the coat is long-tailed, because the picture shows only Captain Duncan's upper half, and in fact the coat has a decidedly civilian cut, with a handkerchief flopping from its breast pocket—a surprisingly landlubberly touch—and only two buttons showing instead of the many that usually decorated a sea captain's tunic in the 1860s. Since the portrait is in black and white, we don't know if the buttons are brass or if the coat is blue or black. A photograph of Captain Duncan in Dewey Ganzel's *Mark Twain Abroad; the Cruise of the Quaker City* shows a rather saintly old gentleman, white-haired and white-bearded, wearing what appears to be a civilian suit of black broadcloth tailored in much the same fashion as the supposed "uniform" in *The Innocents Abroad*.

Finally, Professor Blair omits an important detail from Huck's description of the King. Huck does not say that the con man wore "an old longtailed blue coat." He says he wore "an old longtailed blue *jeans* coat." (Again, my italics.) A deckhand might have worn the durable twilled cotton cloth called blue jean, but a ship's captain was more likely to wear blue serge.

Emperor Norton, who invariably wore an old blue army coat, long-tailed and brass-buttoned, fits Huckleberry Finn's description of the King almost exactly. The only difference of any importance lies in their natures. Twain called the Emperor a "lovable old humbug," whereas Looy is a most unlovable old humbug.

"Sometimes," Twain told the *Oregonian*, "like a composite photograph, an author's presentation of a character may possibly be from the blending of two or more real characters in his recollection." With that in mind, Professor Blair theorizes that there might be just a touch of the Reverend Eleazer Williams in Looy. The Reverend Williams, a missionary among the Iroquois, claimed to be the missing Dauphin. It is Blair's contention that, though Twain based Looy on Captain Duncan, he made the con man pose as the long-lost Louis because he had read the missionary's memoirs and borrowed the idea for his own characterization. But Twain had no need to borrow an idea from a book. He had personally known Emperor Norton, who also claimed to be a French prince.

Let's be fair. Let's just say that Looy the Seventeen was probably about ninety percent Norton, five percent Duncan, and five percent Eleazer Williams. And that's being generous. I really can't yield more than ten percent of Norton to anyone, but I realize that I must leave something for literary scholars to squabble about.

Let the debate begin.

Sources

Proclamations by Joshua Norton or composed by others, but signed with his name, and news items about Emperor Norton, were found in the following newspapers, literary journals, and magazines published between 1859 and 1880:

In San Francisco
Alta California, Morning Call, Evening Bulletin, Evening Herald, Chronicle, News-Letter, Mining & Scientific Press, Pacific Appeal, Jewish Progress, Illustrated Wasp, Overland Monthly, Argonaut, Golden Era, Thistleton's Jolly Giant.

Other Journals
The New York Times, New York *Tribune,* Cincinnati *Enquirer,* Cincinnati *American Israelite,* Philadelphia *Public Ledger,* Denver *Rocky Mountain News,* Portland *Oregonian,* Seattle *Daily Intelligencer,* Los Angeles *Evening Express,* Vancouver *British Colonist,* Sacramento *Union,* Oakland *Daily News,* Marysville *Californian Express,* Marysville *Weekly Appeal,* Petaluma *Argus.*

Bibliography

Asbury, Herbert. *The Barbary Coast.* New York: Alfred A. Knopf, 1933.

Barker, Malcolm E. *Bummer & Lazarus.* San Francisco: Londonborn Publications, 1984.

Branch, Edgar M. *Clemens of the Call.* Berkeley: University of California Press, 1969.

Blair, Walter. *Mark Twain and Huck Finn.* Berkeley: University of California Press, 1960.

Clarke, Dwight L. *William Tecumseh Sherman, Gold Rush Banker.* San Francisco: California Historical Society, 1969.

Collins, Carvel, ed. *Sam Ward in the Gold Rush.* Palo Alto: Stanford University Press, 1949.

Cowan, Robert E. et al. *The Forgotten Characters of Old San Francisco.* Los Angeles: The Ward Ritchie Press, 1964.

Cummins, Ella Sterling (Mighels). *The Story of the Files.* San Francisco: Cooperative Printing Company, 1892.

Dane, George. *Ghost Town.* New York: Alfred A. Knopf, 1941.

Dillon, Richard. *Humbugs and Heroes.* New York: Doubleday, 1970.

Dressler, Albert. *Emperor Norton of United States.* Sacramento: Dressler, 1927.

Ellis, William Turner. *Memories; My Seventy-two Years in the Romantic County of Yuba, California.* Eugene: University of Oregon, 1939.

Fatout, Paul. *Mark Twain on the Lecture Circuit.* Bloomington, Ind.: Indiana University Press, 1960.

Field, Isobel. *This Life I've Loved.* New York: Longmans, Green, 1937.

Fitzgerald, O.P. *California Sketches; New Series.* Nashville, Tenn.: Southern Methodist Publishing House, 1881.

Ganzel, Dewey. *Mark Twain Abroad; The Cruise of the Quaker City.* Chicago: University of Chicago Press, 1968.

Greeley, Horace. *An Overland Journey.* New York: Alfred A. Knopf, 1963.

Bibliography

Hansen, Gladys. *San Francisco Almanac.* San Francisco: Chronicle Books, 1975.

Herrman, Louis. *A History of the Jews in South Africa.* London: Victor Gollancz, 1930.

Johnson, Alva. *The Legendary Mizners.* New York: Farrar, Straus & Young, 1953.

Kahn, Edgar M. *Cable Car Days in San Francisco.* Palo Alto: Stanford University Press, 1940.

Kaplan, Justin. *Mr. Clemens and Mark Twain.* New York: Simon & Schuster, 1966.

Kirchhoff, Theodor. *Californische Kulturbilder.* Germany: 1886. Translated by Rudolph Jordan, Jr., under the title "Norton the First" in *The Society of California Pioneers Quarterly,* December 1928.

Kramer, William M. *Emperor Norton of San Francisco.* Santa Monica: Norton B. Stern, 1974.

Lane, Allen Stanley. *Emperor Norton, Mad Monarch of America.* Caldwell, Ida.: Caxton Printers, 1939.

Lennon, Nigey. *Mark Twain in California.* San Francisco: Chronicle Books, 1982.

Lloyd, B.E. *Lights and Shades in San Francisco.* San Francisco: A.L. Bancroft, 1876.

Lynch, Jeremiah. *The Life of David C. Broderick; A Senator of the Fifties.* New York: Baker & Taylor, 1911.

Mitchell, A.R.K. *Schizophrenia; the Meaning of Madness.* New York: Taplinger, 1972.

Mizner, Addison. *The Many Mizners.* New York: Sears Publishing Company, 1932.

Murdock, Charles A. *A Backward Glance at Eighty.* San Francisco: Paul Elder, 1921.

———. *Horatio Stebbins, His Ministry and His Personality.* Boston: Houghton Mifflin, 1921.

Myers, John Myers. *San Francisco's Reign of Terror.* New York: Doubleday, 1966.

Neville, Amelia Ransome. *The Fantastic City.* Boston: Houghton Mifflin, 1932.

Nickerson, Roy. *Robert Louis Stevenson in California.* San Francisco: Chronicle Books, 1982.

Older, Cora. *San Francisco, Magic City.* New York: Longmans, Green, 1961.

Older, Fremont. *Growing Up.* San Francisco: MacMillan, 1931.

Ryder, David Warren. *San Francisco's Emperor Norton.* San Francisco: Ryder, 1939.

Sherman, William T. *Memoirs.* 2 vols. New York: D. Appleton, 1875.

Soulé, Frank, Dr. John H. Gihon, and James Nisbet. *The Annals of San Francisco*. New York: D. Appleton, 1855.

Stevenson, Robert Louis, and Lloyd Osbourne. *The Wrecker*. New York: Charles Scribner's Sons, 1892.

Stewart, George R. *Committee of Vigilance; Revolution in San Francisco*. Boston: Houghton Mifflin, 1964.

Taper, Bernard. *Mark Twain's San Francisco*. Boston: McGraw-Hill, 1963.

Thomas, Lately. *Between Two Empires*. Boston: Houghton Mifflin, 1969.

———. *Sam Ward, King of the Lobby*. Boston: Houghton Mifflin, 1965.

Timberlake, Craig. *The Bishop of Broadway*. New York: Library Publishers, 1954.

Trollope, Anthony. *The Tireless Traveler*. Berkeley: University of California Press, 1941.

Twain, Mark [Samuel L. Clemens]. *The Autobiography of Mark Twain*. Edited by Charles Neider. New York: Harper, 1975.

———. *Mark Twain's Notebooks & Journals*. Vol. 1. Edited by Frederick Anderson, et al. Berkeley: University of California Press, 1975.

———. *Mark Twain to Mrs. Fairbanks*. Edited by Dixon Wecter. San Marino, Calif.: Huntington Library, 1949.

———. *Mark Twain–William Dean Howells Letters*. Edited by Henry Nash Smith and William M. Gibson. Cambridge: Harvard University Press, 1960.

———. *The Adventures of Huckleberry Finn*. New York: Harper, 1962.

———. *The Innocents Abroad*. New York: MacMillan, 1897.

Walker, Franklin. *San Francisco's Literary Frontier*. Seattle, Wash.: University of Washington Press, 1969.

Wakeman, Edgar. *The Log of an Ancient Mariner*. San Francisco: A.L. Bancroft, 1876.

Index

A

Adelaide, 184
Adventures of Huckleberry Finn, The (Twain), 14
Aerial Steam Navigation Company, 153
Ah How, 92, 127
Ah Toy's bagnio, 45
Alice's Adventures in Wonderland (Carroll), 115, 134
Alta California. See *Daily Alta California.*
Altamonte. *See* Evans, Albert S.
American Flag, 94, 118–19
American Israelite, The, 13, 204
American Publishing Company, 105
Amigo. *See* Evans, Albert S.
Anderson, Peter; *Pacific Appeal* as royal gazette of Emperor and, 145–47, 156, 169, 176, 191–92; Mark Twain and, 147, 149
Argonaut (magazine), 4
Argus, 94
Arthur Andrews Clark Library, 144
Asbury, Herbert, 171
Astor, Emily, 36
Astor, William B., 36
Atlantic Monthly, The, 198
Aurignace, Marcelin, 92, 171

B

Babcock, Alfred, 90–91, 148
Backward Glance at Eighty, A (Murdock), 166
Baldwin Theatre, 196
Ballou, Addie Lucia, 180–82
Bank Exchange, 90, 93–94, 205
Barbary Coast, The (Asbury), 171
Barbier, Armand, 124–25, 127–28
Barnes, George, 104–6, 119, 149
Barrett, Lawrence, 184
Beecher, Henry Ward, 135
Belasco, David, 179, 196
Bella Union, 91, 95, 154, 165–67, 169–71
Benicia, 40–41
Bennett, James Gordon, 114
Bierce, Ambrose, 9, 130–31; legend of the Emperor and, 4, 199; Leland Stanford denounced by, 173; in Marriott's *News-Letter,* 155
Biggelow, Harry, 5–6, 9, 199
Bliss, Elisha, 105, 135
Bluxome, Isaac, 32
Bohemian Club, 188–89, 200, 202, 205
Booker, Sir William Lane, 35, 66
Booth, Edwin, 96, 184
Booth, John Wilkes, 111
Boston *Traveller,* 113
Bowman, Jimmy, 5–7, 9–10, 72, 94; on death of Bummer, 119, 199–201
Bourbon restoration, 18–19
Bradley & Ruloffson, 139–40, 159, 162, 175
Brewster, Rolla, 199
Broderick, David C., 57, 89, 111; killed in dual, 56, 60; San Francisco under, 46–47; Tammany Hall henchmen imported by, 46
Broglie, Madame de, 18
Brown, John, 52, 60–61
Brown Derby, 39
Buchanan, James, 67
Bugbee, Norman, 44–45

228 Index

Bummer, 81–84, 90; death of, 117–19; said to be Emperor's companion, 120–23
Buntline, Ned, 37
Burch, John, 55
Burke, Martin J., 108, 115, 124, 126; Twain and, 116, 126, 128
Burney, Fanny, 18
Burnside, Ambrose, 88

C

Californian, The, 105, 118
California State University, 203
Californische Kulturbilder (Kirchhoff), 174
Camp Allen, 97, 144
Cape Town, South Africa, 11–13, 22–23, 58, 88
Captain Stormfield's Visit to Heaven (Twain), 30, 180
Carlotta, Empress of Mexico, 129, 167, 182
Carroll, Lewis, 134
Carswell, Mrs. 54–55, 66
Casey, James P., 47–49, 91
Central Pacific Railroad, 6, 137, 172–75
Champlin, Charles C., 150–51
Champlin, Charles Chaffee, 150–51
Champlin, Sarah, 150–51
Chapman, Blanche, 179
Chapman, Ella, 179
Charles X, King of France, 13, 19–21, 63
Charles Scribner's Sons, 71
Chicago *Tribune,* 78
Christian Enquirer, 115
Church, William, 91
Cincinnati *Enquirer,* 3, 138, 200
Civil Rights Act of 1866, 133
Civil War, 7, 52, 55, 67–68, 92–93
Clemens, Livy, 183
Clemens, Samuel Langhorne. *See* Twain, Mark.
Cleveland *Herald,* 136
Cleveland *Plain Dealer,* 3
Cobwebs from an Empty Skull (Bierce), 131
Cole, Nellie, 165; the Emperor's marriage plans and, 166–67, 169; known as Lady Peacock, 166–67, 171; as Sam Tetlow's leading lady, 91–92, 95, 154, 166
Cole, Willis, 165
Constock, Henry, 59
Coombs, Freddie. *See* Washington, George, the Second.
Coon, Henry, 106

Cora, Charles, 49, 91
Cowan, Robert Ernest, 143–44
Crowley, Patrick, 124, 126–27
Cuddy & Hughes, 140–41, 167–68
Cummins, Ella Sterling, 57
Currier, Nathaniel, 83, 152
Curtis, William Bostwick, 186

D

Daily Alta California, 68, 70, 81, 85, 100, 116, 130, 159; Albert Evans given byline in, 104–5; Andrew Johnson denounced by, 133; Bummer and Lazarus and, 82, 117; Eastland quoted in, 38; 1851 San Francisco fire described in, 29; on Emperor's death, 2; Emperor viewed as exclusive property of, 107; fake proclamations published by, 76, 78, 89, 110, 112, 129; Fremont Older and, 121; Joshua Norton & Co. and, 31; Norton ridiculed in, 95, 131; Norton's business ads in, 54; Oakland Guard incident and, 97–98; read by Norton, 91; slavery issues and, 55; on Stellifer the King, 113; Mark Twain in, 106, 134–35, 182; on transcontinental railroad, 136–37; as Union paper, 111
Daily California Express, 99
Daily Intelligencer, 201
Davis, Jefferson, 67, 101–2
Deach, Nicholas, 26
Democratic Press, 94
De Young, Charles, 119
De Young, Michael, 119
Dodge, Judge, 115
Douglas, William A., 197
Dramatic Chronicle, 118
Dressler, Albert, 143
Drum, Colonel, 108
Duncan, Charles C., 135, 160

E

Early, Jubal, 92
Eastland, Joseph, 39, 154, 189–90; Emperor's burial and, 199–201; in Masonic Lodge with Norton, 66, 200; Mechanics Institute and, 150; on Norton, 7, 38
Edison, Thomas, 190
1820 Settlers, 15

El Dorado, or Adventures in the Path of Empire (Taylor), 38
Ellis, Alfred J., 27–28
Emma, Queen of Sandwich Islands, 117, 129, 182, 196
Emperor Norton (opera), 205
Emperor Norton, Mad Monarch of America (Lane), 144
Emperor Norton Inn, 205
Emperor Norton Memorial Association, 203
Emperor Norton of San Francisco (Kramer), 203
Emperor Norton of United States (Dressler), 143
Emperor of the United States. *See* Norton, Joshua Abraham.
Eugenie, Empress of France, 170, 182, 196
Eureka Lodgings, 10, 90–91, 109, 127, 130, 148–49, 182, 196–97
Evans, Albert S., 70–71, 89, 92, 136, 145; Bummer and Lazarus and, 83; called Colonel Moustache, 78–79; Emperor as described by, 85, 103, 115–16, 127, 139; fake proclamations published by, 76–78, 131–33; Andrew Johnson denounced by, 133; on Adah Menken, 93; the *Morning Call* and, 104–5; Norton depicted as calculating sham by, 94–95; Oakland Guard incident and, 97–98; pen names used by, 78; retired from the *Alta*, 147; Mark Twain and, 105–7, 111–12, 116–17, 147; George Washington the Second and, 81, 115–16
Evening Bulletin, 47, 63, 94, 107, 145, 194; arrest of Emperor for lunacy and, 124, 126; Bummer and Lazarus and, 82, 89, 117; Emperor's proclamations in, 58–62, 68, 107, 112; on Emperor's wardrobe needs, 130–31; under Fitch, 56–59, 131; Fremont Older and, 120–21; on Pony Express, 65; Vigilance Committee and, 52–53

F

Fairbanks, Mary Mason, 136
Fantastic City, The (Neville), 75
Fennimore, James (Old Virginny), 59
Field, Isobel, 5, 184–85
Figaro, 179
Fisherman's Wharf, 39, 44, 205
Fitch, George Kenyon, 63, 65, 80; on arrest of Emperor, 126–27; death of Lazarus and, 89; Emperor's proclamations published by, 58–62, 68, 112; *Evening Bulletin* under, 56–59, 131; Robert Louis Stevenson and, 194
Fitzgerald, O. P., 87
Forgotten Characters of Old San Francisco, The, (Cowan) 145
Fort Gunnybags, 49, 53
Freemasons, 35, 44, 66, 200
Fremont, John Charles, 40
Fugitive Slave Law, 51

G

Gallagher, Marty, 47
Genessee, 28, 31, 35, 42, 54
George III, King of England, 18, 66
Githens, William, 10, 201
Godeffroy, Alfred, 41, 45, 74–76, 78
Godeffroy & Sillem, 41, 44
Gold Demon, The (play), 179
Golden Era, The (journal) 69; Bret Harte in, 103, 105; Mark Twain in, 94–95, 104
Gold Hill *Evening News*, 78, 93–94, 116
Gold Rush era, 26, 37–38, 59, 74, 91, 189
Graham's Town, 15–17, 19, 22, 24, 55, 58
Grand Hotel, 166–67, 190
Grant, Ulysses S., 111, 135, 137
Greeley, Horace, 56, 114, 122, 137–38
Greenbacks, 100
Gross, Frank, 70–71; Bummer and Lazarus and, 82–83, 89, 117; Twain and, 94, 107, 126
Grubb, C. C., 16–17
Grubb's Academy, 16
Grymes, Medora, 36–37, 74
Gwin, William McKendree, 111

H

Halleck, Henry W., 117
Hallidie, Andrew, 149, 153, 156, 177–79
Harper's Weekly (magazine), 190
Harte, Francis Brett (Bret Harte), 189; in *The Golden Era*, 103, 105; Twain and, 105, 112, 135; *Californian* put out by, 105, 118
Hastings Society, 195
Hauser, Kaspar, 20, 22
Hayne, Julia Dean, 104
Hearst, William Randolph, 120

230 Index

Henessey, Jim, 47
Heuston & Hastings, 85–86
Hill, J. Ellis, 164
Hoboken Democrat, 192
Hopkins, Old Mammy, 165–66
Hopkins, Sterling, 53, 91, 165
Horatio Stebbins, His Ministry and His Personality (Murdock), 161
Horton, Tom, 71
Howe, Julia Ward, 36
Howells, William Dean, 107, 198
Hutchinson, David, 12, 90, 148, 164, 197
Hutchinson, Eva, 10, 148, 197

I

Innocents Abroad, The (Twain), 105, 135
International Hotel, 48–49
Irwin, Benoni, 200
Ives, James Merritt, 152
Ivy Green Saloon, 108

J

Jenkins, John, 29–30, 183
Jewish community and faith, 10–13, 15, 17–18, 20, 22–23, 201–4
Jewish Progress, The, 203
Johns, Tremenhere Lanyon, 94
Johnson, Andrew, 36, 133–35
Jolly Giant (magazine), 175
Jones Hotel, 28–29, 36, 49
Jordan, Dorothea, 9
Jordan, Rudolph, 174
Joseph, King of Naples and Spain, 74
Joshua Norton & Company, 22, 27, 31, 37
Juarez, Benito, 129
Jump, Edward E., 80–81, 83, 89, 126, 128; death of Bummer and, 118–19; legend of Emperor and, 81, 84, 90, 94, 175

K

Kansas-Nebraska Act, 52
Kavanaugh, Hubbard H., 108–9
Keating, Jim, 108
Kerr, Orpheus C., 104
King, Thomas Sim, 52, 55–56
King of Pain, 76–77, 81, 84
King of William, James, 47–49, 52, 89, 120, 200
Kirch, Henry, 22, 58

Kirchhoff, Theodor, 174
Koenig, George, 70
Kossuth, Louis, 85
Kramer, William M., 203–4

L

Lane, Allen Stanley, 144
Lazarus, 81–84, 200; death of, 89–90, 118–19; said to be Emperor's companion, 120–23
Lee, Robert E., 88, 108, 111
Leland, Lewis, 108
Leonard, Major, 77
Leopold, Grand Duke, 20
Leslie's Weekly Illustrated (magazine), 91, 128
Lick, James, 27–29, 31, 35, 43, 95
Lick House, 93, 95
Lick Observatory, 27
Life in San Francisco (play), 84
Lights and Shades in San Francisco (Lloyd), 72, 150
Lincoln, Abraham, 101, 111, 128, 132–34, 151; slavery issues and, 54, 65, 67, 88–89
Liverpool *Mercury*, 158
Lloyd, Benjamin E., 72–73, 96, 150, 189
Log of an Ancient Mariner, The (Wakeman), 30, 33, 183
Longfellow, Henry Wadsworth, 36
Los Angeles *Evening Express*, 138
Louis XVI, King of France, 17–18, 21
Louis XVIII, King of France, 18–19, 21
Louis Philippe, King of France, 19–21, 73
Lucas, James, 73
Lucas, Turner & Company, 43–44
Lynch, Jeremiah, 46

M

McAllister, Hall, 36–37, 45, 74, 154, 189
McAllister, Ward, 36–37, 39, 41, 74
McClellan, George, 133
McComb, John, 94
McCready, Irene, 45
MacCrellish, Frederick: *Alta California* under, 81, 104, 111–12, 116, 131, 135; Civil War loyalties and, 111; Twain and, 135
McDowell, Irving, 108–9
McGowan, Edward, 45–49, 55–56
McGuire, Jack, 47
McHenry, R. H., 94

Index   231

McKenzie, Bob, 32
Magilder, Philip, 169
Maguire's Opera House, 90, 106, 159
Mailliard, Adolphe, 74
Mailliard, Louis, 74
Mailliard, Louis Napoleon, 74
Maloney, Rube, 47
Mansion, The, hotel, 205
Many Mizners, The (Mizner), 41
Marie Antoinette, Queen of France, 18, 21
Marig, B., 187
Marriot, Frederick, 149, 153, 191
Martin, Clark, 71, 83, 89–90
Martin, William: as Emperor's devoted follower, 127–28, 149, 197; on police force, 115, 124, 126–27
Martin & Horton's, 70–73, 82, 90, 121
Marysville *Express*, 100
Mason, General, 108
Masonic Cemetery, 200, 203
Masons, 35, 44, 66, 200
Maximilian, Archduke of Austria, 111, 128–29
Mazeppa; or The Wild Horse of Tartary (play), 93, 95
Mechanics Institute, 149–50, 156, 159
Meiggs, Henry, 39, 43, 47, 75
Menken, Adah Isaacs, 93, 104
Mercantile Library, 189
Metropolitan Hotel, 66
Metropolitan Theater, 84, 179
Mexico, 62, 73, 111, 128–29
Mining and Scientific Press, The (journal), 156, 177
Minturn, Charles, 151–52
Mitchell, Alexander R. K., 72
Mizner, Addison, 39, 41
Mizner, Ella Watson, 39
Mizner, Lansing Bond, 39–41, 45
Mizner, Wilson, 39
Money King, 81, 84
Morning Call, 103, 135, 165, 181; anti-Chinese bias of, 148–49; on business dealings of Norton, 49; called "Morning Squeak" by Twain, 118; Charles Murdock and, 168; on the Emperor and the ladies, 180; on Emperor's death, 2, 197; Emperor's contemplated marriage and, 167; Fremont Older and, 120–23, 168; on Jump's lithograph of Bummer, 118–19; Mark Twain in, 104–9, 149; on Norton's origins, 9–10; origins and development of, 104; on previous wealth of Norton, 6–7; read by Norton, 91; on temperate habits of Emperor, 72
Morse, Salmi, 202–3
Moses, Isaac, 23–24
Moulton, D. Stellifer, 6, 110, 113–16
Mulligan, Billy, 47–48
Mulloy, Tom, 47
Murdock, Charles A., 161, 177; on Emperor's religious views, 160; imperial scrip printed by, 168, 195; on marriage plans of the Emperor, 166
Murray, Larry, 169
Muybridge, Eardweard, 149

N

Napoleon Bonaparte, 15, 18, 74
Napoleon III, 10, 73–74, 78, 111, 117, 128, 170
Naundorff, Karl Wilhelm, 21–22
Neville, Amelia Ransome, 74–76, 81, 156
Newborough, Maria Stella, Countess of, 20–22
Newell, Robert H., 104
New York *Herald*, 114
New York Times, The, 3, 79, 188; Emperor's obituary in, 198
New York *Tribune*, 56, 88, 114, 137
Norden, Benjamin, 15–16, 22
Norton, Benjamin John, 22
Norton, Esther, 15, 22
Norton, Henry, 22
Norton, John, 14–20, 22–24, 54–55, 59, 88
Norton, Joshua Abraham, 2–6, 9–13, 39–41, 48–49, 66, 70–71, 75–79, 81, 84–86, 90, 91, 93–97, 103, 109, 115–16, 120–23, 127, 130–31, 133, 138–46, 148–49, 151–57, 159, 162, 164, 166–67, 169, 175–77, 181–82, 188–90, 193, 196–200; arrested for lunacy, 124–28; birth and childhood of, 11, 14–23, 25; Ambrose Bierce on, 130; the Bohemian Club and, 188–89, 200, 202, 205; on John Brown, 61; business endeavors of, 27–28, 31, 35–42, 44, 49, 53; daily routine of, 91–92, 148–49; death and funeral of, 1–4, 7–8, 10, 195–97, 199–203; fake proclamations printed over name of, 76–78, 89, 110–12, 114–15, 129, 131–33, 169; Imperial bonds sold by, 140–41, 162–64, 167–68, 195, 199; Jewish origins of, 23, 204; madness of,

Norton, Joshua Abraham (*continued*)
15, 19, 23, 24, 39, 56, 72–73, 164, 198; at Martin & Horton's, 70–73; *New York Times* obituary of, 198; Oakland Guard incident and, 97–98; Petaluma Creek project and, 150–52; in Port Elizabeth, South Africa, 22–24; railroad switch invented by, 156–57; religious observances of, 87–88, 160–62; Robert Louis Stevenson on, 4–5, 9, 71–72, 78, 194–95, 198–99; "royal proclamations" issued by, 6, 56–63, 65–66, 68, 76–77, 80, 88–89, 98–99, 112, 116, 140, 142–47, 150, 153–54, 156, 161–64, 166, 170, 173–77, 190–92; San Francisco Committee of Vigilance and, 31–33; San Francisco–Oakland Bay Bridge proposal and, 142–46; Serpent Scepter of, 6, 132, 182, 200; Sherman and, 7, 44–45, 53–54; Stellifer the King and, 110, 113–15; Twain on, 1, 3, 6, 87, 95, 106–9, 135, 137, 198; uniform of, 3, 12–13, 67, 75–78, 91, 130–32, 138, 141, 200; on universal religion, 161–62; George Washington the Second and, 115–16; western tours by, 97–102; women and, 166–67, 169, 181–82, 184–87
Norton, Louis, 15–18, 24
Norton, Louisa, 19, 22
Norton, Mary Ann, 22
Norton, Philip, 15, 17–18, 24
Norton, Sarah, 14–15, 17–20, 22–24, 54–55, 59
Norton, Selina, 22
Norton & Thorne, 44

O

Oakland, 142–46, 190
Oakland *Daily News*, 142–43
Oakland Guard incident, 97–98
Oakland High School, 185
Oakland *Tribune*, 151
Occidental Hotel, 108
Older, Cora, 120, 122
Older, Fremont, 120–23, 141, 164, 168
Orleans, Philippe Eqalité, Duke of, 21
Osbourne, Fanny, 190, 195
Osbourne, Lloyd, 4–5, 71
Overland Monthly, 189

P

Pacific Appeal: Emperor's proclamations in, 145–47, 156, 161–64, 166, 170, 175–76, 191–92; fake proclamation printed in, 169
Pacific Club, 7, 199–200
Pacific Gas & Electric Company, 190
Pacific Mail Steamship Company, 35, 40
Palace Hotel, 125–26, 190, 192–93, 205
Palace of Truth, The (play), 196
Parker, George, 90, 93–94
Pedro II, Emperor of Brazil, 193
Peiser, Nathan, 10–14, 20, 23–24, 88
Perkins, George C., 2
Perriere, Fanny, 45, 75
Perry, Edward C., 106
Petaluma *Argus*, 101–2
Petaluma Creek project, 150–52
Peters, Charles R., 191–92
Philadelphia *Public Record*, 3
Pierce, Franklin, 40, 52
Pinkerton, Allan, 184
Pinkerton's National Detective Agency, 184
Points, The, 27–28
Pomeroy, Jesse, 181
Pony Express, 64–65, 67
Popley, David, 117
Port Elizabeth, 22–24, 58
Porter, Rufus, 152–53
Porter's Spirit of the Times, 37
Portland *Oregonian*, 3
Proll, William, 195–96
Puck (magazine), 94
Pulver, Isaac, 25

R

Ralston, William C., 190
Rassette Hotel, 36
Reardon, Timothy, 189
Red Hot, Hottest (play), 154
Rice, "Old Unreliable," 93
Rio de Janeiro, 25–26
Rippey, Henry, 117
Ritchie, Ward, 144–45
Robertson, Peter, 27, 37
Rocky Mountain News, 3
Roos, Joseph, 83–84, 117
Rossi, Angelo, 203
Roughing It (Twain), 136
Ruiz brothers, 41–42, 44

Index 233

Rutledge, Mrs., 48–49
Ryan, Belle, 45, 49, 55–56

S

Sacramento, 40–41, 55, 98
Sacramento *Phoenix*, 56
Sacramento *Union*, 116, 121
Sawyer, Tom, 93
San Francisco, 23, 50, 68, 76; aristocracy in, in 1850's, 36; Broderick and, 46–47; called 'Frisco, 176–77; city and county united in, 45–46; city warrants forged by Meiggs in, 44; eccentricity tolerated in, 81; 1851 fire in, 28–29; Emperor legend still alive in, 205; Emperor's death in, 1–4, 195–97; in Gold Rush era, 27–28; Norton as mascot of, 96–97; Norton as tourist attraction in, 3–6, 122–23, 140–41, 159, 175–77, 193; San Francisco-Oakland Bridge proposal and, 142–46; slavery issues and, 50, 65; streetcars introduced in, 177–79; transcontinental railroad and, 98; Vigilance Committee in, 29–33, 48–49, 52–53
San Francisco Chronicle, The, 2, 122, 163–64; Emperor's contemplated marriage and, 167; Jimmy Bowman of, 5, 7, 10, 72, 94, 119, 199; Mark Twain in, 118
San Francisco Committee of Vigilance, 29–33, 48–49, 52–53, 165, 183
San Francisco *Daily Herald*, 55, 152, 154; Norton's business ad in, 49; vigilante justice recommended by, 29
San Francisco Examiner, 5, 122, 131, 188
San Francisco Gas Lighting Company, 7, 43, 53, 190
San Francisco *News-Letter*, 149
San Francisco-Oakland Bay Bridge, 142–46
San Francisco Opera Company, 205
San Francisco *Sunday Times*, 47
Scannell, David, 47–48
Schizophrenia, 15, 19, 72
Schizophrenia; The Meaning of Madness (Mitchell), 72
Scientific American, 152–53
Scott, Winfield, 62
Scribner's Monthly Magazine, 70–71
Seattle *Intelligencer*, 3
Seeligsohn, Abe, 203
Semple, Robert, 40

Senator of the Fifties, A (Lynch), 46
Serpent Scepter, 6, 132, 182, 200
Seward, William H., 129
Sharon, William, 190, 192
Sheraton-Palace Hotel, 205
Sherman, John, 158
Sherman, William T., 54, 73, 158; bank founded by, 43–44; the Civil War and, 7, 52, 55; the Meiggs fraud and, 43–44, 47; Norton's mortgage held by, 7, 44; the Vigilance Committee and, 48–49; Sam Ward and, 42
Sibley, Alexander, 37–38
Sillem, Willy, 41, 45, 75
Sim, William, 37–38, 42
Skeantlebury, Billy, 171
Slavery issues, 51, 54–55, 63, 65, 67, 88–89
Sloman, Mark, 15
Sloman, Morris, 15, 17
Sloman, Phyllis, 15, 17
Smythe, Fitz. *See* Evans, Albert S.
Society of California Pioneers, 182, 200
Soulé, Franklin, 105, 135
South African College, 16
Stanton, Edwin M., 134
Stanford, Leland, 149, 181; denounced as robber baron, 172–73; Emperor given railroad pass by, 6, 174; transcontinental railroad and, 98, 137, 140; Yerba Buena Island and, 142, 144
Stanford University, 6
Stebbins, Horatio, 160–61, 166
Stellifer the King, 6, 110, 113–16
Stevenson, Robert Louis, 6, 184–85, 190; Emperor scarcely known by, 5, 72; on Norton, 4–5, 9, 71–72, 78, 194–95, 198–99
Story of the Files, The (Cummins), 57
Streetcars, 177–79
Stuart, James (English Jim), 31–32, 183
Stuart, Jeb, 92
Sullivan, Francis, 47
Swain, Robert, 103, 105, 130
Sydney Ducks, the, 29–32
Sydney *Herald*, 33

T

Tammany Hall, 46
Taylor, Bayard, 38
Tehama House, 49
Telegraph, 67, 113

234 Index

Temple Emanu-El, 87
Territorial Enterprise: Fremont Older and, 121; Mark Twain in, 93–94, 104, 112, 116, 118, 160
Terry, David S., 53, 56, 60, 91, 165
Tetlow, Sam, 167, 169–71; Nellie Cole promoted by, 91–92, 95, 154, 166
This Life I've Loved (Field), 5, 185
Thorne, Isaac, 44
Thumb, Tom, 159
Tikvath Israel, 22, 24
Transamerica Pyramid, 205
Transcontinental railroad, 113, 122, 172–73; completion of, 136–37; Leland Stanford and, 98, 137, 140; Oakland-San Francisco rivalry and, 98
Trollope, Anthony, 158
Turner, Henry, 73
Twain, Mark, 10, 168; anti-Chinese bias of *Morning Call* and, 149; Bret Harte and, 105, 112, 135; Bummer's obituary written by, 118–19; Martin Burke and, 116, 126, 128; Evans and, 105–7, 111–12, 116–17, 147; in the *Morning Call,* 3, 6, 104–9, 149; on Norton, 1, 3, 6, 87, 95, 106–9, 135, 137, 198; in San Francisco, 93–95, 109; on Horatio Stebbins, 160–61; on streetcar safety, 177–79; in the *Territorial Enterprise,* 93–94, 104, 112, 116, 118, 160; Ned Wakeman and, 30, 128, 160, 182–84; on George Washington the Second, 134–35

U

Union Pacific Railroad, 136
University of California, 27; at Berkeley, 132, 187; at Los Angeles, 144
University of Cape Town, 16

V

Vallejo, Donna Francesca Benicia, 40
Vallejo, Mariano, 40
Vallejo *Chronicle,* 10–11
Van Bergen's Saloon, 121, 141

Van Bokkelen, 108
Victoria, Queen of England, 35, 75, 88, 167; portrait of, hung in Emperor's room, 91, 109, 117, 129, 182
Vigilance Committee, 29–33, 48–49, 52–53

W

Wakeman, Adelaide Seaborn, 184
Wakeman, Eddie, 184, 186
Wakeman, Edgar, 34; memoirs of, 183–84; Mark Twain and, 30, 128, 133, 160, 182–84; on Vigilance Committee, 30, 32–33, 53
Wakeman, Keith, 184, 186
Wakeman, Mary Lincoln, 184–85
Wakeman, Minnie, 184–87
Walter & Thompkins, 77
Ward, Annie, 74
Ward, Sam, 42, 73; as King of the Lobby, 36, 134; the McAllisters and, 36–37; Adolphe Mailliard and, 74
Warren, Lavinia, 159
Washington, George, the Second, 81–82, 84, 90, 115–16; Mark Twain on, 134–35
Wasp (magazine), 202
Watson, Ella, 45
Webb, Charles Henry, 105
Weekly News-Letter, 153, 155, 191
Weller, John B., 55
Whittaker, Sam, 32–33
Wilde, Oscar, 39, 188
Wild Horse of Tartary, The (play), 95
William IV, King of England, 9–10
Williams, Albert, 32
Williams, Virgil, 188–90, 200
Wilson, Professor, 152
Wise, Isaac Mayer, 13, 204
Wrecker, The (Stevenson and Osbourne), 4, 71, 198–99
Wunderlich, Albert, 83–84

Y

Yerba Buena Island, 142–44, 146
Yerkes, Charles Tyson, widow of, 39